D1380591

FIRST CHILDHOOD

and

FAR FROM
THE MADDING WAR

CONTENTS

FIRST CHILDHOOD

and

FAR FROM
THE MADDING WAR

Lord Berners

Oxford New York

OXFORD UNIVERSITY PRESS

1983

Oxford University Press, Walton Street, Oxford OX2 6DP

London Glasgow New York Toronto
Delhi Bombay Calcutta Madras Karachi
Kuala Lumpur Singapore Hong Kong Tokyo
Nairobi Dar es Salaam Cape Town
Melbourne Auckland
and associated companies in
Beirut Berlin Ibadan Mexico City Nicosia

Oxford is a trade mark of Oxford University Press

Preface © Harold Acton 1983
First Childhood first published by Constable & Co. Ltd. 1934
Far from the Madding War first published by Constable & Co. Ltd. 1941
First issued in one volume as an Oxford University Press paperback 1983

This book has been published with subsidy from
the Arts Council of Great Britain

British Library Cataloguing in Publication Data

Berners, Gerald Hugh Tyrwhitt-Wilson, Baron
First childhood; and, Far from the madding
war.—(Oxford paperbacks)
I. Berners, Gerald Hugh Tyrwhitt-Wilson, Baron
I. Title
780'.92'4 ML410.B/
ISBN 0-19-281417-6

Library of Congress Cataloging in Publication Data

Berners, Gerald Hugh Tyrwhitt-Wilson, Baron, 1883–1950.
First childhood and Far from the madding war.
(Oxford paperbacks)
1. Berners, Gerald Hugh Tyrwhitt-Wilson, Baron, 1883–
1950—Biography—Youth. 2. Novelists, English—20th
century—Biography. 3. Diplomats—England—Biography.
4. Composers—England—Biography. 5. World War, 1939–
1945—Fiction. I. Berners, Gerald Hugh Tyrwhitt-Wilson,
Baron, 1883–1950. Far from the madding war. 1983.
II. Title.
PR6003.E7425Z464 1983 823'.912 [B] 83-7277
ISBN 0-19-281417-6 (pbk.)

Printed in Great Britain by
Richard Clay (The Chaucer Press) Ltd.
Bungay, Suffolk

PREFACE

'Every artist,' wrote Emerson, 'was first an amateur.' In the 14th Lord Berners we behold a consummate example of the amateur in its truest sense, though he was too conscientious a craftsman to practise the arts as a mere recreation. The paintbrush and the fountain-pen vied in bravura with the ivory keys, and in my view the latter finally won the competition. His individual fun and fantasy are most dazzling in his music; they are more restrained and delicate in his prose.

It is hard for me to realize that he would have been a centenarian in 1983, for he always seemed a youthful spirit, almost a contemporary. He was an honorary attaché at the British Embassy in Rome when I first met him as Gerald Tyrwhitt in my boyhood – I suppose in 1917, for he succeeded to the title of Lord Berners in 1918. He was already attracted to Stravinsky and Casella in music and to the Italian Futurists in painting. His 'Three Little Funeral Marches' had been brilliantly performed by Alfredo Casella at the Accademia Santa Cecilia, and by Depero at the famous Roman theatre of marionettes, Il Teatro dei Piccoli. He was a *cicisbeo* of the glamorous Marchesa Casati and a patron of the Futurist Balla, whose whirling compositions brightened his spacious studio. I remember tin goldfish glittering in big-bellied bowls, some of which were filled with blue and green water like those in chemists' windows, and transparent Javanese puppets on strings. He created the atmosphere of a toyshop where the toys might spring to life and dance wild tarantellas, as in *Boutique Fantasque*. In fact he belonged to an avant-garde which had barely ruffled the surface of England before the Sitwells launched *Wheels* and *Façade*. Later on he was drawn to Surrealism and purchased a picture by Salvador Dali, which inspired a poem containing the lines:

> On the pale yellow sands
> There's a pair of clasped Hands
> And an Eyeball entangled with string . . .
> And a Bicycle Seat
> And a Plate of Raw Meat
> And a Thing that is hardly a Thing.

The art of the colourist is obviously related to music, and in his own painting Lord Berners was a disciple of the early Corot, which is surprising for an admirer of Balla and Dali, but he was always prodigal of surprises. His writings also had the subtle tonality of Corot's landscapes.

An only child of incompatible parents, his father a jaunty sailor and man-about-town when on land, and his mother a passionate equestrienne of conventional mentality, Gerald Berners was born in 1883 at Arley, the country home of his maternal grandparents where most of his early childhood was spent. He was disarmingly conservative in appearance, with a neat moustache and quizzical eyes, a bowler hat when out of doors and a monocle for careful scrutiny. Sometimes he wore his mother's diamond horseshoe tie-pin. His manner was detached and urbane, and he was modest to a fault about his achievements. He could make startling remarks in a matter-of-fact voice. Nancy Mitford introduced him as Lord Merlin into *The Pursuit of Love*, and he caricatured himself as Lord FitzCricket in his novel *Far from the Madding War*. Because he wrote and painted as well as composed music he was treated as a dilettante by the gossip-column hacks. Yet he was fundamentally serious though never solemn, especially in his satire. He revealed himself more in his music than in his books with the exception of his charming autobiographical *First Childhood*, in which he confessed: 'I have always taken an almost intoxicating delight in "perilous laughter", that is to say laughter which, either from good manners or fear, has to be controlled at all costs. The kind of laughter which, on solemn occasions, or in the presence of the great, sometimes wells up within one with such violence that the human frame is nearly shattered in the course of its suppression.'

Lord Berners was fifty-one years old when *First Childhood* was published in 1934. How fresh and funny it still remains today! The narrative meanders in a clear and easy style which combines grace with gusto, studded with felicitous phrases and memorable anecdotes. At any rate the child was father to the man. Here we find many of the ingredients of his music, for the humour is delicate and bitter-sweet. He is a master of understatement. *Schadenfreude* is turned inwards towards his childish misfortunes without self-pity: one is reminded of the pathos of Charlie Chaplin's early films. For example, in the account of a schoolboy 'crush' which ends in disaster on the roof (his hero has invited him to smoke and he is violently sick as a result): 'At last I recovered a little and was able to stagger to my feet. I made for the skylight with faltering steps and managed to get down the ladder. Longworth [his hero] followed me. As we parted to return to our respective dormitories he gave me a look in which fury was mingled with contempt.' He was invariably the anti-hero of his anecdotes.

'As for my immediate ancestry', he stated, 'I am unable to trace any single one of my distinctive traits to my grandparents, and still less to either of my parents. The only conclusive fact that I have learnt about heredity is that, in the later Victorian era, there were certain disadvantages in being born a sport (in the biological sense) in an exclusively sporting environment.' His discovery of music in an unmusical country house was quite fortuitous, as he relates in Chapter VI, 'Introduction to Euterpe'. Strangely, he was first attracted by its graphic symbolization: 'The aural side of music held, at first, no charms for me. Cousin Emily's singing was not of a kind to inspire enthusiasm; it was, in fact, more calculated to put one off music for ever, and it was no doubt due to this fatal association that, once, when I was taken to a village concert, I created a violent disturbance and had to be removed.' An old volume of 'Pieces for the Harp' in the house library, 'compositions which seemed to consist for the most part of arpeggios, glissandos and cadenzas', suggested 'surging waves of melody and rhythm, an ideal music of which, as yet, I had had no conscious experience'. Then, as in later life, the visual sense predominated. He was too modest to trace any distinctive trait to his remote ancestor, the 2nd Lord Berners (1467–1533), one of the founders of the Tudor prose style who translated Froissart at the request of Henry VIII. His own literary style was far from grandiloquent or high-flown, but the subjects of his fiction were highly artificial. They have little in common with Ronald Firbank's, however; Lord Berners used to see him in Rome, perhaps his only friend there before his death at the age of thirty-nine.

Personally I prefer *First Childhood* to his novels. It is dedicated somewhat whimsically to Mr Robert Heber-Percy, who keeps his memory green at Faringdon in Oxfordshire. But each of his major fictions, *Far from the Madding War*, *Count Omega*, *The Camel*, and *The Romance of a Nose*, has a quiet grace and absurdity entirely *sui generis*.

Oxford in wartime provides the setting for *Far from the Madding War*, and one is occasionally reminded of *Zuleika Dobson* in its pages. Emmeline Pocock, the demure heroine, daughter of the Warden of All Saints, 'looked like a nymph in one of the less licentious pictures of Fragonard', and as her contribution to war work she perversely decides to ruin an immense and valuable piece of German embroidery bequeathed to her by an aunt. 'It occurred to her that certain war occupations were of so secret a character that they could not be divulged. That, she decided, would be the line that she would take about hers.'

The author caricatured himself in the portrait of Lord Fitz-Cricket, introducing some factual details into the caricature. For instance:

He composed music, he wrote books, he painted; he did a great many things with a certain facile talent. He was astute enough to realise that, in Anglo-Saxon countries, art is more highly appreciated if accompanied by a certain measure of eccentric publicity. This fitted in well with his natural inclinations.

He had a collection of strange masks that he used to wear when motoring. He dyed his fantail pigeons all colours of the rainbow, so that they flew over the countryside causing bewilderment to neighbouring farmers. He was always surrounded by odd animals and birds. When travelling on the Continent he had a small piano in his motor car . . .

By contrast with another composer, Francis Paltry, who holds that art should be austere and 'believed in catharsis through boredom', FitzCricket 'had always been interested in the pleasurable aspects of art, and he thought that a work of art should never be tedious'. As if in answer to carping critics, he is made to observe: ' "The English have a tendency to judge art by size and weight." '

Lord Berners's own compositions were neither long nor heavy. I remember my keen enjoyment of his ballet, *The Triumph of Neptune*, which was produced superbly by Diaghilev in 1926, as well as his refreshingly varied compositions for the piano and his versatile lyrics, notably the three groups of songs in the German, French, and English manner. Unfortunately I was unable to hear his opera *Le Carrosse du Saint Sacrement* or see his ballet *The Wedding Bouquet*, in which he collaborated with Gertrude Stein – still in the repertoire of the Royal Ballet at Covent Garden. (A juicy passage from Gertrude Stein is also quoted in Chapter VIII of *Far from the Madding War*. This ends: ' "Exceptions are circular and have little extremities that shake and are less than more and fewer than something." ')

In his biography of Diaghilev Mr Richard Buckle has described *The Triumph of Neptune* as a 'mixture of naive Victorian pantomime, Jules Verne, and modern satire'. Sir Sacheverell Sitwell provided the scenario; the décor and costumes were enlargements of Pollock's toy theatres and hand-painted prints in Hoxton. 'In the Schottische,' writes Mr Buckle, 'there was an imitation of bagpipes, and the wild yelping of Highlanders. The "Waltz of Cloudland" seemed to be by an English member of "Les Six" but had some Ravellian overtones. The interruption of the polka of the Sailor's Wife and the Dandy by a drunken voice singing "The Last Rose of Summer" from Flotow's *Martha* was a funny surprise. The musical numbers for four Harlequins, for the Hornpipe and for the Apotheosis were smash hits.' Jules Verne had been Berners's favourite author at his private school as opposed to the popular Henty, and Mr Buckle is perceptive in his comparison with 'Les Six', for Lord Berners was temperamentally more akin to them than to his fellow English composers, though I am sure Lord Nelson would have approved of *The Triumph of Neptune*, forgetting his French phobia during its performance.

In spite of his penchant for 'perilous laughter' it would be a mistake to pigeonhole Berners as a musical humorist. His *Fragments Psychologiques* ('Hatred', 'Laughter', and 'A Sigh') have dramatically effective depth; his musical parodies are far more than parodies of other composers, they are stylistic reflections of his moods in a multi-coloured mirror. Contemporary critics remarked on their revolutionary audacity, less revolutionary nowadays, perhaps, since the age of Stockhausen and the dodecaphonics.

Count Omega is his only novel whose hero, Emanuel Smith, is a composer. Smith becomes infatuated with a gorgeous young giantess called Madam Gloria, whose virtuosity on a trombone seems to offer the perfect climax to a symphony he is composing.

Madam Gloria is jealously kept by a mysterious millionaire with a mania for practical jokes, and guarded by a eunuch, but a fashionable dressmaker who is a reincarnation of Joan of Arc acts as a secret go-between. This elaborate fantasy reads as if it had been written after a series of vivid nightmares, yet I suspect Emanuel Smith provided a vehicle for some of the author's private opinions:

He thought that the actual state of music was far from satisfactory. The atmosphere of the concert room, he considered, had become like that of a museum and the works of even the greatest composers only called forth the same kind of emotions as those aroused by museum pieces. Serious music had ceased to be vital. People were moved by it, sensually or intellectually, and then returned to their ordinary state of mind. It had become a mere temporary drug of which the effects soon wore off. In this insensitive and blasé world, absolute music was inadequate. Something more was needed to enhance its message, to galvanise its votaries into new life.

For the student of allegory and the subconscious *The Camel* is a rococo pastiche of a Victorian moral tale with macabre undertones. The humped quadruped appears at an English country vicarage in mid-winter and takes a furious fancy to the vicar's wife. As L. P. Hartley wrote of it, 'Lord Berners has a genius for finding grotesque juxtapositions, and for startling us with an incongruity so violent as to be really frightening.'

Having written the words and music of a haunting song called 'Red Roses and Red Noses', Lord Berners continued to be obsessed by that important feature, for his next and last novel was *The Romance of a Nose*. This is a fantasy about Cleopatra, who wishes to emulate Helen of Troy but her nose is so long that she decides to devote herself to philosophy and culture and become a highbrow. Eventually her nose is shortened by plastic surgery, which produces a change in her character. She soon becomes Caesar's mistress and a byword for feminine witchery.

One episode in the book reminds me of a luncheon I enjoyed with the author in a public restaurant, when he blew iridescent soap bubbles which floated across the crowded tables of astonished diners. After a banquet in honour of Kallimachos, the hostile governor of the Thebaid whom she is determined to fascinate, Cleopatra 'had prepared a little surprise. Thousands of large flies had been caught and enclosed in papyrus boxes, each one having a tiny streamer of brightly coloured silk attached to it. She beckoned to her steward. "You may release the flies," she whispered. Like miniature birds of paradise they filled the air with swirling colour as they flew out into the courtyard and settled on the trees.' The image is adaptable to Lord Berners, who opened a cage-door for a bevy of brilliant birds, the tinted fantail pigeons of Faringdon. These are still wheeling in the luminous air for our delight. Nine of them are particularly splendid: they symbolize the Muses of whom Lord Berners was ever a faithful, if wayward, votary.

Having been a guest at Faringdon, I cannot forbear to mention his hospitality. Even during and after the last World War, when edible dainties were scarce on the market, he offered us dishes of memorable succulence, for he was the most generous of gourmets. Violet Trefusis used to tell a story, much embroidered as was her wont, of how he discovered a sturgeon 'as long as a submarine', at a fishmonger's in Yeovil. It contained a precious bag full of caviare which went bad as nobody in the house could cope with it. The sturgeon was too big for the frigidaire and was placed on a chaise-longue in the hall. A sad story, the point of which seems to be that only Lord Berners could discover a sturgeon in Yeovil. His various health fads betrayed a latent hypochondria. When he stayed with Mrs George Keppel in Florence, where most of her guests played card games after dinner, he would walk rapidly from room to room without stopping for twenty minutes or longer. This would now be called 'jogging'. He said it was for his digestion, but I suspect it was a ruse to escape the bridge-fiends.

An unabashed hedonist, in revolt against the brands of boredom he had had to endure at his grandmother Lady Bourchier's in his childhood, he gave immense pleasure and constant amusement to his friends. His talent for provoking laughter even after his death would gratify his genial soul. Last but not least he wrote for his epitaph

> Here lies Lord Berners,
> One of the learners.
> His great love of learning
> May earn him a burning
> But, praise to the Lord,
> He seldom was bored.

Harold Acton

CONTENTS

FIRST CHILDHOOD

To

ROBERT HEBER-PERCY

*whose knowledge of orthography
and literary style has proved
invaluable*

I

The Screen

I can remember very vividly the first time I became aware of my
existence; how for the first time I realised that I was a sentient
human being in a perceptible world. I seem to have acquired this
state of self-consciousness very much in the way in which one
masters the technique of riding a bicycle or of performing some
trick of juggling, when, at a given moment and without any
apparent reason, it is suddenly found that the thing can be done.

This awakening of my perception was not brought about by any
very remarkable incident. There was no salamander in the fire, no
tolling of bells to announce some famous victory or the accession of
a monarch. Much as it would enhance the interest of my story and
lend it a touch of the picturesque, a strict regard for truth forbids me
to connect the circumstance with any occurrence of national or even
of local importance. The conditions in which this epoch-making
event in my mental career took place could not possibly have been
more trivial. I was merely standing beside a table in the library at
Arley, when, all at once, what had hitherto been a blurred
background became distinct, just as when someone who is
shortsighted puts on spectacles. Objects and individuals assumed
definite shapes, grouping themselves into an ordered whole, and
from that moment I understood that I formed part of it – without,
of course, a full premonition of all that this exactly entailed. The
commonplace features of this first landmark in my experience
remain clearly recorded in my mind's eye; the massive mahogany
table with its cloth of crimson velvet, the fat photograph album with
gilt clasps that could be locked up as though it were a receptacle for
obscene pictures, whereas in reality it contained nothing worse than
family portraits; the china bowl full of Christmas roses, slightly
frost-bitten as those flowers usually are, a pastel portrait of my
grandmother as a girl; in the middle distance my grandmother
herself, my mother and a few aunts and, in the doorway, my nurse

waiting to take me out for a walk. An ensemble which, you will agree, was entirely devoid of any kind of poignancy, although it may have had a certain charm as a Victorian conversation piece.

People I have questioned on the subject of the first awakening of their consciousness, have proved strangely uninformative. They could in most cases remember some particular incident that had occurred at an early stage in their lives, but none of them were able to recall the exact moment in which they had realised for the first time that they were human beings. Some even confessed that, as far as they knew, it had never happened to them at all. And I daresay they have managed to get through life just as happily.

The phenomenon I have described took place when I was three and a half years old. Up to that point my life had not been wholly uneventful. I had travelled to Malta and back, I had been dropped into the Mediterranean by my nurse, and had appeared at a children's party attired as the Infant Bacchus. But, as far as my memory goes, these things have passed into oblivion. They lie buried in my subconsciousness and I can only be thankful that they do not seem to have given rise to any very serious complexes, inhibitions or repressions.

We are told, however, that the things which happen to us after our birth are of less importance in the moulding of our character than those that occur during our prenatal history, and that it is in this mysterious, elusive period that the impulses are determined which drive us through our brief span of life. With regard to heredity I am unable to discover any very evident genealogy for my own character. My ancestors, for several generations back, appear to have been country squires or business men with recreations of an exclusively sporting nature; although, of course, it is quite possible that there may have been among them a few artistic ladies who painted in water-colours, visited Italy or played on the harp. It appears that, many years ago, some gipsy blood came into the family. The fact was hushed up more or less successfully, but nevertheless there have been indications that it has continued to flow, like a subterranean stream, coming now and then to the surface with disconcerting results.

As for my immediate ancestry I am unable to trace any single one of my distinctive traits to my grandparents, and still less to either of my parents. The only conclusive fact that I have learnt about heredity is that, in the later Victorian era, there were certain disadvantages in being born a sport (in the biological sense) in an exclusively sporting environment.

I was born in 1883 at Arley, the home of my maternal grandparents, and it was here that most of my early childhood was spent. Arley was a huge neo-Gothic house of grey stone, built towards the end of the eighteenth century. It was a little like Strawberry Hill in appearance and, if not so airy and fantastic in its architecture, was quite as adequately turreted and castellated. Its atmosphere was highly romantic and I think that Horace Walpole, Monk Lewis or the authoress of *The Mysteries of Udolpho* would have approved of it. It was surrounded by a very lovely park, undulating and well-timbered, a wide valley through which the river Severn flowed. The house itself stood on a height overlooking the river, and the gardens were laid out with slopes and stone balustrades descending to the water's edge. The most striking feature of the park was a range of heavily wooded hills following the line of the river in the direction of Southbridge, the picturesque and rather foreign-looking local town. This range was known as the Terrace. It was an earthly paradise for children, and the precipitous sandstone cliffs that stood out here and there from among the trees provided an inexhaustible field for exploration and adventure.

One of these cliffs appealed strongly to my childish imagination. It was known as the Tarpeian Rock, the name being no doubt a relic of the classical taste of a bygone generation. It was a sheer wall of red sandstone encrusted with lichen and overhung with tall fir trees. The fascination the Tarpeian Rock exercised over me was due, no doubt, to an early craving for the 'terrible and sublime,' together with a certain interest aroused by the sadistic associations of the name. I remember being bitterly disappointed when I learnt that Tarpeia, instead of having been hurled from a rock as I had imagined, had in reality been crushed by the shields of the Sabine soldiers who had meanly taken advantage of an ambiguous phrase.

However, the Tarpeian Rock was only one among the many interesting things to be found in the park. There was, for instance, the little pool known as the 'bottomless pit,' where an attempt had once been made to find coal, and now the disused mine-shaft was filled to the brim with stagnant water. It stood in a coppice of gloomy aspect in which, so it was rumoured, no birds ever built their nests; a fact that greatly increased the sinister reputation of the place. But I am afraid that to anyone unacquainted with the legend of its bottomlessness and its nestlessness it would have seemed just a very ordinary pond.

The Ice-house provided another thrill. In the days before the general use of artificial ice, the frozen surface of one of the pools would be broken up every winter and stored away in a circular, semi-underground chamber covered with a thick layer of bracken. Once or twice, as a special treat, I was allowed to have the door of the Ice-house opened so that I might peer into the chilly depths, where the ice we had skated upon lay slumbering in its bracken nest until the time when it should emerge once more to cool our drinks and provide us with sherbets and ices.

But it is in Arley itself that the most vivid of my early reminiscences are concentrated. The house, with its stairways and passages, its mysterious nooks, cupboards and attics, each place having a distinct atmosphere of its own, formed a microcosm where I was able to find ample nourishment for my budding tastes and sensibilities.

The two rooms I preferred above all others were the library and the drawing-room. These two rooms contained the greatest and most varied horde of treasures.

I loved the library for its rows of tawny-coloured books in the high Gothic bookcases surmounted by niches containing the busts of Eminent Men of Letters (or were they Roman Emperors?); its elaborate gas chandeliers with their luminous globes like gigantic incandescent fruit on Gothic branches; the massive marble fireplace with the porphyry urns on the mantelpiece; the cavernous leather armchairs and the silver reading lamps with their bright green glass shades. The whole room seemed to radiate warmth and security in those snug Victorian days.

The drawing-room appealed to me in a different way. It was gayer, more feminine, more frivolous. Here the Gothic decorations were less austere and the traceries were picked out with light blue and gold. From the fan-vaulted ceiling, like an inverted fountain, there hung a huge crystal chandelier with drops and pendants that flashed and glittered with rainbow hues and were reflected by the tall mirrors between the windows. The curtains were looped up in a labyrinth of folds and tassels. The chairs and sofas of pale blue satin were plentifully punctuated with buttons, and there was a kind of double settee in the form of an S, called a 'Sociable.' (Anything less conducive to sociability it would be difficult to imagine, however advantageous it might have proved to people who were proud of their profiles.) In one of the corners of the room stood a monstrous grand piano, which seemed to be used more as a repository for odds and ends than for any musical purpose. In front of the fireplace lay a thick white woolly hearthrug and on one side there stood a fire-shield made of a stuffed Himalayan pheasant with outspread wings, whose iridescent breast and plumed tiara used to fill me with joy.

But what fascinated me more than any other object in the room was a tall folding screen of brightly-coloured pictures cut out and pasted on at random, the joint handiwork of my mother and her sisters who, between them, must have mutilated a whole library of illustrated books and coloured prints in the course of its construction.

Under a transparent layer of yellow varnish there lay an entrancing world of flowers, birds and landscapes all jumbled together in kaleidoscopic confusion. Here you could see 'Doves of Siam, Lima mice and legless Birds of Paradise' and countless other things as well. Views of Italian lakes and towns were framed in sprays of orchids. Against a background of Swiss mountains, chamois and chalets, glittering humming-birds thrust their rapier-like beaks into the calyxes of tropical flowers. A gigantic green and crimson parakeet appeared to have alighted on the spire of Cologne cathedral, whilst a company of mediæval knights on richly caparisoned horses caracoled in front of the Sphinx and the Pyramids. The whole thing was without rhyme or reason, but it conjured up a magical vision of some fantastic fairy paradise and, whenever I got a chance, I would creep into the drawing-room and remain before this screen in rapt attention, vainly endeavouring to memorise the innumerable objects depicted on it.

Such was the impression the screen made upon me in my early

childhood. But when, many years afterwards, I came upon it again, stored away in a lumber room whither the purist taste of a later age had banished it, I was amazed to find that it was composed for the most part of political caricatures and sporting scenes. The well-remembered continental landscapes, the exotic birds and tropical flowers formed but a comparatively small portion of the whole. Neither did they, as one might suppose, feature more especially in the lower panels of the screen which, in those days, would have lain within my natural range of vision. In fact, in order to get at some of them I must have been obliged to stand on a chair.

The discovery was a surprising one, and it would seem to prove that at the time when the screen aroused my infantile enthusiasm, an inborn selective force must have already been at work, concentrating on certain things and excluding others, a selective force which continued to function in spite of the strenuous efforts of parents, nurses, governesses and schoolmasters to divert its activity into channels more favoured by themselves.

II

The Inhabitants of Arley

Places, when I think of them, have a way of connecting themselves in my memory with definite aspects of weather and with certain times of the day. Whenever I think of Arley I invariably see it under grey, wintry skies and in the afternoon. Sometimes these climatic and temporal associations seem to be merely arbitrary, but in this particular instance they are probably due to the fact that it was in the winter and at this time of day that the emotions the place aroused in me were most intense. It was always in the late afternoon that my mother and I used to arrive at Arley. The most vivid emotion is that of immediate anticipation, and I can even to this day recall the thrill of delight I always used to feel when, upon approaching the house, I caught the first glimpse of its grey battlemented towers looming through the trees; the delicious anticipation of tea in the library after a long and tedious journey, of seeing my small cousins again after a protracted period of loneliness, and of all the Christmas fun that was to follow.

The station was about a quarter of a mile from the house on the other side of the river. One crossed over in a ferry-boat, a method of approach which added a further excitement to the arrival. When the river was flooded, as it very often was at that time of year, the crossing was even fraught with a certain amount of danger, and one day the boat actually capsized, hurling passengers and their luggage into the swirling waters. After this incident the ferry-boat was replaced by a handsome, but less romantic, suspension bridge.

The winter visits to Arley were always the pleasantest. At that time of year the house was enlivened by the presence of four or five small cousins, children of about the same age as myself. An atmosphere of festivity prevailed, and I was allowed more licence than at other seasons when I stayed there alone with my mother.

My grandmother, Mrs Farmer, was all that one could possibly wish a grandmother to be. In the eighteen-eighties women used to assume the aspect of a grandmother as soon as the first grandchild was born, whereas in 1930 they would be much more likely to celebrate the event by having their faces lifted and spending the evening in a night-club, triumph over old age being one of the many remarkable advances of the present generation over the last.

Mrs Farmer, who, at that time, cannot have been much more than fifty, certainly made every effort to look the part of a grandmother. She always dressed herself in ample flowing gowns of sombre-hued silk or satin. On her head she wore a lace cap (as did also my other grandmother, Lady Bourchier, but with a vastly different effect). Her silvery hair was parted symmetrically over her forehead. Altogether she had the air of an elderly Madonna, placid and matriarchal. Her early life had been singularly exempt from excesses of joy and sorrow, and her features were equally free from the traces that such excesses leave. Although her views on life were limited and rather rigid, she had never been known to utter an unkind word or a hasty judgment. She was essentially one of those whose sober thoughts had never learnt to stray. Her answers were so soft that they turned away not only wrath but many other things besides. Virtue, backed by charm, is more successful as a repressive influence than when virtue stands alone and, in the presence of Mrs Farmer, sentiments and impulses that were quite reasonable in themselves often had to be stifled because they were not strictly orthodox. This is perhaps the only charge that could be brought against her, if indeed it be a charge at all; for most people will agree that it is a good thing for revolutionaries to control their opinions within the home-circle and, in any case, in our home-circle there were no revolutionaries to speak of.

In the dining-room at Arley there hung a full-length portrait of my grandmother, painted about 1870, which showed her dressed in a rather elaborate evening gown of the period, smiling benevolently in complete disregard of a terrific thunderstorm that was approaching her in the background. The picture might, in fact, have stood for an allegory of the later Victorian era.

One Christmas Eve, as we were in the very act of drinking her health, this picture suddenly fell to the ground, an accident which very naturally cast a gloom, filling us with obvious forebodings. But, as my grandmother continued to live for another thirty years or so, I can only imagine that Providence relented or else that a mistake had been made by the angel in charge of Prognostics.

Mrs Farmer's early life had, as I have said, been singularly free from care but, later on, a shadow crept into her hitherto sunny existence. My grandfather, who had always been the sanest, most normal of men, was stricken down with a strange mental affliction. I never quite understood what it was and what had caused it. By my grandmother and by the rest of the family it was looked upon as an 'act of God' – though what particular sin the poor old man could possibly be supposed to be expiating God only knows. He had proved himself a devoted husband and an excellent father. But in those days every calamity that was not properly understood, from an earthquake to a blunder on the part of the Government, was attributed to the capricious temperament of the Deity. And that is no doubt why so many people, who were outwardly religious, detested Him in secret.

My grandfather used to sit all day long in a darkened room. From his lips there came forth a stream of never ending groans and curses. His cries were often so loud that they could be heard all over the house. There were moments when he seemed able to control himself but, although he sometimes ceased to cry out, I never saw him smile or take an interest in anything. At meals he always occupied his place at the head of the table, even when there were visitors, and every Sunday he went to church. But these public appearances involved many anxious moments, and I remember him once, in the parish church at Arley, bursting out into so violent a storm of expletives in the middle of the sermon that the service had to be hastily concluded.

The curious thing was that he should have been allowed by the family to continue the ordinary routine of daily life just as though he were normal. I suppose the patriarchal idea was so firmly established that, so long as he continued to live and his physical condition allowed him to move about, he was still looked upon as nominally the head of the house and was treated as such.

Apart from the natural awe I felt for a grandparent, I do not remember ever being at all frightened by his abnormal state. One might have thought that those dreadful groans and curses issuing from that darkened room would have filled a child's heart with fear, but both I and my cousins soon grew accustomed to hearing them. We knew that it was 'only Grandpapa.' I even remember listening with curiosity to some of the more peculiar oaths he occasionally employed, although I never attempted to make any practical use of them myself in daily conversation. I suppose I must have realised that such rhetorical delicacies were exclusively for the use of grown-ups. However, in the privacy of the nursery, I would sometimes entertain my small cousins by giving them a realistic imitation of my grandfather's peculiarities, a performance which relied for its effectiveness chiefly on the fact of its being in the worst possible taste and, if overheard by nurses or parents, of its being immediately and severely punished.

Besides my grandparents, there were two other permanent residents at Arley, Uncle Luke and Aunt Flora. They were both of them unmarried. Uncle Luke, it was rumoured, had suffered in his youth from what is known as 'an unfortunate love affair.' Whether the young lady he had been engaged to had died or whether she had jilted him I was never able to discover, but anyhow the result was 'unfortunate.' Incidentally I recommend the fiction of 'an unfortunate love affair' to anyone wishing to remain a bachelor without being interfered with. It excites compassion among the sentimental and affords a protection against too insistent matchmakers. Uncle Luke never married nor did he show signs of being seriously attracted by any woman during the remainder of his life.

Aunt Flora was a chronic invalid. In her youth she had met with a hunting accident which had injured her spine and obliged her to spend most of her time reclining on a sofa in her sitting-room. For although she was able to stand up and was even able to walk about a little with the aid of a stick, any prolonged movement exhausted her. She was extremely pretty, and before the accident occurred she had been passionately fond of every form of social gaiety. Mrs Matchett, the housekeeper, used to say that if only she had been able to get about like other girls she would undoubtedly have made a brilliant marriage.

I was devoted to Aunt Flora and, had I been allowed to do so, I would willingly have spent most of my time in her company. She occupied a little suite of rooms on the ground floor of one of the towers. The room she sat in was octagonal in shape and had high French windows opening directly on to the garden. The windows faced south, and it was one of the sunniest rooms in the house. Even on grey, wintry days its yellow wall-paper and striped hangings of apricot-coloured silk gave an impression of sunshine.

Aunt Flora loved flowers and birds. The tables were always laden with flowering plants, and in one of the windows there stood a large domed cage that looked like the model of a mosque made of wire, in which there fluttered and chirped a number of brightly-coloured waxbills and singing finches. What with the fragrance of the flowers, the twittering of the birds, the gay wall-paper and Aunt Flora's own flower-like personality, the place always seemed to me a haven of perpetual spring. Just outside the windows there grew a shrub of the early-blossoming chimonanthus. (Winter-sweet it was called in the days before gardeners grew so refined.) The tiny mauve and yellow blossoms nestling in the leafless branches always used to remind me of Aunt Flora herself. She had very fair hair and her white skin had a slightly shrivelled appearance as though it were almost too delicate for the cold, northern climate in which she seemed to be existing in a state of precarious acclimatisation.

Aunt Flora was not very clever, but she had an appealing, bird-like silliness that, in its way, was a good deal more attractive than a great many other people's intelligence. She read very little, neither did she care for any of the usual indoor occupations. She was entirely dependent on company for her amusement. Thus, instinctively, she would exercise all the charm within her power to retain her visitors as long as possible, and the sensation that she was not bored, and indeed never could be bored, infected them with an equal desire to stay.

Debarred, as she was, from participation in any wider form of social entertainment, she retained nevertheless a passion for clothes. She would spend as long a time as she was able – before exhaustion compelled her to stop – in front of her mirror, rather pathetically trying on new dresses and hats that were sent to her from Paris and London. She often allowed me to help her to undo the parcels that arrived from the dressmakers and, with an almost equal delight, we would examine the delicate fabrics, the feathers and the artificial flowers as they emerged from their wrappings of tissue-paper. One day she made me a present of a bird of paradise plume which I religiously preserved as though it were a holy relic for many months, until at last it went the way of most of one's childish treasures and mysteriously disappeared. Apart from purely æsthetic reasons I was attracted, I suppose, by this finery because it seemed to afford a glimpse into that glittering realm of festivity I vaguely apprehended from the illustrated papers and from overheard fragments of conversation. Aunt Flora appreciated my admiration, and one evening she put on, for my benefit, a dress she had worn some years previously at Court, before her accident had obliged her to retire from the gay world. As she stood before me in the lamplight with curling ostrich feathers on her head and a long, billowy train of some transparent, silvery material, I felt almost afraid. It was as though she had been transformed into some strange, unearthly being from another world.

Like all children, I used to ask a great many questions. Aunt Flora was patient in answering them, but she was inclined to take her revenge by giving me information that was incorrect or misleading. When I asked her what was really the matter with my grandfather, she told me quite gravely that he was bewitched, that he was under a spell. I asked her if a counter-spell, a magic charm, could be found, would he get all right again? She said Yes.

The idea lay for some days incubating in my brain until one day I happened to read in a volume of Russian Fairy Stories about a man who was delivered from a ban the Ice-Maiden had laid upon him by being crowned with a wreath of snowdrops. It seemed a simple matter. I asked my grandmother if it had ever been tried and was told not to talk nonsense. But by that time I had already discovered that, when grown-ups told one not to talk nonsense, it was in nine cases out of ten merely a device for setting aside an embarrassing suggestion. I began to harbour the gravest suspicions, and finally became convinced that, for some reason or other, my poor grandfather was being deliberately held in thrall.

Come what might, I was determined to make the experiment, which was facilitated by its happening to be the snowdrop season. I gathered a large bunch of those self-righteous little flowers and, with the help of some wire and some cotton thread, I managed to construct a clumsy wreath. Secreting myself in the library with my talisman, I waited until the sound of snoring announced the fact that my grandfather had fallen asleep. I then stole into his room on tiptoe, succeeded in deftly placing the wreath on the old gentleman's head, and returned to my hiding-place to await the result.

Shortly afterwards I heard my grandmother enter the room. Her startled exclamation at the strange vision of my grandfather sitting with his mouth open, snoring loudly and decked out like Ophelia, must have roused him from his slumbers, for it was followed by a bellow of rage and a great commotion.

I guessed that my experiment had failed. My hopes of being acclaimed as a miracle-worker were dashed to the ground. I was now terrified by what I had done, for I realised that, after having mentioned the subject of snowdrops to my grandmother, I should at once be suspected. I fled to Aunt Flora's room as to the horns of the altar, and besought her protection. She was, I fancy, amused by my account of the unfortunate experiment, and no doubt she felt a trifle guilty for having put the idea in my head, and for having been indirectly the cause of all the trouble. Knowing also that, however good my intentions may have been, they would most certainly be misjudged by the rest of the family, she willingly undertook my defence, and I got off with a caution never again under any circumstances to enter my grandfather's room without permission.

III

The Fairy Godmother

Another and rather similar incursion into the realm of magic had consequences that were equally disastrous.

As a child I was not encouraged to believe in the more frivolous elements of the supernatural world. On the few occasions when my mother or my nurse had told me fairy tales, their narrative style had seemed to be almost deliberately lacking in conviction. But, in spite of this materialistic policy on their part, I succeeded in amassing quite a substantial collection of fairy-story books, Grimm, Perrault, Madame d'Aulnoy, a volume of Russian folk-lore and an edition of the *Arabian Nights*, in which the fact that the text had been so carefully expurgated that it resembled a plum-pudding without the plums was amply compensated for by the Oriental voluptuousness of the illustrations. These books I used to devour with ecstatic enjoyment until at last I became completely engrossed in the fantastic world they chronicled. But I remember that I was always more interested in the pageantry of fairyland than in the personality of its inhabitants. In the story of Cinderella I was far more thrilled by the pumpkin coach, by the glass slipper, than by the young woman who rode in the former and wore the latter. Ali Baba meant less to me than the cave of the Forty Thieves; I thought more of the Chinese setting of Aladdin, of the Lamp, of the Palace of the Genii than of Aladdin himself; Rapunzel remained a vague and hazy figure while I could visualize clearly the tower from which she let down her hair.

Mrs Matchett, the housekeeper at Arley, held different views to those of my nurse and my mother. She thought that it was right and salutary for children to believe in fairies. She used to regale me with the most incredibly nonsensical tales. Not content with merely playing the part of Mother Goose, she actually contrived to bring into my life, for a short while, one of the denizens of fairyland.

Although Mrs Matchett was a squat, Gamp-like little person, she possessed nevertheless a certain Victorian dignity of deportment. She had a great admiration for my grandmother and a still greater one for Queen Victoria. These two women were her models as regards both costume and manners. The solid respectability of Victorian furniture was reflected in her attire, and her protuberant bust had the tight rotundity of an over-stuffed sofa cushion. I often longed to slap it. The act, I felt sure, would have afforded the same sort of tactile pleasure as the stroking of velvet or marble.

I am afraid Mrs Matchett was rather a snob. She would pronounce the names of titled personages with an unction akin to the syrups she kept in jars on the shelves of her cupboards together with boxes of candies, spices and crystallised fruits. In the same cupboards she treasured up ornaments from the wedding, christening and birthday cakes of the various members of the family; flowers, fruit, cornucopias and figures made of some white substance that looked insidiously like sugar but was in reality a sort of hard, chalk-like plaster, as I found out to my cost when once I attempted to eat a particularly luscious-looking cupid.

Just as Aunt Flora's room was a gilded cage, an ornamental conservatory for her flower-and-birdlike personality, so was the housekeeper's room a tea-cosy, a Victorian glass case for the comfortable, Victorian, four-square Mrs Matchett. In the housekeeper's room Time seemed to have been excluded. The Past had been shaken out, brushed, folded up neatly and put away in a drawer. The Future, one felt, with all its dangers and uncertainties, would never venture to come knocking at the door of so impregnable a stronghold. The air of solidity and security which everything in that room exhaled was a defiance to the ravages of Time, and the enemy itself, represented by an elaborate gilt clock, was imprisoned and immobilised under a glass dome.

Over the mantelpiece there hung a large photogravure of the beloved Queen and a smaller one of my grandmother. On a work-table beside Mrs Matchett's own particular armchair reposed her two favourite books, the Peerage and the Bible, while the centre table with its cloth of scarlet rep was laden with volumes of the *Leisure Hour*, *Sunday at Home* and a monumental Cookery Book in which most of the recipes began with such instructions as 'Take two pints of cream, two dozen eggs and one pint of old liqueur brandy.' At all times of the year, even in the warmest months, there was a blazing fire in the grate and a kettle simmering on the hob.

From the adjoining still-room there came a delicious smell of baking bread and hot fresh cakes. But the housekeeper's room itself had the slightly stuffy atmosphere of an unventilated eating-place, for it was the custom of the upper servants to quit the servants' hall at the end of a meal with their pudding, and eat it there, as a subtle distinction of their rank.

Mrs Matchett, as I have said, was my Mother Goose; but, being a practical woman, a woman of action, she did not confine herself to mere verbal descriptions of Fairyland. She invented for my benefit a Fairy Godmother, and she would speak of her just as though she were a real live person – as it might be my grandmother or Aunt Flora. This supernatural being was supposed to dwell behind the wainscoting, from which she would emerge from time to time and confer benefits upon those she favoured. Mrs Matchett was continually producing gifts, generally of an edible nature, which she said the Fairy Godmother had left for me. But of my benefactress herself I was never able to catch even the most fleeting glimpse. Like events in the novels of Henry James, she was always 'just round the corner.'

The actual personality of the Fairy (who, owing to a certain lack of imagination on the part of her authoress appeared to me to be not so very different to some of the human beings I knew, and indeed just a little too much like Mrs Matchett herself) interested me less than her alleged supernatural powers. She was able, I was told, by means of her magic wand to perform acts of transmutation. She could, if she wished, transform lumps of coal or common stones into chocolate or crystallised fruits. If irritated she could also change human beings into animals and reptiles of the lowest kind. Small boys who were naughty and disobeyed their elders were frequently turned into toads. So I imagine that Mrs Matchett foresaw the possibility of putting the fiction of the Fairy God-mother to comminatory uses if necessary.

In response to my reiterated questions about the magic wand, Mrs Matchett carried her deception still further into the regions of reality by actually producing, one day, a staff covered with silver paper and tipped with a glittering tinsel star. (It had been used in an amateur Christmas pantomime performed at Arley a few years before.) Much as I had been thrilled by the idea of the Fairy

Godmother I now felt that I was in touch with a concrete fact. The exhibit enraptured me. But, although I was allowed to finger it, the magic wand was never actually left in my hands, nor did Mrs Matchett attempt to perform any miracles with it in my presence. And so I made up my mind to get possession of it and to test its powers myself. Excitement blinded me to reason, and no thought ever entered my head as to whether the wand would prove effective in other hands than those of the Fairy and, if so, why she had been so careless as to leave it behind for Mrs Matchett or anyone else to get hold of.

Here, in the shape of a parenthesis, let me introduce my cousin Emily.

Emily Pearson was a distant cousin. She was an orphan, a condition which, for one reason and another, seems to excite sympathy, and my grandmother had befriended her. She used to come to Arley on long visits, and when she was there she acted in the capacity of secretary to my grandmother and helped her to run the house. She was about twenty-five, and my small cousins and I naturally looked upon her as one of the grown-ups. We also looked upon her as a very disagreeable young woman. Indeed we hated her. She was a spoil-sport and a sneak. She was of small stature, lean and cross-eyed. She looked a good deal older than her twenty-five years. She had a rather tight little face with thin lips and small eyes, and her clothes always seemed to have a far larger number of buttons than were really necessary. We were told that her childhood had been an unhappy one, but we felt it must have been her own fault, and even if it were not, it was no excuse for her trying to spoil ours. Her one object in life seemed to be to throw cold water on anything that one suggested, particularly if it had anything to do with amusement.

Cousin Emily was supposed by the family (who knew nothing whatever of such matters) to possess musical talents. But, such as they were, they were very meagre, and contributed more to diffuse gloom than anything else. She played a few pieces on the piano and she also sang. She used to shut herself up in the billiard-room for an hour every day in order to practise her singing. These manifestations would generally be the sign for the banging of doors all over the house, for her voice had a peculiarly penetrating quality; its high quavering tones would mingle strangely with the cries and groans of my grandfather. I have often wondered about her singing, and why she did it. It was perhaps her own method of communing with God. But what pleasure it can possibly have afforded either to God or to herself it is difficult to imagine.

To return to the magic wand. It was not long before I was able to track it to its secret hiding-place and I managed to get possession of it during the temporary absence of Mrs Matchett. My first thought was for my cousin Emily. If only I could succeed in turning her into a toad! How marvellous it would be! How I should go up in the estimation of my cousins! It was true my grandmother might be angry but, if the worst came to the worst, I could always restore my disagreeable cousin to her original form, and at any rate it would have given her a good lesson.

I found Cousin Emily in the drawing-room, reading. Stealthily creeping up behind her, I began making what I imagined to be the requisite cabalistic passes, at the same time willing with all my might that she should be transformed into a toad of loathsome aspect. Unluckily she chanced to look up and catch sight of me in one of the mirrors. She was, I fancy, rather taken aback and not a little alarmed by the malignancy of my gestures. She inquired, with some surprise, what on earth I was doing. I told her, with bravado, that I was in possession of a magic wand and that I was about to turn her into a toad. She snatched it out of my hand and, exclaiming furiously, 'Who has been telling you this nonsense?' went off to report the matter to my grandmother. I was sent for and put through a cross-examination ('cross' in every sense of the word), in the course of which the whole history of the Fairy Godmother was revealed. Mrs Matchett was rebuked and the poor fairy, assailed by universal derision, perished like a poisoned rat behind the wainscoting.

This unfortunate experiment, following on the affair of the snowdrops, convinced me that I had no real aptitude for Magic.

IV

Lady Bourchier

My paternal grandmother, Lady Bourchier, was a very different person to the kindly, angelic-featured Mrs Farmer. She was actually one of the most forbidding, awe-inspiring women I have ever known, and my two grandmothers might have served as twin allegorical figures representing the brighter and darker aspects of Divine Charity.

Lady Bourchier was intensely religious and violently low-church. She went so far as to have herself described in *Who's Who* as 'distinctly low,' an epithet which must have caused some surprise to those who were unaware of its sectarian significance.

While quite a young woman she became acquainted with Lord Radstock and was 'converted' by him. I was told that, in the unregenerate period before her conversion, she had, like Saint Augustine, led a frivolous and mundane life, had enjoyed dancing and social festivities. But I am inclined to doubt this legend. I feel sure that she must have been born with the seeds of a baleful asceticism in her heart, for not even conversion could have succeeded in so permanently embittering any human being.

Lady Bourchier lived at a place called Stackwell about three miles from Arley on the other side of the river. It was a gloomy unattractive house. Originally Elizabethan in style, it had been deformed by later additions out of all recognition. It was surrounded by a moat which was generally half-dry and always rather smelly, and the house was shut in on all sides by tall fir trees. Even under a blue sky and when the sun shone its brightest Stackwell looked as grim as an ogre's castle. I was always thankful that I never had to stay there often, and never for any length of time.

Lady Bourchier had brought up her children on the principle that respect is preferable to love. As a precept of education this may perhaps be valuable, but in her particular case she succeeded in obtaining neither; her children merely came to regard her with a sullen aversion. Anyone so bigoted could hardly inspire respect and she was lacking in any single lovable quality. On the other hand, she had a forcible personality and a will of iron. She dominated and repressed all those with whom she came into contact. There was something a little tragic about all this waste of energy. You felt that, if only some interest had possessed her, other than this narrow intolerant religion which cramped and stultified her whole being, she might have been quite a remarkable woman. Even with her total lack of amenity, she might have distinguished herself in some capacity for which amenity is not an absolute necessity. She might have become a Florence Nightingale, a Lady Astor.

Somebody once asked my father if Lady Bourchier were not a Baroness in her own right. He replied, 'Yes, but she is everything else in her own wrong.'

In appearance Lady Bourchier was not unlike Holbein's portrait of Bloody Mary with just a touch of Charley's Aunt. In fact her coiffure might have been modelled upon that of the latter, and she wore a lace cap with two large, melancholy black bows on it, which always made me think of a couple of crows perching on the roof of a Methodist chapel. There was indeed something very peculiar about all her clothes. Though she usually wore a simple costume of black silk resembling in style the dresses worn by Queen Victoria in her later years, the garment was not as simple as it looked. It appeared to possess the faculty of increasing or diminishing in volume like the sails of a ship. It was rumoured that, concealed beneath her skirts, there was an elaborate system of strings and pulleys for raising her petticoats off the ground whenever she walked in the garden. Whether this was the case or not I imagine nobody had ever ventured to probe. It is certain that, whenever she went out of doors, her clothes used to assume a curious bunched-up appearance behind, which made her look like an emu.

In fact my cousins and I always used to refer to her among ourselves as 'The Emu,' and I remember that once, when she took us to visit the Zoo, we contrived to confront her with the bird itself. Our little joke was not particularly successful, because she guessed immediately what we were up to and said with a sour smile, 'I suppose you imagine it looks like me.' It was among her many alarming characteristics that she seemed to be able to read your inmost thoughts and to be endowed with the same sort of inquisitorial omniscience as the dour God she worshipped and with whom she gave one the impression of being on terms of exclusive amity.

My grandfather, a pleasant easy-going individual with the air of a Paterfamilias out of one of John Leech's drawings in *Punch*, was completely under her thumb. He had a mild liking for politics in which, however, he was never permitted to indulge. The only subjects Lady Bourchier allowed to be discussed in her presence were the less sensational items of general news and those preferably of a theological nature. It must be confessed she sometimes appeared to take an interest in local scandals. She seemed to derive a certain pleasure from hearing instances of other people's godlessness. It gave her satisfaction, no doubt, to hear of yet another of God's creatures obviously destined for Hell.

Whenever conversation strayed into one of the many paths of which she disapproved, my grandmother had a remarkable faculty of making her disapproval felt. Without saying a single word she managed to radiate disapproval. The air seemed to grow heavy with it, and the most audacious, the most garrulous talker would wilt and be silent. You may imagine that conversation under such circumstances was not likely to attain a very high level of interest.

There was, however, one note of humanity in Lady Bourchier's nature, and that was her fondness for birds. She used to encourage robins, tits, nuthatches and sparrows to come to her windows and be fed. She had succeeded in taming a pair of blue-tits, so that they would come on to the window-sill and take food out of her hands. At least that was what she said. We had to take her word for it because nobody had ever seen them do it. She used to say rather pointedly that this famous pair of blue-tits would never come to her if a stranger were present. In fact she always referred to them in a mysterious, exclusive fashion rather in the manner in which Elijah might have spoken of his ravens. However, one day I was privileged to catch a glimpse of the birds, and I remember causing a mild sensation by rushing into the drawing-room where several members of the family were sitting, and crying out excitedly, 'I say! I've just seen Grandmother's tits!'

Lady Bourchier spent a good deal of her time in paying minatory visits to the sick and the poor. She would set out on these charitable raids in a small pony-chaise which she used to drive herself, armed with soup and propaganda. The rest of the day she passed in meditation in her grim little study overlooking the moat. There was always an immense pile of cheap, ill-bound Bibles on the table and these she would give away whenever she got a chance. 'Let me see, child, have I given you a Bible?' 'Yes, Grandmother,' one would hastily reply. But you never managed to get out of the room without having one of them thrust into your hand. Disposing of a bible was no easy matter. It would, of course, be sacrilegious to burn it. If deliberately left behind or lost it would invariably be returned because she always took the precaution of writing one's name and address on the title-page. I remember once when I dropped one of them into the moat being horrified to find that it refused to sink and continued to bob up and down on the surface like a life-buoy. Even this contingency, I felt, must have been foreseen by my grandmother and in consequence she had had it lined with cork.

Before I take leave of Stackwell and its grim châtelaine I must speak of the dreary rite that took place twice a day and was known as Family Prayers. I imagine that in 1930 there are very few households where this practice still lingers. In those days it was customary in nearly every home. But at Stackwell, family prayers took on a peculiarly drastic form and the institution seemed to be resented equally by the family and by the servants. I remember, as a child, being impressed by the annoyance and ill-feeling it caused among the domestics, who were obliged to quit whatever work they were engaged upon, dress themselves in tidy clothes and troop into the dining-room in order to sit upon hard benches for twenty minutes or more, listening to my grandmother declaiming scriptural exhortations in a voice that seemed to hold out very little hope of salvation for the lower classes.

Samuel Butler, in *The Way of All Flesh*, likens the family prayers of the Pontifex household to a swarm of bees he saw fruitlessly attacking the painted bunches of flowers on the wall-paper, 'so many of the associated ideas present but the main idea hopelessly lacking.' Of the family prayers at Stackwell one could not even say that there was a question of associated ideas. The ceremony appeared to be devised solely for my grandmother's benefit. It was a sort of daily rite to emphasise her own intimacy with God at the expense of her audience.

I think that my grandmother and I were the only two people who got any real pleasure out of the Stackwell family prayers, but for vastly different reasons. I have always taken an almost intoxicating delight in 'perilous laughter,' that is to say laughter which, either from good manners or fear, has to be controlled at all costs. The kind of laughter which, on solemn occasions or in the presence of the great, sometimes wells up within one with such violence that the human frame is nearly shattered in the course of its suppression. The vision of that grave row of domestics sitting bolt upright on the benches opposite to me was irresistible. I used to try to disturb their deadly seriousness by making surreptitious grimaces at them, and on one occasion I scored a memorable triumph by laying on the place occupied by the butler a notice bearing the words 'Stand for one donkey.' This masterpiece of humour was successful in producing an explosion of muffled snorts, and one of the footmen was obliged to leave the room with his handkerchief to his face.

Towards the end of her life my grandmother's reading of family prayers developed into a sort of macabre farce. With the gradual failing of her intellect, the collects and lessons became more and more seasoned with spoonerisms and every form of ludicrous mistake. I remember her starting off one morning with the alarming request, 'Oh, Lord, bear down upon us from on high!' and on another occasion she got horribly mixed up in the prayer in which the words 'true joys' occur, and kept on referring to 'Jew's toys.' But it was really more pathetic than funny. Poor Lady Bourchier! What a dreary, unprofitable existence! If only her religion had proved some sort of consolation to her instead of merely serving to fill her soul with bitterness. How different were my two grandmothers! The one brimming over with the milk of human kindness, the other soured by the vinegar and gall of a cramped Protestant intolerance.

V

My Parents

Fox-hunting was the dominant interest in my mother's life. Horsemanship was the one thing she excelled in. She came of a hunting family. Her brothers and sisters were crazy about fox-hunting. Aunt Flora, though practically a cripple, took a passionate interest in it, and I think her inability to follow the hounds was an even greater sorrow to her than not being able to wear her lovely dresses at parties. Even the hidebound Cousin Emily, with her dislike of active enjoyment, would never have dared to cast aspersions on fox-hunting. That was the one sport she would never have ventured to spoil. I think that if my mother had been asked, at my christening, by a benevolent Fairy, 'With what gifts shall I endow your child? Shall he be a distinguished politician, a great writer, an eminent composer, a painter of renown or a good rider?' there is no doubt as to what her answer would have been.

My mother's outlook on life was such as one might expect to find in any member of a well-to-do mid-Victorian county family. In spite of a certain amount of rivalry and friction she believed very firmly in the sanctity of family ties. She was a little ostentatiously devoted to all the other members of her clan. 'Blood is thicker than water' was a phrase that was continually on her lips, until my father put a stop to it by remarking that it was not so thick as the water in the moat at Stackwell.

She had been brought up in luxurious surroundings by parents who were kind and easy-going, ready at all times to indulge their children in any reasonable pleasure. My mother and her brothers and sisters were not, in any case, very difficult children to deal with. Well-behaved, devoid of any excessive fantasy or eccentricity, they had a wholesome respect for the commandment which exhorts us to honour our fathers and mothers.

They used to spend most of the year at Arley, pursuing their rural sports, hunting, shooting and fishing. Golf had not yet come into vogue. Every summer the whole family moved, rather reluctantly, to London for the season. My grandfather's house in Belgrave Square was, in atmosphere if not in style, an almost exact replica of Arley. It had the same air of solid, Victorian comfort. The rooms were large and well-proportioned, and from the windows one saw nothing but the tall trees in the square. One might have been in the country. Belgrave Square, in those days, was not the vortex of traffic it is now. The aristocratic silence was only disturbed by the occasional passing of an elegant victoria, a landau or a hansom, and the sound of high-stepping horses.

Once the Farmers embarked upon one of those very British excursions to the Continent. A sort of Grand Tour. It was a great adventure. They started off with a few days in Paris. Then they proceeded to Milan, Venice, Bologna, Florence and Rome. They were accompanied by a courier and a whole retinue of servants. I am not sure if sun-helmets and green veils formed part of their outfit; I should think it was quite likely. But although they brought back a lot of lovely souvenirs, alabaster models of the leaning tower of Pisa, goblets of Venetian glass, slabs of mosaic made of coloured marble representing birds, flowers and Italian peasants, which encumbered the tables at Arley for many years afterwards, I am not sure that they really enjoyed being abroad. It rained in Venice, Uncle Luke caught a sunstroke in Florence, my mother lost a bracelet at the opera in Milan, and my grandmother found a bug in her bed at Bologna. These mishaps were often referred to when anyone spoke too enthusiastically of foreign travel.

My mother, as a girl, seems to have had vague leanings towards romanticism. But it was a nice, well-trimmed, landscape-gardener's kind of romanticism. She preferred Walter Scott to Byron. But as soon as she was married, one of the first things she did was to go out and buy a copy of *Don Juan*, which she had previously been forbidden to read. Another thing she did on the same occasion was to walk down Bond Street unaccompanied. However, I fancy that both these acts were more in the nature of a gesture than a real craving for adventure.

Amongst some old papers I discovered the manuscript of a story my mother had once written. It was, I believe, her only literary effort. The story was about a young woman (obviously a self-portrait) who lived in a Gothic castle, surrounded by dogs and horses. It was not a very exciting story. Nothing very unusual seemed to have happened to the heroine. But then I fancy that there was nothing my mother would have disliked more than to have something very unusual happening to her. Although she displayed considerable courage on horseback, and I have no doubt that she would have been brave in a shipwreck or a railway accident, I am sure that in the ordinary course of life she never would have gone out of her way to look for trouble.

If she ever indulged in day-dreams about a future married state, it is probable that she pictured to herself an existence which should be more or less a continuation of the life she was then leading, and a husband who should be somewhat similar to Uncle Luke, whom she adored, or possibly a youthful edition of her father as she had first known him.

Her marriage, when it came, proved a bitter disillusion. At the time when my father became engaged to my mother, he was a lieutenant in the navy, and he was deeply in debt; a situation that was largely due to one of Lady Bourchier's many errors of education. For although she bullied and terrorised her children she accustomed them to a far more expensive standard of living than they would be able to afford later on; at the same time she refused to allow them to adopt any profession in which it might be possible for them to make money. The family was numerous, and the Bourchiers were not rich enough to give their children anything but a very small allowance. My father's was barely sufficient to pay for his annual consumption of cigars.

Far be it from me to cast aspersions on one of the partners who were kind enough to bring me into the world; nevertheless, I must confess that I have a shrewd suspicion that my grandfather's great wealth had some influence upon my father's choice. It is difficult to believe that he could ever have been seriously in love with my mother. But it is only fair to add that he did not seem to be the kind of man who could ever have been seriously in love with anyone.

Whatever hopes may have been raised, it soon became apparent that my mother would not be nearly as well off as had been expected. The allowance my grandfather gave her on her marriage was disappointingly small. However, he paid off all my father's debts.

It was some time before I came to understand the lack of affection that existed between my two parents. I thought at first that it was the normal relationship between husbands and wives. Later on, when I grew more sophisticated, I was able to diagnose more accurately the hopelessness of the case. My father was worldly, cynical, intolerant of any kind of inferiority, reserved and self-possessed. My mother was unworldly, naïve, impulsive and undecided, and in my father's presence she was always at her worst. It was, of course, just possible that such contrasting characteristics might have dovetailed. But, alas! they never did. My mother and father were like two cogwheels that for ever failed to engage.

My father was a curious, moody, rather brilliant creature. He was wrapped up in his career. He was essentially a man of action, and thought was distasteful to him except on purely practical matters. He had no sympathy with art and literature. My mother, in moments of irritation, used to say of him that he was a snob. It was undoubtedly true that he would only put himself out for people who could be of some use to him. But, on the other hand, he could be very charming when he wished, and he had a great many devoted friends.

As a child, I saw very little of my father. He was nearly always away at sea. My discrimination was acute enough to let me realise that, of my two parents, he was by far the more interesting. But association with and dependence on my mother led me to give her all my affection and to take her side rather than his.

I used to admire and enjoy my father's occasional flashes of wit. But I feared and disliked the long periods of silence and moodiness that intervened, and even his wit, within the family circle, was only exercised, as a rule, at the expense of my mother or her friends.

I remember one instance of this, which made me laugh very much at the time. My mother had rather a tendency to encourage bores. There was one friend of hers whom my father particularly disliked, a certain Colonel Stokes, a foolish old fellow who seemed to live in a perpetual state of righteous indignation. He used to write letters to the papers and he had a red, military face that looked as if it might go off bang at any moment. Colonel Stokes was always bubbling over with local gossip and, with the subtle instinct bores always seem to possess for the inapposite, he would invariably insist on recounting his grievances to my father. One day a dreadful thing happened. One of our neighbours, it appeared, had lost his temper and kicked his wife in public. This had upset the Colonel very much. 'I mean to say,' he protested. 'To kick your wife! And in public too! It's not cricket, is it?'

'No,' said my father, stifling a yawn; 'it seems to me more like football.'

I was always very much impressed by my father's elegance. He took a good deal of trouble about his clothes. He was a small, well-built man. He wore a neat, pointed beard and he walked with an imposing swagger. He had that easy superiority of manner which enables people to command respectful attention whether on a battleship or in a restaurant. Anyone meeting him for the first time might have mistaken him for a minor royalty.

It gradually became obvious to me that my father had a life quite of his own, about which my mother and I knew nothing, and that, when he was in our company, he was wearing, in a figurative sense, his old clothes; a deportmental négligé, a dishabille of manners which he no doubt felt would do well enough for home life.

He never attempted to take any active part in my education. Once, when my mother suggested that, for some offence or other, he should beat me, he merely said that he couldn't be bothered. I suppose I ought to have been grateful to him, but I remember feeling a little offended by his lack of interest.

It is said that a child's idea of God is often based on the characteristics of its male parent. If this is the case, it may perhaps account for the somewhat peculiar ideas I entertained, in my childhood, with regard to the Deity. I remember, on an occasion when I was misbehaving, my nurse said, 'If you're not careful, one of these days God will jump out from behind a cloud and catch you such a whack!' The threat was an alarming one, but I was not perturbed, and retorted, 'Nonsense! God doesn't care WHAT we do.'

VI

Introduction to Euterpe

Both in the earliest developments of my individual taste, as also in later life, the visual sense has always predominated. Even to music I was first attracted by its graphic symbolisation. The aural side of music held, at first, no charms for me. Cousin Emily's singing was not of the kind to inspire enthusiasm; it was, in fact, more calculated to put one off music for ever, and it was no doubt due to this fatal association that, once, when I was taken to a village concert, I created a violent disturbance and had to be removed.

One day, however, I unearthed in the library at Arley an old volume of 'Pieces for the Harp,' compositions which seemed to consist for the most part of arpeggios, glissandos and cadenzas. My imagination was strangely moved by the sight of these black waves of notes undulating across the pages, and, having collected all the blank sheets of paper I could find, I set to work to cover them with imitation cadenzas. At first I omitted staves and clefs, for it was chiefly the notes and the heavy triple and quadruple lines of the notation that stirred my fancy with their forms almost architectural in design. In the beginning there was only a faint connection between these symbols and any idea of tone, but after a while, helped no doubt by the romantic character of the titles, they came to suggest surging waves of melody and rhythm, an ideal music of which, as yet, I had had no conscious experience. About this time there came to stay at Arley a young woman who was a very fine pianist. She had the additional advantage of being of a prepossessing appearance. None of the household (with the possible exception of Emily) cared in the least about music, but, out of politeness no doubt, the visitor was asked to perform. Owing to the possibility of my making a hostile demonstration I was told to leave the room. This I did without protest, for as yet I felt no very definite association between the cadenzas I had copied out of the book of 'Pieces for the Harp' and the severe-looking grand piano in the drawing-room that was only played on by Emily. Nevertheless, the strains I heard through the half-open door compelled my attention. It was the Fantaisie Impromptu by Chopin. Here at last was the realisation in sound of the magic signs that I had so eagerly transcribed. The upward rush of semiquavers at the beginning of the piece, followed by a shower of golden rain, burst like a rocket in my imagination, and I remained spellbound beside the door.

When the performance was over and I was able to approach the pianist, I begged her to play once more that wonderful piece of music. She was, I fancy, struck by the contrast of my very real enthusiasm with the somewhat perfunctory appreciations of her grown-up audience and, as soon as the room was empty, she willingly complied. During the rest of her visit the unfortunate young woman had no peace. With childish persistence I never stopped imploring her to play over and over again this magic music, and, with infinite patience, she even managed to teach me to render, after a fashion, the first few bars of the Fantaisie Impromptu. She also played to me the works of other composers, but she obviously preferred those of Chopin; and so did I. The mere appearance of his name printed in thick black letters on the covers used to fill my heart with ecstasy.

In the billiard-room at Arley there was a small cottage piano, decrepit in appearance and uncertain in tone. Here, whenever I was able to escape from my nurse, I would spend my time playing over and over again the first few bars of the Fantaisie Impromptu, which I had learnt by heart, interspersed with a few extemporisations of my own.

The billiard-room was a vast and rather gloomy apartment, separated from the main body of the house by a long, narrow corridor. The only illumination came from a skylight, and the light, falling from above, created the impression of an aquarium. The centre of the room was occupied by the billiard-table, and over it six gas-jets with opaque green shades concentrated the light upon its surface. In the daytime, under the melancholy skylight, there was something peculiarly depressing about that empty expanse of green cloth and those green shades which seemed to annihilate even the greenest of thoughts.

As though to accentuate the grimness of the place, the walls, papered in dull magenta, bristled with antlers, wart-hogs, elephant

tusks, and over the fireplace there was a large trophy composed of
assegais and other barbarous weapons. On one side there was a
raised dais upon which the ladies could sit and watch the gentlemen
playing billiards.

Except when there happened to be a house-party, the billiard-
room was deserted, and when Cousin Emily was not indulging in
one of her musical soliloquies, I was allowed to strum undisturbed
'amid the encircling gloom' and the smell of stale tobacco smoke. So
violent was my enthusiasm for this newly-discovered pleasure that
it rendered me impervious to atmosphere; the billiard-room, with
its assegais and wart-hogs, was transformed into a paradise by the
presence of that discordant, moribund cottage piano.

This unexpected penchant for music was not entirely approved
of. My mother's attitude, when she saw me 'taking to music,' was
(to use a familiar phrase) a little like that of a hen when a duckling
she has hatched out takes to the water, an attitude of alarm,
tempered with pride. She was assured, however, by the rest of the
family that it was quite a harmless pursuit, so long as it took place
out of hearing, and that it would at any rate keep me from mischief
until the time came for me to apply myself seriously to sport. One
of my aunts even went so far as to provide me with a Music Primer,
a thick volume bound in scarlet cloth containing a very elementary
exposition of the theory of music, followed by a series of
progressive pieces beginning with a simplified Mozart minuet and
ending up, in a flourish of glory, with a mazurka of Chopin. The
local piano-tuner was called in to give me a few piano lessons. As
soon as I was able to read I started to work on the pieces at the end
of the Primer. With the impatience and self-confidence of extreme
youth I attacked the mazurka first of all and eventually succeeded in
playing it more or less correctly.

My growing proficiency began to excite comment. I was
sometimes made to show off my talents to visitors, which I did with
an almost excessive alacrity. The Chopin Mazurka was my *cheval
de bataille*. Unluckily it happened also to be one of Cousin Emily's
stock pieces, and every time I played it in public I used to notice
that she either left the room or else would remain seated with a look
of marked disapproval on her face. I imagine that, ultimately, she
must have spoken about it to my mother, for I was told not to play

the mazurka when Emily was present, and that it would be a good thing if I were to try and learn another piece.

VII

Althrey

When I was about six years old, my mother and I went to live in a small house called Althrey, on the borders of Shropshire and Wales. It was an unpretentious house and, after the spaciousness and grandeur of Arley, it seemed to me cramped and unattractive. To begin with, it had only two storeys. The fact that Arley had three gave rise in my mind to an odd sort of architectural snobbishness. I considered that a house with only two storeys was lacking in distinction. However, there were certain features in the surrounding scenery that had a consoling affinity with Arley. The actual situation of the house was pleasant enough. It stood on a grassy slope, facing a wide expanse of meadow-land, enclosed on three sides, like a stadium, by low, thickly-wooded slopes which reminded me of the terraces at Arley. In this arena the river Dee, a winding, picturesque stream, not unlike the Severn, made an almost complete circle, leaving in the same direction as that in which it entered, as though it had met with some geological opposition and was not going to insist. In the spring and early summer the meadows were spangled with every kind of wild flower – cowslip, fritillary, cuckoo-flower and bright marsh-marigold, that edition de luxe of the common buttercup, and in the woods and hedgerows there was a greater variety of bird-life than even Arley could provide. As a child, ornithology was one of my principal hobbies. At a very early age I became a bird bore.

On a distant hill there stood a grey, ivy-clad house, bearing the romantic name of Gwyn Hylerd. For years this house had been uninhabited. It was beginning to fall into ruin and had acquired a sort of Walter de la Mare atmosphere of eeriness. The serpentine course of the river placed it beyond the range of our daily walks and, despite the curiosity the place aroused in me, during the four or five years I lived at Althrey, I never managed to get more closely acquainted with it. It continued to retain for me all the charm of an unreached goal. 'Yarrow unvisited' is often the most satisfactory for the idealist, and, whenever I think of that particular landscape, the forlorn grey house on the distant hill always figures as a little Valhalla of mystery and romance

> 'We have a vision of our own;
> Ah, why should we undo it?'

At Althrey I led a rather solitary life. It is said that an only child has less fun but better fare. I know that, in my early youth, I suffered a good deal from boredom. I occasionally met other children and I had several small friends in the immediate neighbour-hood whom I saw fairly often, but it is in the daily routine of a child's life that solitude tells. For such important functions as getting up, going to bed, meals and lessons, I had no other company than my nurse and my mother.

Every afternoon after luncheon I used to have to rest. This entailed lying on a bed in a darkened room for about an hour. At this time of the day I always felt unusually wide awake, and I used to find this enforced suspension of my activities rather irksome. At the same time this hour of repose was not without its charm. I was never able to sleep, and on a summer afternoon it was pleasant to lie in idleness and think of all the lovely things one could do when the siesta was over and the hour of liberation came. A pause in which one could 'reculer pour mieux sauter.' But one afternoon my day-dreams were interrupted by an extraordinary phenomenon that took place on the ceiling. Everything that was happening outside the house within a certain radius appeared upon it, mirrored in vivid shadow-play. As I lay on my bed I could see, reproduced on the ceiling, the moving figures of servants, gardeners or grooms. A dog trotted across and a cat appeared and sat licking itself. I saw the carriage coming up to the door and my mother going out for a drive. It was a complete cinematographic representation in silhou-ette. The curtains had been drawn in a certain way which allowed a small shaft of light to penetrate, and the ceiling of the room had been converted into a cinema screen.

Alas! as soon as the curtains were touched the vision disappeared and I was never able to recapture it. Every afternoon I used to pull the curtains backwards and forwards hoping to produce the effect once more, but I was never able to get more than a blurred picture that resembled a cinema out of focus. The clarity of the first vision was a miracle that never repeated itself. It depended, I suppose, upon a very exact spacing of the curtains, the intensity of the light outside and other details of arrangement that ought to have been carried out with scientific precision. I was also a little nervous of experimenting too openly with the curtains lest I should be detected and made to divulge my discovery. I had an instinctive objection to grown-ups getting to know about any unusual form of pleasure for fear it should be promptly condemned as immoral and forbidden. One never knew.

Most of my time at Althrey was passed in the study of bird-life. My enthusiasm for ornithology had been originally aroused by the coloured illustrations of Gould's *British Birds*, huge volumes bound in dark green morocco which, as a special treat, I was sometimes allowed to take out of the library at Arley. For some obscure reason birds of the swallow tribe appealed to me most of all; especially sand-martins; and it was a source of sorrow to me that, although there was a sandy cliff in the neighbourhood which seemed pre-eminently suitable for the habitation of sand-martins, not one ever built its nest there. I should have liked to have been able to boast of having sand-martins' nests on the property. Finally, I was reduced to burrowing holes myself in the face of the cliff and pointing them out to people as the genuine article. I carried on this innocent deception until, one day, the son of one of our neighbours, a disagreeably spry youth with a highly technical knowledge of natural history, detected the imposture and proclaimed it from the housetops. It was a horrible humiliation. I never liked that boy since, and I am glad to say that he came to a bad end.

Ornithology had its pitfalls and false doctrines, just like any other branch of scientific research. In an apparently authoritative book on birds written by a clergyman (not, I may say, the Vicar of Selborne) I found it stated that the tree-creeper was of so sensitive and nervous a disposition that if one were to throw a stone at the tree upon which it was creeping, a few feet below it, it would fall to the ground senseless. I wasted a great deal of time stalking tree-creepers and throwing stones in the manner indicated, but each time the bird merely flew away and I was left feeling rather foolish. When I complained about it to my father, he said that the clerical naturalist who had recorded the phenomenon had very probably made a bad shot and hit the bird itself. Plausible as this explanation seemed to be, my faith both in clergymen and in the written word was severely shaken. The first seeds of scepticism were sown in my heart. In the same book I read that the capercailzie, during the mating season, became so engrossed in its love-song that you could steal up behind it while it was singing and hit it over the head with a bludgeon. This statement I never had the chance to verify. In any case the author, in contradiction to his calling, seems to have been rather bloodthirsty in his attitude towards the feathered tribe, and it would have been just as well had he been a little more animated with the spirit of St. Francis.

Those who say that their childhood was the happiest period of their lives must, one suspects, have been the victims of perpetual misfortune in later years. For there is no reason to suppose that the period of childhood is inevitably happier than any other. The only thing for which children are to be envied is their exuberant vitality. This is apt to be mistaken for happiness. For true happiness, however, there must be a certain degree of experience. The ordinary pleasures of childhood are similar to those of a dog when it is given its dinner or taken out for a walk, a behaviouristic, tail-wagging business, and, as for childhood being care-free, I know from my own experience, that black care can sit behind us even on our rocking-horses.

I was subject, as a child, to outbursts of temper so tumultuous, so unbridled as to cause those who witnessed them to expect at any moment an attack of apoplexy. I often regret that I am unable any longer to lose my temper in so spectacular a fashion. I have noticed that people with a reputation for violent irascibility generally succeed in getting their own way, and it is not in the least necessary for outbreaks of bad temper to have the backing of superior physical strength. The wrath of the lamb is notoriously terrible and even the rabbit, when it stamps its foot, is alarming enough. A really good display of fury is always impressive; there is something mystical, something demonic in its quality. There is no doubt that, during my early childhood, the violence of my temper was very useful in preserving me from punishment. It certainly did so on the occasion of my first and only experience of corporal chastisement.

This took place when I threw my mother's spaniel out of the window. Let me hasten to assure dog-lovers that this action was not inspired by innate cruelty or even by a hatred for dogs in general. It was due, rather, to a false association of ideas, an erroneous form of reasoning to which the human mind is particularly prone. I had heard somebody say that if you threw a dog into water it would instinctively swim. Reflection upon this biological fact led me to wonder if a dog, when thrown into the air, would also instinctively fly. Happening to see my mother's spaniel lying near an open window on the first floor, I felt that here was a good opportunity to make the experiment. It was a fat dog, and I had some difficulty in lifting it up on to the window-sill. After giving it an encouraging pat, I pushed it off. I watched the unfortunate animal gyrating in the air, its long ringleted ears and tail spread out by centrifugal force. (Incidentally it bore a strong resemblance to Elizabeth Barrett Browning.) But it appeared to be making no effort whatever to fly.

My mother was excusably infuriated by what appeared to be an act of wanton cruelty (although the animal had fallen unscathed into a lilac bush) and I failed to convince her of the scientific aspect of the experiment. She made up her mind to cross the educational Rubicon and to give me my first thrashing. This was the occasion on which she appealed in vain to my father. By the time she had selected a convenient implement (which happened to be a bedroom slipper) I fancy her resolution had already weakened. She set about it in a half-hearted fashion. Nevertheless, the first blow acted upon me as a spark in a powder magazine. With empurpled face, foaming at the mouth, I wrested the slipper from her hand and began belabouring her throat and bosom with such violence that she ended by flying in terror from the room.

Flagellation having proved a failure, other methods of correction were attempted. Returning, one day, from a picnic, I made myself very objectionable and was put out of the pony-cart and compelled to run behind it. Whereupon I gave vent to an access of fury so appalling, both to the eyes and to the ears, that the cart was promptly stopped and I had to be taken in again. When another offence was punished by confinement in a dark cupboard, I retaliated by locking up all the water-closets and throwing the keys into a pond. As there happened to be visitors staying in the house at the time, the confusion and discomfort caused in the household can be easily imagined. The only corrections that had any real effect upon me were those of a moral nature. Curtailments of liberty or of food I merely regarded as strictly personal disputes between myself and my nurse or my mother. When, however, I was 'sent to Coventry,' when the servants declined to speak to me, when my mother refused to 'kiss me good-night,' the fact that I had offended against the rules of order and decency was brought home to me far more acutely, and I was made to feel that I was up against the forces of convention and public opinion that keep the ordinary citizen in his proper place.

VIII

Mother and Child

Reflection on the subject of parental affection has led me to the cynical conclusion that the love of parents for their children is, more often than not, heavily alloyed with unconscious egoism. It is the secret wish of most parents that their offspring should grow up into replicas of themselves and carry on their own ideals to a higher state of perfection. At the same time they would probably be surprised and offended if they were to find them doing it too successfully.

Parents, as a rule, find a certain difficulty in living down the fact that they once had a greater knowledge of the world than their children. And, even if they continue to retain an intellectual predominance, they are apt to forget that their advice has, in many cases, become less valuable through conditions being no longer quite the same. Thus it comes about that it is not always the children who are hostages to fortune.

A really satisfactory relationship is only possible in cases where children and parents are equally intelligent (or equally stupid) and have more or less the same tastes. If you do not enjoy this happy condition, the safest course is to dissociate yourself as much as possible from your children, to maintain a benevolent aloofness, and to leave them to find salvation as best they may. You will then be in a stronger position when disasters occur. You will have the pleasure of being able to say, 'There, you see! We let you have your own way, and look what has come of it!'

In the education of children, as in many other matters, the wisest maxim is 'Surtout point de zèle.' It was certainly the one that governed my own father's attitude towards my own upbringing. Of course, owing to his profession, he was a good deal away from home. But in the brief intervals of his return I never remember his taking anything beyond a very mild interest in my mental or physical development. Consequently the task of my early training devolved upon my mother.

The keystone of my mother's character was an artless simplicity. She was devoid of any kind of affectation. She was one of the most natural people I have ever known. In her speech she was uncalculating and spontaneous. Like most of her generation she never attempted to analyse her motives. She had very little knowledge of the world and little psychological judgment. She had a vacillating nature, and she was for ever changing her mind. But beneath this shifting surface there was a solid bedrock of all the traditional ideas and conventions she had absorbed in her youth, ideas she never questioned and which she deliberately refused to put to the test of reality.

In this my mother was typical of her class and her period. A certain rigidity of mind is one of the things that particularly distinguished her generation. Nowadays people are more willing, sometimes even too willing, to indulge in experiment. To take a trivial example (which, however, can be taken as symbolical of wider issues), my mother had been brought up to believe that reading in bed was bad for the eyes. Consequently in her house there were never any lights beside the beds. In order to read one was obliged to erect a little altar of candles on the *table de nuit*.

In literature and art my mother's tastes were conventional but at

the same time catholic. She admired indiscriminately Keats and
Longfellow, Jane Austen and Marie Corelli. Paintings by Leader
and Luke Fildes gave her the same emotions as those by Raphael
and Titian. In the drawing-room at Althrey there hung a copy of a
Raphael Madonna bought by her during the famous Italian tour,
and two Siennese primitives given her as a wedding present. There
was also a photogravure of a picture called 'The Soul's Awakening,'
showing the effect the reading of a religious book can have on a nice
young girl. The picture represented a young woman holding a book
in her hand which may have been the Bible, the Prayer Book or St.
Thomas à Kempis. She was obviously very much struck by some
passage in it and was raising her eyes to heaven and looking as if
butter wouldn't melt in her mouth. There was another engraving of
a young lady seated at an organ. It was called 'The Lost Chord,' and
one felt that it was just as well that she had lost it. There was also an
equestrian portrait of the Empress of Austria jumping a fence with
the greatest imaginable elegance.

My mother's taste in furniture and decoration was characterised
by the same catholic insouciance. The house contained a bewilder-
ing jumble of good and bad. Oriental fretwork and rather crude
specimens of late Victorian furniture stood side by side with
Chippendale and Sheraton. My mother's taste was also influenced
by sentiment, and she often grew attached to objects that were
entirely lacking in artistic value just because they happened to have
been given to her by people she liked. Notwithstanding certain
regrettable lapses of judgment, there was an inner harmony of her
soul that reflected itself in the arrangement of her home. In the
drawing-room at Althrey there prevailed so delightful an atmosphere of peace and content that people would exclaim upon entering
it for the first time, 'What a charming room!'

My mother had, in spite of her diffident nature, a very good
opinion of her own judgment. She had been brought up in
conditions of complete unworldliness and had been accustomed to
depend on others. When, after her marriage, she was obliged to
manage for herself and discovered that she was able to do so more
or less successfully, she began to take a rather exaggerated pride in
her efficiency. She knew that she rode well and that she looked well
on horseback. For this she had some justification. But she was also

convinced that her taste was impeccable and that her opinions on life were infallible.

My father, also, was convinced of the infallibility of his own judgment. His outlook, however, was a vastly different one from that of my mother. He was apt to scoff at all the dogmas my mother held most sacred, such as the superiority of simple faith over Norman blood, of kind hearts over coronets. My mother's lack of dialectic skill often set her at a disadvantage. With a single caustic phrase my father would demolish my mother's humble but soundly constructed philosophies.

This led her to entrench herself more and more in her inward sense of right. She grew to distrust clever and fashionable people. She preferred reigning in a hell of mediocrities to serving in a heaven populated by the élite. For, in spite of the intellectual subordination and the constant humiliations my father both consciously and unconsciously enforced upon her, there lay concealed within her a desire to dominate, and if my father had happened to be a man of weak character he would probably have been subjected to a certain amount of bullying.

My mother was almost entirely devoid of that questionable asset, a sense of humour. Comedy and tragedy were, for her, two completely separate things. That the two Muses walked, at times, arm-in-arm, she absolutely refused to admit. Nevertheless, she often expressed her views in a way that was distinctly humorous, although she herself was quite unconscious of the fact. And although she was unable to detect humour in herself or in others she never minded being laughed at. When her ingenuous remarks were greeted with uproarious laughter, she was often rather surprised, but never in the least offended or abashed. And she would remark quite complacently, 'People are always telling me I am so amusing.'

My mother was very fond of dogs. There were four of them at Althrey. A spaniel (who has already figured in these pages), a collie, a fox-terrier and a bloodhound. The collie's pedigree was far from distinguished but he had perfect manners. The fox-terrier possessed the longest ears I have ever seen growing on any dog. The mild, dignified bloodhound, with rugged face and bloodshot eyes, would sit and stare at one with such an air of reproach that, after a time, one began to feel that one must have done something frightfully unkind.

Dogs that are much in the company of their owners often end by acquiring a similarity of temperament. By a kind of telepathic transfusion the characteristics of their masters are transmitted to them. The dogs of hearty people have a tendency to grow hearty, the dogs of lethargic people to spend most of their time sleeping, the dogs of fierce people to bark and bite.

The dogs at Althrey, although of widely different breeds, had, all four of them, many of my mother's distinguishing characteristics. They were loyal. They only cared for my mother and hardly took any notice of the other members of the household. They formed certain definite habits from which they never departed. They were upset by any novelty. They were obedient, but at the same time rather independent. They often seemed unable to make up their minds and would hesitate about such actions as entering a room or going upstairs. They were serious dogs. They had no sense of humour. They were always going off into the woods to hunt but they never got lost.

Taking all things into consideration, I should say my life at Althrey was pleasant enough. My mother and I were constantly together. Every day we used to go for long rambles through the fields, or by the river side, or else we would drive about the lanes in a pony-cart. Sometimes my mother would allow me to help her when she was gardening. My help consisted, for the most part, in destroying valuable flowers or in planting weeds with great care in conspicuous places. In return, she would take an active but not very expert interest in my ornithological studies. Indeed her participation in this latter pursuit often resulted in serious dissensions. I once accused her of having caused a golden-crested wren to desert its nest, and there was one altercation that lasted for several weeks, as to whether a bird we had seen in the distance was a cuckoo or a sparrow-hawk. However, notwithstanding these occasional disputes, we were very happy in one another's company.

On the subject of riding lessons and horsemanship in general our harmonious relationship was in far greater danger of being marred. Here an insidious undercurrent of mutual grievances aggravated the essential divergence between my mother's character and my own. It was her ambition that I should excel in horsemanship and be a credit to the family tradition. Consequently she was over-anxious, and my early training in the art of riding was mismanaged through excess of zeal.

I am glad to say that I am singularly free from complexes and repressions and, if I have any at all, they are assuredly connected with my early experiences on horseback. I was made to begin riding almost as soon as I could walk. I fell off my pony more often than not, and as I was generally laughed at when I did so, the combined effects of fear and humiliation inspired me with a distaste for riding which the equally potent dread of derision obliged me to dissimulate. I never ventured to dispute the point of view that to ride well was the main object of life; that to be a bad rider meant that one could never hope to attain to any measure of success or popularity. All my cousins and most of my small friends seemed to have inherited sporting tastes, and in this respect I was the one black sheep of the family.

IX

Nesta

My mother was particularly anxious for me to make friends with other children in the neighbourhood who had sporting proclivities. One or two of the little playmates who were thrust upon me I actively disliked. The most objectionable of them all was a little girl called Nesta, the daughter of an amateur horse-coper. She was what is known as a tom-boy. She was a braggart and a swashbuckler and, unfortunately, in her case boastfulness was supported by facts. She was as strong as an ox, she rode beautifully and she could climb trees in a way that was both efficient and ostentatious. She patronised me with contemptuous arrogance. She was for ever telling me that I was a 'muff' and that I ought to have been a little girl, to which I would reply, 'If I had to be one like you, thank Heavens I'm not.'

Amongst my toys there was a very lifelike horse equipped with real harness and a detachable tail. Nesta had among hers a large doll which could be dressed and undressed. It also had articulated joints and it could open and shut its eyes. One day, in a spirit of mockery, she suggested that we should exchange the horse and the doll. I eagerly assented, and the next time I went to see her I took the horse with me and brought back the doll. This created a violent scandal at home. My mother was very much upset. She intimated to me that it was a terrible mortification for a mother to have a little boy who preferred dolls to horses. She continued for some time afterwards to comment on the fact in scathing terms in the presence of visitors. Nesta was of course delighted. It was just the effect she had hoped to produce.

A little later, however, I did manage to get even with her, though I am obliged to confess that the manner of doing so was due not so much to my own ingenuity or bravery as to the sheeplike behaviour of my pony and the consequence of equine sex-appeal.

In one of the paddocks adjoining the house where Nesta lived there was a miniature hippodrome consisting of a series of fences and a small water-jump. One day, after I had been out riding with Nesta and some other small friends, she took us to the paddock in order to treat us to an exhibition of her skill in jumping. I had a feeling that, among other things, her performance was designed for my special humiliation.

After a preliminary harangue in which she laid stress on the difficulty some of the fences presented and the ease and efficiency with which she was going to jump them, she set off round the course. Whereupon my pony started to follow. In spite of all my efforts, I was unable to hold it back. Hard upon her pony's heels, and in mortal fear, I was carried over all the fences, including the water-jump. How I contrived not to fall off I cannot imagine.

Her equestrian act completed, Nesta turned with a triumphant air to take the applause of her audience and was stupefied to find me just behind her. I had spoilt her show. Luckily for me, nobody guessed the true explanation of my feat, and, shaken as I was by the awful ordeal I had just been through, I was nevertheless able to pull myself together and pass the matter off as though I had acted of my own free will.

As a result of this incident, Nesta's attitude towards me was slightly modified. But not for long. Her boastfulness, her contempt for those less proficient than herself were so essential a part of her character that she soon returned to her old ways, and continued to provoke me to sullen anger with her crude assumption of superiority, her taunts and jeers whenever I came to grief on horseback. And this happened more frequently than ever, for my mother, hearing of my involuntary jockey-act, the truth about which I naturally concealed from her, had a miniature steeplechase course set up, where I was obliged to practise jumping every day.

I grew to dislike riding more and more, but the idea of 'manliness' was constantly held up to me, and manfully I persevered.

Manliness was a virtue in which one had to be laboriously instructed. Like so many other virtues, it did not seem to correspond with the natural instincts of the human being. I came to the conclusion that 'manliness' was a very complicated ideal. Why, for instance, was it considered unmanly to cling to the pommels of the saddle when it seemed such a very obvious thing to do? Why was it manly to kill a rook or a rabbit or even to ill-treat a cat, while it was unmanly to hurt a dog or a horse, who were much larger and apparently better able to retaliate? Why were music and painting held to be effeminate when all the greatest painters and composers had been men? And how could Nesta, who was a girl, be more manly than I was? Why was she held up to me as an example? Was manliness an ideal for both sexes?

I gave up the attempt to unravel the various problems connected with manliness, and set out to try and do, within limits, what was expected of me. I began to understand that the lot of small boys resembled that of the heroes of the Light Brigade, 'Theirs not to reason why.'

My pony began to develop a tendency to friskiness, and kicked me off several times in succession. Nesta, hearing of this, said, 'Let me ride him. I will tame him for you.'

She rode him and was promptly kicked off herself. I was overjoyed. This was her second defeat in the War of Liberation. Her Waterloo was shortly to follow.

One day my mother invited two small boys to spend the afternoon with me. They were the sons of the Colonel Stokes whom my father so much disliked. Both were good riders, but in every other respect they were as uninteresting as their father. My mother had thrust them upon me with a view to encouraging my taste for sport. Nesta had also been invited, not without protests on my part. She arrived in a particularly aggressive mood. I felt that I was in a minority. The Stokes boys were definitely in her hemisphere rather than in mine. Despite the fact that they too were occasionally subjected to her taunts and overbearing patronage, they admired her and were fond of her, a circumstance that makes the part they played in the dénouement of this story all the more mysterious.

We had climbed up on to the top of a haystack. I rather diffidently suggested playing at smugglers. Nesta invariably turned down any game not suggested by herself. 'I don't care,' she said, 'about the sort of baby games you like.'

She was standing near the edge of the rick. I gave her a violent push. She fell on to the shaft of a cart below and cut her leg. She broke out into a torrent of abuse, at the same time pulling down her stocking to examine the wound. Then a very odd thing happened. For a moment the air seemed full of electricity. We were beset by that same primeval panic that brings about mass hysteria, pogroms or stampedes. I jumped down from the haystack, followed by the two boys. We all three fell upon Nesta simultaneously and, tearing away her clothes, each of us gave her a resounding smack on her bare bottom.

It all seemed to have happened in a flash, just as if we had been moved by some extraneous force, as though we were marionettes worked by a common impulse. After it was over, we relapsed once more into a normal state.

For a few minutes Nesta lay speechless on the ground. Then she burst into tears. Her three aggressors stood by, rather sheepishly watching her while she picked herself up and, still sobbing, made for the house.

Although the outrage had been committed with complete unanimity, the responsibility for it rested, I felt, upon my shoulders alone. Nesta was my guest and the incident had taken place at my home. The only thing to do, I thought, was to follow her indoors and to endeavour to repair matters as best I could. As we approached the house we saw her driving away.

My mother, fortunately, was out at the time. For this I was thankful, although it only meant trouble deferred. For the moment

I only had to face the reproaches and recriminations of my nurse.

We sat down to tea in silence. The two remaining guests seemed utterly dumbfounded. Their stolid faces were flushed and sullen. As I have said, they were more Nesta's friends than mine. But in the odd psychological turmoil that had just taken place, it seemed as though the rage Nesta had provoked in me had been so violent that it burst out and overflowed through telepathic channels, compelling the two boys to act almost automatically, as if under the influence of some sort of hypnotic suggestion. Or it may have been that, subconsciously, they resented Nesta's domination as much as I did, and her momentary abasement aroused some primitive instinct of revolt and savagery.

I was ashamed of myself. I was suffering from a guilty conscience. None the less I now hated Nesta more than ever, after what had happened. I hated her for having caused me to behave like a cad.

The issue had been of too complicated a nature to clear the air. My emotional tension found relief at last in a hysterical outbreak. I laid my head on the table and gave vent to peals of shrill laughter, unchecked by the expression of complete bewilderment on the sheeplike faces of the Stokes boys, and by my nurse's horrified interjections of 'For shame!' 'How can you?' and 'Well, I never!' Finally, I flung myself on a sofa, and the laughter gave place to a most lamentable howling, while the two boys were hurried away.

When my mother returned and was told of the events of this agitated afternoon, to my surprise she received the news with unexpected placidity. The ways of grown-ups were ever unaccountable! Beyond impressing me with the fact that one should never, under any circumstances, strike a woman, she did not seem to attach any very serious importance to my misconduct. She even remarked, 'Well, I hope it will be a lesson to her not to be so bumptious.' My mother's complacency on this occasion may have been in some measure due to the fact that Nesta's father had, a few days before, succeeded in selling her a very unsatisfactory horse.

At all events, I had contrived to get Nesta out of my life for good. She never came over to Althrey again, and whenever I saw her at children's parties she always looked the other way. Once at the dancing class I came face to face with her in a passage. I put out my tongue at her (it seemed the thing to do) and she went off muttering, 'Nasty cowardly little muff!'

Soon afterwards Nesta's parents left the neighbourhood, and I never saw her or heard of her again.

X

Neighbours

At Althrey we had a great many neighbours. The countryside was dotted with 'gentlemen's houses' and an occasional 'stately home.' The occupants were just what one might have expected them to be; the men hunted and shot, the women hunted, gossiped and played croquet. A visit to London was, for most of them, a hectic interlude in their peaceful rural lives, and it generally coincided with some such event as the opening of the Royal Academy or the Eton and Harrow match.

I was, in those days, too young to be able to extract much pleasure from the foibles and eccentricities of mankind; however, the characteristics of some of the people I used to know remain vividly impressed on my memory.

About four miles away there lived an elderly lady, Mrs Lafontaine, and her companion, Miss Goby. They were devoted to children, and they seemed to have taken a particular fancy to me. I was often invited to go over and spend the afternoon with them.

The tastes of these ladies were the reverse of sporting, but my mother allowed, and encouraged me to go and see them whenever they asked me. Mrs Lafontaine had a charming house and she was very rich. Even the most high-minded parents may be allowed to have worldly ambitions for their children, and Mrs Lafontaine had no heirs. (However, I may say at once that nothing came of it. When Mrs Lafontaine died, most of her money went to charities and the remainder to Miss Goby.)

At that time I had never been abroad and Mrs Lafontaine represented for me the glamour of foreign travel. Each year she and Miss Goby went for a tour on the Continent. They were enthusiastic water-colour artists, and they always brought back portfolios full of sketches of France, Italy or Switzerland, executed with a skilful combination of accuracy and romance.

Mrs Lafontaine and her companion were the apotheosis of a certain type of Englishwoman still happily to be met with on the Continent. Both of them had the slightly prominent teeth of the traditional 'fille d'Albion.' Their high fringes in the Queen Alexandra style were crowned with hats perched at a slanting angle which made them look as though they were just about to loop the loop. The gestures of the two ladies were brisk and decided, their voices rather loud and authoritative. One could visualise them moving through foreign crowds, oblivious of mockery, wholly concentrated on the enjoyment of 'being abroad.'

For them the Continent was still the Continent of the eighteenth-century Grand Tour, with a touch of Mark Twain's 'Innocents Abroad.' Their Germany was still the Germany of Goethe, their France was the France of the first English settlers on the Riviera, their Switzerland, devoid of Sanatoriums and Winter Sports, the Switzerland of William Tell, edelweiss and the Merry Swiss Boy.

Mrs Lafontaine's house was called Rose Hill. It stood, as its name implied, on a hill, and its trellised porches were festooned with roses. The park descended in a gentle slope to the river Dee, and the banks of the river were thick with chestnut trees and larches. In the summer the two ladies would often take me with them to picnic by the river side. We would drive down across the grass in a pony-chaise, followed by a footman in another cart laden with a large hamper, a tea-kettle and sketching appliances.

The pictures they made of the neighbourhood had the same romantic qualities as the ones they painted abroad, and Rose Hill came to figure more and more in my imagination as a foretaste of the continental world I so longed to know.

My mother was a little apt to censure Mrs Lafontaine's exaggerated partiality for everything foreign. A very pronounced Italian atmosphere prevailed at Rose Hill. The rooms were full of mosaic cabinets, bright striped fabrics from Naples and Sorrento, inlaid wooden boxes, painted Venetian cupboards, chandeliers and goblets of Murano glass. In the hall there was a huge stone fire-place transported from Bologna. Even the food was Italian, and there were risottos, macaroni and, a thing I especially delighted in, little packets of raisins folded up in vine leaves and tasting like wedding cake.

Mrs Lafontaine was a great authority on Italian literature, and once when my mother gave a 'book tea' (a rather dreary entertainment in which everyone had to come dressed as the title of a well-known novel), the two ladies of Rose Hill appeared, the one wearing a top hat, the other a veil, as 'I promessi sposi.' In a more sophisticated neighbourhood this entrée might possibly have occasioned ribald comment and given birth to sinister rumours. As it was, it merely baffled everyone, and Mrs Lafontaine was obliged to disclose what they were supposed to represent.

Both the ladies were intensely young at heart. Mrs Lafontaine appeared to be growing younger every day. She adored giving children's parties, and surrounding herself with very young people. In their midst she seemed to become herself a child. Miss Goby, in order to ingratiate herself with her patroness, or perhaps with a view to keeping her in countenance, would enter with an even greater zest into the infantile revels. I remember, on one occasion, in a hayfield, Miss Goby, throwing decorum to the winds, rushed forward and tried to stand on her head in a haycock. It was due to this incident that I first got an inkling that the two ladies were slightly ludicrous.

As I grew older I grew, at the same time, to be a little ashamed of my friendship with Mrs Lafontaine. I discovered that most of my contemporaries looked upon her and Miss Goby as figures of fun. In the transition from childhood to adolescence, independence of spirit is liable to diminish. My judgment of people and things became more and more influenced by public opinion. The memory of the happy afternoons I had spent at Rose Hill in the company of the two ladies, the pleasant picnics by the river, the excitement of examining a new batch of continental landscapes, the delicious Italian food, all this was temporarily obliterated by a growing sense of the ridiculous which, in its immaturity, made me self-conscious and afraid of being associated with anything or anybody generally considered to be absurd. A sense of humour, to be of any real value to its possessor, must be untrammelled by any kind of conventional bias, and I was, at that time, very far from having attained to the enlightened state in which it is possible to combine mockery with affection, and to disentangle the sublime from the ridiculous. Not that there was very much that was sublime about the ladies of Rose Hill, but there was a good deal that was lovable and, from my own point of view, particularly stimulating.

Now that they are dead and gone, the record of all the happy hours I spent in their company, of all they represented for me at a certain period of my childhood, of their kindness, of their absurdity and of my ingratitude, remains in my memory as an aftermath tinged with melancholy and regret.

Another neighbour of ours who stood out from the background of more ordinary county folk was Mr Vivian Pratt.

Distantly related to a ducal family, he enjoyed a greater consideration in the county than he might otherwise have done. Mr Vivian Pratt was considered eccentric, but nothing more. In those days people were more naïve with regard to certain aspects of life than they are now. It was said of him that he had odd mannerisms, that he was inclined to be effeminate, and there criticism ceased. Mr Vivian Pratt had a mincingly ingratiating voice and he moved with an undulating gait. When walking through a room he looked as though he were trying to avoid imaginary chairs and tables, and he would describe elaborate circles with the middle portion of his body. His clothes had a fashion-plate neatness and always seemed a little inappropriate to the country, but when he appeared on horseback nobody could present a more dapper picture of horsiness. His get-up, however, like that of Miss Lucy Glitters when she appeared in the hunting-field, looked as if it could not have weathered even the mildest of rain-storms.

His manners were excessive in their courtliness and he used to annoy my mother by addressing her as 'Dear lady.' His conversational repertoire consisted of a number of more or less amusing anecdotes relating to London society or to the theatrical world. He was inclined to be sententious and epigrammatic.

I gathered that my father did not care very much for Mr Pratt, and certainly his behaviour, when Mr Pratt was present, and his comments after he had left, seemed to suggest that he understood him better than my mother appeared to do. I remember one day Mr

Pratt saying, 'I often think that the best things in life are behind us.' My mother was inclined to agree with the sentiment and was a little puzzled when my father broke into a malignant guffaw of laughter which seemed hardly justified by the innocent nature of the remark.

I had an impression that Mr Pratt was not very interested in children. When he came to the house my presence appeared to embarrass him and he seemed almost studiously to avoid noticing me. But once, when I rode over to take him a note from my mother, he made himself unexpectedly agreeable. He showed me his collection of jade and his orchid houses, and when I left he presented me with a magnificent cattleya. When I showed the orchid to my mother on my return the gift appeared to cause her an unaccountable irritation. She said it was a ridiculous thing to have given a child. It is possible that the incongruity of the gesture aroused some dim apprehension slumbering at the back of her unsophisticated mind. I was accompanied, when I paid this visit to Mr Pratt, by a rather good-looking groom, and I remember thinking that, after all, Mr Pratt must be a nice man as he seemed so amiable in his manner to servants.

After we left Althrey I lost sight of Mr Vivian Pratt for many years. During the last months of the war I met him again. He was working for the Red Cross in Paris. An officer in the same department told me that he had made himself extremely useful. However, he qualified his eulogy by adding, 'It's extraordinary what a lot of that sort there are in the Red Cross. I suppose it provides an opportunity for exploiting the "feminine touch."'

In contradiction to the generally expressed opinion that such people grow more repulsive with age, Mr Pratt, when I saw him again, seemed to have been decidedly improved by the patina of time. There were still unmistakable indications for the pathologist, but his voice had grown less mincing, his gait less undulating. The impression I had may, of course, have been due to the fact that he was wearing a uniform, which (as the term implies) has a tendency to minimise irregular characteristics; or possibly it was because I had grown more accustomed to a type which, in the intervening years, had come into its own.

XI

Educational

When I reached the age of seven my mother thought it would be a good idea to amplify my education by employing the services of the local curate.

Mr Allen was a meek and gentle young man. He wore his hair parted in the middle, and this, together with his beard and his general air of mildness, gave him a strong resemblance to the traditional portraits of Our Saviour. It was, I am sure, quite unintentional on his part, for he had so humble and unassuming a nature that he would never have dared. He was indeed so diffident and apologetic in his manner that I took him, at first, to be a perfect specimen of a nincompoop, and I remember saying to my mother, 'I am sure that I could love Jesus better if He were not so dreadfully like Mr Allen.'

However Mr Allen the man and Mr Allen the teacher were two separate individuals and, although I began by despising him as a man I came eventually to revere him as a teacher. In spite of his aggravating demureness, he possessed a real genius for instruction. He made his lessons so interesting that I used to look forward to them. Under his pleasantly persuasive tuition I even enjoyed Latin Grammar, which he encouraged me to look upon in the light of an acrostic or word game. I enjoyed it almost as much as I came to loathe it later on, when, at my preparatory school, it ceased to be a game (as did also games themselves) and was held up as a serious object in life, acquiring a definite moral value, so that a misconstruction of syntax came to be considered a more egregious offence than a misconstruction of the facts of life.

But even Mr Allen, for all his pedagogic charm, was unable to reconcile me to arithmetic. I had an active distaste for figures and the mere sight of the simplest addition sum filled my soul with nausea. When I read in one of my bird books that crows experienced difficulty in counting up to more than six I sympathised with them heartily, and, having previously rather disliked crows, I began to regard them with an almost sentimental interest.

Most children have an immense capacity for resisting information that does not appeal to them, and Mr Allen, like the family doctor, wisely followed the line of least resistance. Thus we skated lightly over mathematics and concentrated on other more agreeable subjects. I conceived a violent passion for Greek and Latin mythology, and Mr Allen was rash enough to lend me a small illustrated Mythological Dictionary. For months afterwards I would startle everyone I met with the most embarrassing questions about Leda and the Swan, the rape of Ganymede, the engendering of Minerva and all the more curious and scandalous episodes of the classical Mythology. Once, upon being shown a very well-furnished sow by its proud owners, I expatiated at length and with a wealth of detail upon the striking resemblance it bore to the many-breasted Diana of the Ephesians.

However, it must not be thought that I was an unduly prurient child. When I was hurried away from a cow that was in the throes of parturition I was not in the least curious to know what it was all about. Indeed I had a presentiment that it was going to be an unappetising spectacle. When children appear to have an unholy flair for pornography it is more often than not merely a puckish instinct for getting even with their elders by embarrassing them.

Mr Allen lived in the village which was about a quarter of a mile distant. His house was situated on the banks of the river, a pleasant little cottage, with trellised porch and diamond-paned windows, that looked as if it had been designed by Kate Greenaway. I used to walk in to my lessons every morning. At the end of two years Mr Allen left the neighbourhood and it was decided to entrust my further education to a professional.

I overheard a certain amount of deliberation as to whether the new governess should be English, French or German. For my own part I secretly hoped that she would be French. I had never been to France, but I had already conceived a very definite opinion about that country. It was based, as far as I can remember, upon conversational allusions to the 'proverbial gaiety' of Paris, a photograph of the Eiffel Tower and a gaily decorated box of sweets that had come, one Christmas, from Boissier. I also hoped that a Frenchwoman in our midst might possibly impart a touch of continental 'légèreté' into our rather dull provincial atmosphere.

The impious wish, however, was destined to be disappointed. In those days the three Rs, Russians, Radicals and Roman Catholics, inspired certain people with an alarm that verged on panic. My mother was assured that it would be most unwise, even criminal, to confide a little Protestant soul to a Papist. And there were equally cogent reasons (I forget what they were were) against employing a German. In the end, as a compromise, it was settled that the governess should be Swiss.

Mademoiselle Bock came from Geneva. She had a wooden, expressionless face that looked like one of the carved sheep one sees in Swiss toyshops. Her shape was suggestive of a chalet, and her hats, constructed for the most part of flannel and braid, completed the illusion by looking as though they were pinned down on to her head by heavy boulders. As for her conversation, it seemed to be regulated on the principle of a cuckoo-clock. At intervals she would emit sentences of varied lengths, but of an unvarying cheerful smugness.

I was frankly disappointed. Nevertheless, although there was nothing in either the character or the appearance of the new governess that could possibly capture a child's imagination, the mere novelty of having a governess was in itself sufficiently exciting; and for a time everything went well. Furthermore, Mademoiselle Bock's descriptions of her native land, despite their aridity, began to rekindle my desire to experience the joys of foreign travel. Dreams of an idealised Switzerland began to weave themselves in my brain, and in my imagination there formed itself a glowing vision of the land of edelweiss and cowbells. Even the scrunched-up appearance of the country on the map delighted me. Names such as Grindelwald, Finsteraarhorn, Pontresina, Interlaken filled me with ecstasy and I would repeat them to myself in a kind of litany.

Near the house there was a little valley. A stream ran through it and terminated in a pond. Out of this locality I created an imaginary Switzerland. The stream was the Rhône and the pond the lake of Geneva. The modest slopes on either side of its muddy waters were given the high-sounding names of Mont Blanc, the Dent du Midi and the Jungfrau. On the banks of the pond I determined the sites of Geneva, Lausanne, Vevey and Montreux. I engineered a waterfall and called it the Pisse Vache, after the famous cascade near Martigny. The frenzy of a demiurgic creation was upon me and I got a delirious enjoyment out of this country of my invention such as the real Switzerland has never been able to afford me.

Mademoiselle Bock's attitude, when I explained it all to her, was distinctly chilling. She appeared to take only the mildest interest in this evocation of her native land, and when I showed her with pride my greatest triumph of all, the Pisse Vache, she merely remarked, 'It is not a very nice name.'

I have subsequently learnt that the Swiss are apt to be a little over-sensitive about their country. It is possible that she may have thought that the whole thing was an elaborate insult. Perhaps, however, it would be more reasonable to attribute her attitude to the instinctive distrust that governesses and schoolmasters are wont to display towards any manifestations on the part of their pupils which do not happen to be included in their own categories of normal subjects for enthusiasm. Anyhow I was deeply wounded by her lack of interest and it was the beginning of the end of my friendly relationship with Mademoiselle Bock.

A few weeks later I had an attack of what I imagine to have been an early form of Weltschmerz. It was brought on, I remember, by my reading a book called *The Island Home*, the story of a remarkable group of boys and girls living on an island off the west coast of Scotland. They led an adventurous, heroic life, sailing on the sea, clambering among the cliffs, battling with eagles in their eyries and rescuing one another, in a world seemingly devoid of parents and governesses. How mean, how unsatisfying seemed, in comparison, my own humdrum existence in the company of my mother and my governess, with nothing more exciting to look forward to than the daily walk or drive! I began to conceive a violent distaste for Mademoiselle Bock's wooden countenance. I felt that it was an unutterable humiliation to be under her control.

The ebullition of my soul found an outlet in literature. I spent the whole of one afternoon in composing a wild Ossianic lament in which Mademoiselle Bock figured as a tyrant and an oppressor. I wrote it in French, for I thought that a foreign language would be a more suitable vehicle for such lofty invective. My command of the French language was, at that time, elementary in the extreme, and it must have been incredibly funny. I can only remember that the first sentence began with the words 'Ah que je suis malheureuse.'

As soon as I had completed the effusion, I fastened it with a drawing-pin to Mademoiselle Bock's desk. I saw myself in the rôle of Luther nailing the Theses to the church door at Wittenburg.

Instead of being annihilated, as I had hoped, by this savage indictment, she merely took the document to my mother and read it aloud to her with sarcastic comments.

Hostilities were now formally declared. I eagerly searched my geography book for some damaging fact about Mademoiselle Bock's native land. At the next geography lesson I opened my atlas at the map of Switzerland, and pointing to it derisively, cried, 'Switzerland is only a third-rate country. It has no coast-line!' I then proceeded to tear the map of Switzerland into small pieces and threw them in her face. Mademoiselle Bock retaliated by boxing my ears, and the lesson ended in sound and fury.

After a day or two of punishments and sulking, a *modus vivendi* was finally arrived at which continued until the unfortunate incident which led to Mademoiselle Bock's departure.

During the summer months, when the weather grew warm, I used to do my lessons in a little summer-house in the garden. Close at hand, concealed in a shrubbery, there was a rustic closet which Mademoiselle Bock, every morning, used to visit with clockwork regularity. The fact that she was the only person of the household to make use of it suggested to my mind a diabolical plan of revenge.

The gardener's son had a natural talent for carpentering and, with his assistance, I constructed a very ingenious booby-trap. By an intricate system of leverage we succeeded in so arranging matters that, when you sat down, a small board came up and hit you a terrific blow on the behind.

As a matter of fact the experience was more alarming than painful.

Next morning I anxiously awaited the moment for Mademoiselle Bock's customary retirement and, as soon as she had set out, I made my way swiftly through the bushes, crept up to the door and listened for the result. I was rewarded by hearing the sound of a dull whack followed by a startled cry. A few moments later Mademoiselle Bock emerged with a distraught countenance.

The practical joke had succeeded only too well and I was now a little alarmed at its possible consequences. There was just a chance, however, that the mishap might be attributed to accident or that Mademoiselle Bock's native prudery might restrain her from mentioning the occurrence. But, alas! the evidence that the seat had been tampered with was too obvious, and smarting Swiss buttocks overcame native prudery. The matter was reported to headquarters and the most horrible row ensued. My ingenuity was condemned in scathing terms. Mademoiselle Bock threw up her situation, declaring that she had not believed it possible that such a detestable child could exist, and it was then and there decided that it was high time for me to be sent to school.

XII

The First Day at School

My preconceptions of school life were based mainly on two books, *Tom Brown's School Days* and *Eric or Little by Little*; I did not, however, find the latter wholly convincing, and I suspected them both of being slightly out of date.

I was able, nevertheless, to construct an imaginary picture of school life in which I could see myself figuring to my own satisfaction. The scene in Tom Brown where the hero successfully defends 'little Arthur' against the bullies who tried to stop him saying his prayers had an especial appeal for me; not that I felt very deeply about prayers, but in this case they seemed as good a pretext for heroism as any other.

The school chosen for me was Elmley. My father and my uncles had been there and it was considered to be one of the best preparatory schools of the day. After the death of the Headmaster, Mr Gambril, Elmley began to go downhill and now it has ceased to exist as a school. When I went to visit the place some years ago with a view to refreshing ancient memories, I noticed a definite alteration in the atmosphere; there was a feeling of gaiety, of irresponsibility in the air that had been absent in the old days, and I was told that it had been converted into a lunatic asylum.

It was settled that I should start my school career with the Summer Term, and at the end of April my mother and I went up to spend a few days in London at my grandfather's house in Belgrave Square. On the eve of the day upon which I was to go to school I was taken to my first play, which was 'Charley's Aunt,' and the excitement of this novel experience distracted my thoughts from the ordeal that was to take place on the morrow.

But next morning I awoke with a sinking sensation of impending misfortune. Waking up in my comfortable bedroom, with the sun streaming in over the tall trees in the square, I was distraught with panic, and I experienced all the vain regret of one who has failed too late to realise when he was well off.

The early part of the morning was spent in a final round of shopping to complete the purchase of my school outfit. I remember having to try on a bowler hat. It was the first time I had ever worn this uncomfortable and slightly ridiculous form of headgear; at the moment it seemed to me to be an emblem of sorrow, almost a crown of thorns.

Elmley was about an hour's journey by train from London. It had been arranged that I should go down early in the day with my mother, so that I might become familiar with my new surroundings before the other boys arrived. The school was quite close to the station. It looked at first sight pleasant enough. A square Georgian house of grey stucco; in front of it a wide asphalt playing-ground enclosed by a low wall and flanked by constructions of more recent date, on one side a rather ugly chapel and on the other a conglomeration of outhouses, fives courts, offices and a swimming-bath. The path from the station led through the playing-fields. A tall row of elms ran parallel to the house, and on the farther side of it (which was really the front) a group of ilexes and conifers sheltered the house from the main road.

Apprehension must have reduced my personality and magnified external objects; for everything at Elmley appeared to me to be of immense size. The elm trees seemed gigantic, the house of Cyclopean dimensions and the playing-fields as vast as the savannahs. For years afterwards I continued to think of everything at Elmley as being over life-size, so that when I visited it again in recent years the scenery seemed to have considerably shrunk.

We were greeted by Mrs Gambril, the Headmaster's wife. Her round face with its rather bare expression and her sleek auburn hair dragged off the forehead reminded me forcibly of a horse-chestnut. She was dressed very fashionably, yet she had the unmistakable air of an 'official' woman, as it might be female warder or the superintendent of a workhouse. She had a sister, Miss Temple, who helped her to run the non-didactic departments of the school. Miss Temple was a replica of her sister, but with the subtle distinction of spinsterhood; she was slightly more angular and less suave.

Mr Gambril joined us at luncheon. His appearance was surprising. I had never in my life seen anyone quite so yellow. His skin was yellow, his hair was yellow and he had a small yellow moustache carefully waxed at the ends. I discovered later that he smoked cigarettes incessantly (indeed one never saw him without a cigarette in his mouth), and that was the cause of his yellowness. I suppose the yellow stains that one sometimes sees on the fingers of cigarette-smokers must have spread over his entire body. He certainly looked as though tobacco juice flowed in his veins, and whenever he grew angry there would be an additional rush of it to his face, which became a deep mahogany. He had very small light blue eyes that appeared all the more striking for being set in their complementary colour. He wore a grey frock-coat and one of those flat, elaborate satin ties folded like a table-napkin and fastened with a large diamond scarf-pin.

At luncheon that day nobody could have been more urbane. He was exercising the charm specially reserved for parents. He patted me on the head, smiled at me and said, 'We shall make a man of him.' (That dreadful 'manliness' again!)

So far it had not been very alarming; a polite and amiable host, two benevolent middle-aged ladies and a pleasant dining-room looking out on to a garden. One might have been visiting neighbours. I felt slightly reassured, and thought that I might perhaps be going to enjoy being at school.

This emotional respite lasted until my mother's departure. Then, as the train steamed out of the station, I was suddenly overcome by the sensation that it was bearing away from me not only my mother but the whole of that home life to which, in spite of a certain ennui and restlessness, I had become fondly attached, leaving me alone in a new and unsympathetic world.

Mr Gambril had accompanied us to the station. On the way back I noticed a distinct change in his manner. He was no longer the amiable friend of the family. An official chasm had opened between us. He seemed all of a sudden to have grown immensely large and I infinitesimally small. The personal note had vanished. He now spoke to me in a voice that might have been directed at any small boy.

On returning to the house he took me to his study, that grim chamber, the scene of many a future agony. My mind, from the stress of emotion, had become a hyper-sensitive retina upon which every detail stood out with an almost painful distinctness. The rows of solemn-looking dictionaries and primers on the book-shelves, the bust of an elderly gentleman of forbidding aspect on the mantelpiece (Mr Gambril Senior, the former Headmaster), and in a corner near the window an ominous group of canes and birches.

Mr Gambril selected a number of books from the shelves and handed them to me. 'These are the books you will require. Put them in your locker and don't lose them! You will be shown where your locker is. Lucy dear!' he called – Mrs Gambril appeared – 'take this boy and show him his locker.'

Mrs Gambril led me through a green baize door that separated the Headmaster's quarters from the rest of the school. She showed me the different classrooms, the huge Assembly Room that could accommodate the entire school (there were over a hundred boys in all) and the Lobby, a wide and rather dark passage running down the middle of the building and leading into the Assembly Room on one side and into the smaller classrooms on the other. At the end of the Lobby there was a large glass door opening on to the playground. My newly-acquired school books were deposited in my locker, including my other belongings and the beloved four volumes of *British Birds* with coloured illustrations, which my mother rather reluctantly had allowed me to take with me.

The barren appearance of the classrooms and the general aspect of the school furniture struck a chill in my heart. I felt as strange, as forlorn as if I had been visiting the mountains of the moon. Everything looked so uncomfortable, so hard and utilitarian, and the air was heavy with the cheerless smell of fresh paint and furniture polish.

In the playground outside I caught sight of two disconsolate figures. 'Those,' said Mrs Gambril, 'are the two other new boys, Arthur and Creeling.'

The name Arthur revived memories of *Tom Brown*. But at that moment I was very far from wishing to have to champion anyone. A 'little Arthur' would have only been an additional embarrassment.

Mrs Gambril left me in their company. Arthur was not in the least like his namesake. To begin with he was one of the ugliest little boys I had ever seen. His face looked as though it belonged to the vegetable rather than to the human anatomy. His features gave one the impression of being bruised and swollen, and his eyes were red with weeping. Creeling was better-looking, but he had a sanctimonious expression that repelled me. He looked like a miniature curate.

Upon seeing me they both made a visible effort to pull themselves together and to appear a little less despondent, but it was not very successful. I, myself, was hovering on the brink of tears.

Creeling, who was a little older than Arthur and myself, tried to assume a moral leadership. 'You must never,' he advised us, 'let other fellows find out the Christian names of your sisters.'

'I haven't any sisters,' I replied with some asperity. In spite of my woefully flagging spirits I resented his attitude of Mentor.

As Arthur appeared to be practically speechless, the conversation, such as it was, was carried on between Creeling and myself. Timidly and as though we felt we were trespassing, we visited the playing-fields, the cricket pavilion, the fives courts, the lavatories, the swimming bath, and Creeling made an unsuccessful attempt to get into the chapel.

'They have a service every day,' he remarked, 'and on Sundays three times.'

The prospect seemed to cheer him, but Arthur gulped and said

'How awful!' in a horror-stricken voice, and his face grew more swollen and bruised in appearance than ever.

After a time the other boys began to arrive. Creeling, Arthur and I clung together disconsolately in a corner in the Lobby. I prayed that we might remain unobserved for as long as possible. Hitherto the presence of my contemporaries at children's parties had never inspired me with the slightest feeling of shyness; the background of home life had given me a certain sense of security, and on such occasions there had always been a mother, a nurse or a governess in the offing. Now, however, I was bereft of these aids to confidence, and I knew that I would have to fend for myself.

It was not long before we were noticed. A group of boys from the far end of the Lobby bore down upon us with whoops and cries of 'New boys!' It was an awful moment; a moment of suspense such as explorers must go through on the appearance of an unknown savage tribe.

These cannibals, however, proved comparatively friendly. It is true there were one or two youths whose practice it was to kick new boys, but it was done with an absence of malice that made me realise that it was a formality rather than an act of hostility. The ordeal of being asked one's name was not so terrible after all, and I began to gather confidence.

I created a favourable impression by exhibiting my books of British birds. Next to being good at games a taste for natural history was highest in popular esteem; but I was not aware of this at the time, and I fear it was merely one of those impulses which sometimes tempt us to try and enhance our personality by reverting to our possessions. Anyhow the move was a successful one, and the mild popularity I acquired by offering to lend some of the volumes helped to carry me through supper, which would otherwise have depressed me with its long refectory tables covered with coarse linen, the plates and teacups of monumental solidity, the chunks of bread-and-butter and slices of stringy cold meat of a similar calibre and the over-sweetened tepid tea poured out of metal jugs, gulped down to the accompaniment of a deafening roar of conversation.

As soon as supper was over, a bell rang and we all trooped into the chapel. Mr Gambril made his appearance clad in a surplice. He was followed by the assistant masters. After a short address on the subject of the reassembling of school, to which I listened in a spirit of reverent attention, there followed prayers and a hymn. The lamplight, the music and that odd musty smell peculiar to English Protestant churches combined to work upon my feelings. My eyes filled with tears and everything became a blur.

In my dormitory there were seven or eight small boys of about the same age as myself. Apart from Creeling, Arthur and myself they were all second term boys and they all seemed to be suffering from home-sickness. From the other dormitories there came shouts of hilarity, but in ours depression reigned. After we had undressed and stowed away our clothes in wicker baskets under our beds, a manservant walked through the rooms ringing a bell, the signal for private devotions. Each boy knelt down by his bedside. (There was not going to be any 'little Arthur' nonsense about prayers.) Soon afterwards Mrs Gambril appeared, followed by the Matron, and said good-night to each of us in turn. This was a special act of kindness to new boys on the first evening and the ceremony was not repeated on subsequent nights. Finally, one of the assistant masters came in and turned out the gas.

Misery descended upon me with the darkness. For a long time I lay awake. So apparently did most of the other occupants of the dormitory, for the air was full of the sound of muffled sobbing.

Through a chink in the blinds I could see that there was a bright moonlight outside, and through the half-open window I could hear the nocturnal sounds of the country, the lowing of cattle in a neighbouring field, the cry of a night-bird, the whistle of a distant train (wending its way northwards perhaps, in the direction of Althrey), and from the garden below there came up a faint scent of lilac. Now that the turmoil of human contact had died away, all these things reminded me poignantly of my far-off home. My mother, the servants, the garden with its flowers and its birds, appeared to me like the sad ghosts of a past that was now gone for ever. I even thought regretfully of Mademoiselle Bock.

I remembered the four volumes of *British Birds* in my locker. These seemed now to constitute the only link with home life.

XIII

Sadistic Interlude

I suppose Elmley was a good school in its way. It was expensive. We were well educated (according to the average educational standard of English preparatory schools in those days). The food given us was of a quality to preclude any desire for over-indulgence. Games and religion were both compulsory. The Arts were discouraged. Care was taken of us when we were ill. The only really serious drawback to the school was the fact that the Headmaster happened to be a sadist.

Nobody will deny that the majority of small boys between the ages of nine and fourteen are horrid little beasts and deserve to be frightened and bullied. But I find it difficult to believe that it is necessary for them to be tortured and terrorised to the extent that we were tortured and terrorised by Mr Gambril.

When I say that Mr Gambril was a sadist I am perhaps laying myself open to the charge of inaccuracy. To compare him to the Marquis de Sade, it might be objected, would be doing an injustice to that wayward nobleman. Mr Gambril's cruelty was of a far more inhuman type. It was cruelty for cruelty's sake, pure unadulterated cruelty, and there were no extenuating circumstances of sexual aberration.

Mr Gambril had elevated the faculty for inspiring terror to a fine art. There was, to start with, something peculiarly blood-curdling in this potentiality for frightfulness being concealed beneath so dapper an exterior. Mr Gambril's spruce urbanity would, in a twinkling of an eye, be horribly transformed. It was though a neat-looking bantam's egg were suddenly to hatch forth a viper. The phenomenon (to which I have already referred) of the tobacco-juice rushing to his face, turning it from its habitual yellow to a deep mahogany, was in itself alarming enough. In addition to this, his small light blue eyes would glare with a fixed, snake-like fury, and the ends of his waxed moustache would quiver like twin serpents' tongues. All, without exception, the older and the younger boys alike, were terrified of him, and, long after I had left the school, the memory of him continued to haunt me as an unforgettable horror.

His father, old Mr Gambril, whose bust I had seen on the mantelpiece in the study, and who had been Headmaster before him, was alleged to have been even worse than his son, though it hardly seemed possible. It was recorded of him that he was a perfect old devil. One of the favourite punishments of this charming old gentleman had been to make boys hold up their hands with their fingers bunched together and, on this sensitive apex, he would whack them with a cane or one of those thin Greek Primers bound in cardboard. I imagine that on a cold, frosty morning this mode of correction must have been particularly painful.

The present Headmaster, however, had a stock of tortures that were equally ingenious. He would pull one up by the hair near one's ears. He would hit boys on the shins with a cricket stump. He had a way of pinching his victims that was positively excruciating. Whenever I tried to do the same thing to a boy smaller than myself it never seemed to be quite so effective.

He excelled also in the administration of mental tortures. The mark books were always examined at meal-times. They were laid before him in piles as he sat at luncheon or supper. He would examine them in a leisurely way and call up any boys who had been given bad marks. It would be difficult to describe adequately all the horror and agony that being 'called up' entailed. It nearly always involved the fearful pinching and hair-pulling, but, more often than not, you were sent back to your place with the instructions to come to the Headmaster's study as soon as the meal was over. This meant further tortures, culminating in a caning. The actual punishments, however, were less agonising than the period of anticipation, the suspense of waiting to be called. If one had received a bad mark during the morning, the luncheon hour would be spent in an agony of fear. Mr Gambril looked through the books at random, in no particular order, so that it was a matter of chance whether one would be called up at luncheon or supper. I can still remember that terrible, devastating panic that seemed to paralyse the digestive organs and deprive one of appetite, and if, as often happened, the fatal summons was delayed till supper-time it was impossible to eat anything during either meal. One boy, when the time came for him to be sent for, was actually sick, and it is surprising that this did not happen more frequently. I find it hard to believe that this particular form of terrorisation can really have been good for growing boys.

Mr Gambril occasionally gave vent to a sort of grim humour and invented punishments that were highly capricious and fanciful. I remember that once, in a blithe, Gather-ye-microbes-while-ye-may spirit, he made one of his victims go down on his hands and knees and lick a straight line on the floor in front of the assembled school.

And yet nobody ever dreamt of complaining to his parents. Some years after I had left Elmley, my mother came to hear of Mr Gambril's cruelty. She was surprised and horrified, and said to me, 'Why on earth didn't you tell me? I would have taken you away at once and sent you to another school.' That was perhaps one of the reasons of my suffering Mr Gambril in silence. To be sent to another school! It might have been just as bad, perhaps even worse. And, in any case, my complaints would probably have been discredited at the time and merely led to further punishment. All the grown-ups seemed to be in league against one, and it is this sensation of a hopeless contest that turns most small boys into fatalists. Furthermore, strange as it may seem, there was a sentiment of loyalty to the school.

One can understand a man whose life is devoted to teaching small boys behaving occasionally like a wild beast. It is said that one cannot touch pitch without being defiled, and I suppose it is a difficult task to remain a schoolmaster for any length of time without the temper being permanently damaged and the mind contaminated (although some people seem to have achieved it). But Mr Gambril frankly overshot the mark, and one cannot help feeling that a man so obviously afflicted with blood lust, coupled with an uncontrollable temper, would have done better to choose some other vocation.

XIV

Elmley

The first few days at Elmley I spent in a benumbed condition. It was as though my transplantation from home to strange surroundings and an unaccustomed mode of life required a completely new orientation of nervous energy, bringing into play an entirely different set of muscles and ganglions. The rigid routine, the novelty of having to do my lessons in a class, in competition and under strict discipline, seemed to invest them with an unwonted and formidable aspect. For the first time social discrimination became a matter of importance. One's behaviour had to be adjusted accordingly. It became necessary to exercise a nice judgment between the people to whom deference was due, those whom one could treat on terms of equality and those who might be looked on as inferiors and who could be snubbed and bullied.

The seeds of snobbishness soon began to sprout. One day, during the intervals between the classes, I was sitting in the lobby drearily musing, when a red-headed freckled boy a year or two older than myself approached me. He was a distant relation, and he informed me that he had been deputed by his parents to look after me. He did not seem a particularly attractive youth, nor was he a very prominent member of the school. I was only moderately grateful for his patronage, and, much as I had need of them, I made no attempt to avail myself of his proffered services.

Creeling, Arthur and I were naturally a good deal thrown together at first. They were new boys like me, they were in the same class and in the same dormitory. Of the two I very much preferred Arthur. He was hideous, he was a nonentity, yet there was something peculiarly disarming about his inarticulateness and his dogged resistance to any kind of outside influence, whether for good or for evil. He sank at once to the bottom of the class and seemed perfectly contented to remain there. His clumsiness was almost preternatural. He was always knocking things over. No teacup, no inkpot could resist his devastating approach. Indeed they seemed to crash instinctively to the ground when he drew near, and it was as though inanimate objects, in his presence, were roused to a kind of gravitational frenzy. Once, when we were going into chapel, he contrived to upset the lectern. But this may perhaps have been done deliberately, for he adopted a sort of 'non possumus' attitude towards every form of religious worship. During the service he puffed and groaned, and refused to join in the hymns; upon being ordered to 'sing up' he merely emitted a gruff baa like an asthmatic sheep. At games he was thoroughly inefficient. When playing cricket he invariably managed to hit the stumps with his bat, and whenever he threw the ball he nearly always succeeded in hurting somebody. Abuse and mockery left him equally unmoved.

Creeling was of a very different type. He was a smug, self-satisfied little person and he was extremely religious. He always looked as if he had just risen from prayer. He was fairly intelligent and very hard-working, and he was always second in his class. He never misbehaved himself and never got bad marks. He was a sneak. Whenever he detected an abuse he was quite capable of reporting it to the Matron or to one of the masters, actuated by an overwheening sense of duty. But he was cunning enough never to be caught out.

I ended by taking a violent dislike to him, and remembering the advice he had given me on the first day of the term about not divulging the Christian names of my sisters, I managed to spread the rumour that he had two sisters called Tabitha and Jane. Like Putois, in the story by Anatole France, Tabitha and Jane soon became real personages, and the unfortunate Creeling was never able to live them down. Whenever he was seen writing a letter, he would be assailed by cries of 'Hullo, Creeling! Writing to Tabitha and Jane?'

When I first went to school I seem to have had curiously exaggerated impressions of relative age. I was then nine, and boys of fourteen appeared to me to be immeasurably older, almost grown up; and there seemed to be little difference between the monitors and the masters. Like most small boys I was an ardent hero-worshipper. The particular hero that took my fancy at Elmley was a boy called Longworth. He was the Captain of the Second Eleven. He seemed to me to embody every possible perfection. He was a tall, athletic, fair-haired youth with regular features and an engaging smile. He reminded me of one of Flaxman's illustrations to the

Iliad. In the normal course of school life such a paragon would hardly be likely to pay any attention to so humble an individual as myself, or to be aware even of my existence. Perhaps, if I were to distinguish myself by unusual prowess at cricket . . . but, as far as my skill at cricket was concerned, this would be out of the question for a long time to come. How I wished that it had been Longworth's parents who had asked him to look after me! I wondered if anything might possibly be done through domestic channels. I wrote to my mother, imploring her to make enquiries among her acquaintances as to whether any of them knew some people called Longworth who had a son at Elmley. I tried to find out where he lived. But all this got me no farther. It seeemed a hopeless quest, and I had to resign myself to gazing at him wistfully from afar.

At Elmley the thing I missed more than anything else was the possibility of pursuing my ornithological studies. The playing-fields were extensive and there were a good many likely-looking trees and hedges, but (like the coppice at Arley) no birds ever nested there, and the bird-life, such as it was, merely tended to sadden me and to call forth regretful memories. The swallows that hovered over the cricket-ground, the swifts that flew screaming past the schoolroom windows while we were toiling away at Latin or arithmetic, filled me with an aching desire for home. I pined for the meadows and woods of Althrey. I thought of the play of Schiller I had read so laboriously with Mademoiselle Bock, and the description of how Mary Stuart pined for France. My soul breathed out a message to the swallows for them to bear homeward, just as the unhappy queen commissioned the fleeting clouds with a message for the country that she loved.

One morning, during an arithmetic lesson, there rose up in my mind's eye so vivid a picture of a certain hedgerow at Althrey where, about the same time last year, a golden-crested wren had built its nest, that I burst into tears. I found it impossible to explain what had really upset me, and so I complained of feeling queer in the stomach. The result was that I was sent off to the Matron's room and given a dose of castor-oil. As good a cure as any other, I daresay, for sentimental visions of this kind.

The only form of natural history cultivated at Elmley was the collecting of beetles, cock-chafers, caterpillars and kindred insects. This was known comprehensively as 'bug-hunting.' And, in this connection, an incident arose which may be quoted as a fair example of the ridiculous quandaries in which schoolmasters sometimes find themselves placed.

Late one afternoon, during a half-holiday, the bell tolled and an assembly was called. There was always a mysterious excitement attaching to the calling of an assembly. It generally meant that some grave scandal had occurred. The air would be heavy with an atmosphere of crime. There would be wild speculation as to the nature of the offence and its perpetrators. Even the most righteous would be obsessed by a sense of guilt, for the crimes committed were frequently unconscious ones.

The whole school trooped into the large Assembly Room, where the Headmaster stood at his desk, wearing an air of tremendous gravity.

'Boys,' he said, 'in connection with this new craze for the collecting of insects, a very unfortunate word has arisen. I believe that those who indulge in this practice are known as bug-hunters, and the expression to which I am referring is a contraction of that word. Now, boys, I have not the least doubt that this word has been employed in complete ignorance. I am convinced that its true significance is one that is undreamt of by any of you. But, in point of fact, it is a very horrible and disgraceful expression, one that would bring a blush to the cheeks of your mothers and sisters, and one that no gentleman would ever dream of using.

'The word must henceforth be expunged from your vocabulary, and any boy heard making use of it in future will render himself liable to very severe punishment. Boys, you may go.'

XV

Games and Literature

There were two very large flies in the ointment of my school life. The Headmaster was one of them, the other was the fact that I was not good at games.

At Elmley you were made to feel, by a system of subtle propaganda, that organised games were the touchstone of character and that, unless you happened to excel in them, there was little likelihood of your ever being good for anything in later life. Of course work had its importance too; but it did not carry with it the kind of personal esteem one coveted. Anything like imagination, fantasy or artistic talent was naturally at a discount.

In the beginning I used to enjoy playing cricket. But there was far too much of it, and the games went on far too long. They seemed interminable, and there were so many other interests I found more engrossing. I didn't always feel in a mood to 'play up,' and in the midst of this eternal obsession of games I often longed to be allowed to indulge in other pursuits, such as the study of natural history, reading, drawing, music or even riding. The Elmley creed that games were the criterion of ultimate failure or success often aroused in me a feeling of despair and caused moods of sullen depression. I was fairly popular with both the masters and the boys. (One had, of course, one's ups and downs.) But the fact that I was not good at games thwarted my youthful ambition and prevented me from cutting a figure as I should have liked to do. There became implanted in me a sense of inferiority from which it took me a long time to recover.

There was another thing about school life that affected me disagreeably at first, and that was the entire absence of any kind of privacy. It was impossible ever to be alone. Any signs of wishing to withdraw from the society of one's fellows was looked upon as eccentric and reprehensible. As a matter of fact there were certain hiding-places I discovered to which I could retreat when I wanted to be alone, but I always did so with a sense of guilt and in fear of being found out. I suppose that the desire for solitude on the part of a small boy should be considered abnormal, youth being by nature gregarious, and the saying that an Englishman's home is his castle (which would seem to suggest a certain taste for privacy) only applies to grown-ups. Anyhow it seemed unlucky that I was never able to strike the golden mean. At home, in the early part of my childhood, I had often longed for playmates. Now I longed equally for occasional moments of solitude.

On Sunday afternoons and on wet days we were allowed a respite from games and were able to indulge in reading and other frivolous occupations. Whenever it rained heavily enough to be considered prejudicial to our health, a bell was rung and we had to go indoors. Also in winter, whenever there was a very thick fog. Many a time I welcomed the sound of that bell, which meant a temporary relief from the tedious tyranny of games and a return to some engrossing story-book I was reading, and how often during the Winter Term, I used to watch, with eager interest, the fog growing thicker and thicker until at last one could no longer see the football.

Literature, at Elmley, was not absolutely tabooed. There was a school library from which we could borrow books every Sunday. The two most popular authors of the day were Henty and Jules Verne. They were respectively the Apostles of Manliness and Imagination. Boys could be practically divided into two categories, those who liked Henty and those who preferred Jules Verne. Henty had the larger following. I sampled a few of his works, but I soon found out that there was a disappointing monotony in his literary invention. The stories were, all of them, very much alike; there was for ever the same boy-hero, merely transposed to different historical and geographical backgrounds, in an atmosphere over-charged with a rather mawkish patriotism.

Jules Verne, on the other hand, led one into a new universe of marvels. His books comprised every subject that one could possibly dream of. His readers were introduced to every quarter of the globe, were invited to explore every possibility of the Future. In those days, on the eve of the appearance of motor-cars, submarines and aeroplanes, his novels had a prophetic glamour. In one of them, *The Castle of the Carpathians*, there was even a forecast of the Talkies. Such books as these, one felt, might have been approved of for their

mere educational value. Geography could be learnt more graphical-
ly and more agreeably in a story like *Round the World in Eighty
Days* than in any Primer of the school curriculum. Yet Jules Verne
was not wholly approved of by the school authorities. I suppose it
was feared that his influence might lead to dangerous excesses of the
imagination.

The Imagination! That seemed to be a bugbear at Elmley. The
word 'imagination' was always used in a depreciative sense. In some
of my old school reports I find the sentence 'Too apt to be ruled by
his imagination' occurring several times. The Matron at Elmley,
who had apparently been making a study of my character during a
period of illness when I was confined to the Matron's room,
remarked that my principal defect was that I was too imaginative.
Imagination was certainly no help to me at Elmley, and undoubtedly Jules Verne did a good deal towards fostering this undesirable
quality. I remember once, inspired by *The Clipper of the Clouds*,
spending a wet afternoon trying to construct a model flying
machine. It looked very nice and complicated, but as far as flying
was concerned it was a failure. My effort elicited a reproof from the
Headmaster, who happened to see it. 'Men,' he said, 'were never
meant to fly; otherwise God would have given them wings.' The
argument was convincing, if not strikingly novel, having been used
previously, if I am not mistaken, by Mr Chadband; and a potential
inventor was discouraged.

XVI

Boxhill

Towards the end of the Summer Term there took place the annual
excursion to Boxhill, the great yearly Beano. Early in the morning
the whole school embarked in a special train to spend the day on
that Delectable Mountain. I remember, in those days, before I knew
what the Continent was like, Boxhill always struck me as looking a
very foreign-looking place. The closely-cropped brown turf, the
stunted, thickly foliaged trees and the white, chalky soil were unlike

anything I had ever seen before. I remember thinking that the scenery must have resembled that of Mount Ida or the Sabine hills.

We used to arrive about nine o'clock in the morning, and, until the luncheon hour, we were allowed to pass the time in whatever way we liked. At one o'clock a whistle was blown and we assembled under the trees. Tablecloths were spread upon the ground, and the food, consisting of mutton pies, cold meats, hard-boiled eggs, salads, jam puffs and ginger-beer was surprisingly excellent; which proved that the school cook could, on occasions, rise above the usual low level of his fare. The alfresco meal seemed doubly delightful after the long succession of monotonous, tasteless food, the unappetising course of stringy meats and greasy soups, that detestable concoction known as 'hash,' a sort of scavenger's potpourri, those potatoes that seemed to embody the worst characteristics of both dampness and dryness and, at the same time, to be suffering from every known disease of the vegetable kingdom, and that concomitant horror 'greens,' a tough, tepid packet of some kind of nauseous cabbage, pressed down and cut into squares.

Pretentious but unskilled cooks often seek to disguise their lack of talent under a wealth of ornament and to render it, at least, pleasant to the eye if not to the palate. At Elmley, the cook seemed determined that his handiwork should be no whited sepulchre and that its aspect should be as unpleasant as its taste. Thus, on Boxhill day, the simple, well-cooked food, that both looked and tasted good, came as a glad relief; in addition to which there was the primeval joy of eating in the open air.

As soon as luncheon was over, the traditional battle between two rival armies took place. This was known as 'The Rag.' The school was divided into two camps. One was commanded by the Head Monitor, the other by the Captain of the Cricket Eleven. I found out that the latter camp was considered to be the most elegant, and I felt slightly humiliated when I was told off to be a member of the Monitor's side. I believe that, in this mimic warfare, there were definite rules as to what might or might not be done, but, just as in real warfare, nobody paid the slightest attention to them. The main object was to capture flags and prisoners, and the side that took the greatest number was considered to have won. Fair means and foul were employed both in aggression and in defence, and sometimes boys were quite badly hurt. Nevertheless, it was great fun rushing about in the woods, making as much noise as possible, taking flags and prisoners, eluding would-be captors and rallying to the war-cry of your side.

The festive atmosphere of the day, the general feeling of excitement must, I fancy, have transformed the place into something a little different to what it really was, for, on revisiting it not so many years afterwards, I was unable to locate any of the spots I had thought to be indelibly stamped on my memory. I have noticed that, under the stress of some particular emotion, I am apt to carry away highly coloured visions of places that do not correspond with reality, which is no doubt why, upon revisiting them, I have so often been puzzled and disappointed.

After the battle had been raging for an hour or so I was sent out as a scout, to reconnoitre. The Captain had chosen me, not on account of any prowess I had displayed, but merely because I happened to be on the spot at the time. Nevertheless, I felt very proud at having been selected, and I set out, in a valiant mood, determined to distinguish myself in some way or other. I had not gone far when a figure leapt out upon me from behind a tree. I had just made for myself a formidable cudgel and, with it, I hit my assailant a terrific crack over the head. Almost simultaneously I realised that it was Longworth. He staggered forward and fell to the ground. To my horror I saw blood pouring down his face and on to his shirt. As a matter of fact it was only his nose that was bleeding, but the spectacle of the fallen hero petrified me with fear. I remained rooted to the spot, not knowing what to do.

A crowd of boys appeared, clustering round the murderous scene. I heard someone say 'He's killed Longworth!' A momentary truce was declared, while the resuscitated Longworth struggled to his feet. He gave me an angry glance, and muttering 'You little brute!' walked away, with dignity, through the trees.

He was not really hurt, and the incident was a trivial one in the wear and tear of the afternoon's warfare, but it embittered the rest of the day for me. It seemed a particularly malevolent stroke of ill-fortune that I should have injured just the one person I most wished to propitiate. I had craved for Longworth's attention and only too successfully had I succeeded in attracting it.

It was long past sundown when the school reassembled on the platform of Boxhill station. After this glorious day of liberty the return journey was tinged with an 'after the party' feeling. Most of us were rather exhausted by our activities, although there were one or two boys whose heartiness nothing could tire, and who continued, throughout the journey back, to be uproarious to a weary audience. My unfortunate experience with Longworth continued to haunt me and, although the incident seemed to have passed unnoticed in the general turmoil and was not even mentioned among the various more exciting chronicles of the day's exploits, self-consciousness and remorse magnified it into vast proportions.

Longworth himself showed no desire to chastise my impertinence. I passed close to him on the station platform and I realised, from his attitude of Olympian contempt, that the incident had been dismissed and that I had been consigned once more to the oblivion out of which, for one brief moment, I had poked my head.

However, I was not going to get off as lightly as that. Longworth had a younger brother, about two years older than me. Longworth Minor was almost as good-looking as his brother, but he had not the bland appearance of a Greek hero; he looked more like a well-groomed hawk. He adored his elder brother, and it very soon became obvious that his attitude towards me had become decidedly Corsican. I imagine that Longworth Major, feeling that any further notice of the Boxhill incident would be beneath his dignity, had deputed his younger brother to deal with the situation. The first manifestation of hostility took place on the following morning, and I received a savage kick on the shins as I passed through the lobby on my way to early school.

Longworth Minor had a reputation for being a bully. He was in the Third Form and was a member (if not the actual ringleader) of a very objectionable band of youths in the same form, whose object in life seemed to be to torment and harass the smaller boys whenever they got a chance. They had constituted themselves into a sort of Vehmgericht, a Council of Ten, and the most sinister rumours of their terroristic methods were being circulated.

The Third Form classroom was at the far end of one of the wings and was reached by a flight of stairs leading to that classroom only.

Opening out of it was a smaller room that was never used, partly because it was rather dark and partly because there was no other access to it except through the Third Form classroom itself. This room had been organised by Longworth Minor and his friends as a torture-chamber for the punishment of anyone who happened to incur their displeasure.

Those who had suffered in the torture-chamber gave the most hair-raising accounts of it. One marvelled at their ever having managed to survive. The tortures were various and refined. One of them consisted in placing the victim's wrists in two jagged, semicircular holes cut in the top edge of a locker and then pressing down the lid. Another consisted in tying the victim's hands behind his back and pulling them upwards by means of a rope slung over a beam, a form of torture much favoured by the Spanish Inquisition and in mediæval Germany. In the art of inflicting physical agony even Mr Gambril might have learnt a thing or two.

The dark exploits of the band spread terror among the smaller boys. The staircase leading to the Third Form classroom, up which, one felt, victims might at any moment be dragged to their doom, acquired all the grim associations of the Bridge of Sighs. My own classroom was at the end of the passage, close to the fatal staircase, and I was obliged, in going to and from it, to pass in front of this dangerous spot, where there were always two or three Third Form boys hanging about.

So far I had succeeded in escaping their attentions, but after the Boxhill episode and the evidence of Longworth Minor's hostility I knew I had been marked down. Creeling, who always seemed to be *au courant* of every intrigue, confirmed my fears. 'I should advise you to be on your guard,' he said to me one day. 'You are next on the list.'

It was always one of Creeling's characteristics that he was always warning people of any unpleasantness that might be coming to them. There was no doubt that he meant well, but people who acquire a reputation for 'meaning well' are not as a rule very popular with the recipients of their good intentions.

During the days that followed I crept about the passages with a gnawing fear in my heart, trying to make myself as inconspicuous as possible. The mere appearance in the distance of a Third Form boy filled me with panic. I was unable to keep my mind on my work, nor could I sleep at night. My terror was so great that I seriously contemplated running away from school. I can say that I now know from personal experience what must have been the sensations of those who were marked down by the Inquisition, expecting to be pounced upon at any moment by the 'black-cowled minions of the Church.'

In a school the size of Elmley it was easier for abuses to escape the vigilance of the masters, and a rainy afternoon was always fraught with danger; circumstances were favourable for indoor mischief, for boys were left more or less to their own devices. But there was generally one of the assistant masters on duty in the big schoolroom, and I used to take my book there and read; or else I would go and practise on the piano in the music-room. In both of these places I was comparatively safe from aggression. Anyone of at all a sensitive disposition who has been subjected to bullying at school may, I think, safely look forward to no greater anguish of mind during the rest of his life. The strain of having to be perpetually on my guard was beginning to tell, and had it gone on much longer my health would probably have broken down, which would perhaps have been the best solution, for in the Matron's room I should at least have been immune from aggression.

One day a rumour began to be spread that the evil practices of the Third Form had been discovered. It became known that Longworth Minor and several of his friends had been birched by the Headmaster. In the sermon on the following Sunday there was an indictment of bullying. Although the whole business remained shrouded in mystery, there seemed no doubt that some very drastic steps had been taken to put an end to the activities of the Third Form Camorra. Longworth Minor abandoned his attitude of hostility, the other members of his band seemed thoroughly cowed, and there was no more talk about the torture-chamber.

Later on it transpired that it had been Creeling who had reported the matter to the Headmaster, that he had, in fact, 'sneaked.' When openly accused, he denied it indignantly. But, from what we knew of some of his previous actions, and from other evidence, there seemed no doubt that he had been guilty of this breach of school etiquette. Despite the fact that he ought in reality to have been regarded in the light of a saviour (for he had definitely removed an incubus of terror), any form of sneaking was considered, according to the school code of honour, to be a disgraceful act.

I, who more than anyone had reason to be grateful to him, was particularly violent in the denunciation of his conduct. 'The little beast,' I remember saying, 'it is just the sort of thing one might have expected him to go and do!'

XVII

Summer Holidays

At last the Summer Term came to an end. An infinity of time seemed to have passed since that day when I first stood, small and trembling, upon the threshold of Elmley. In stature I had not grown appreciably larger, but spiritually my outlook had widened. New expansions had taken place within my little soul. The sense of Free Will which, in the nursery, had never given me cause for thought, now seemed to be thwarted at every turn by Predestination in the shape of schoolmasters, school conventions and public opinion. I discovered, however, that physical strength and superiority in games were the most reliable assets of Free Will. Although I had not yet mastered the technique of bluff, so important in our dealings with our fellow human beings, I had already managed to acquire a certain skill in hypocrisy. I was beginning to learn how to adapt the expression of such opinions as I held to their suitability.

During the slow-crawling weeks, home life grew more and more remote until, at last, my only connection with it seemed to be the chain of letters from my mother. But as the holidays drew near, the pleasant vision appeared once more, and began to grow in intensity. I started to number the diminishing days with increasing excitement.

A relaxation of school discipline during the last few days of the term seemed to effect a complete transformation in the nature of school. For the moment Elmley became quite bearable, almost a scholastic Utopia, in which masters and boys were no longer bores or bullies, and the memory of the long school hours, the tedious afternoons of cricket, and Mr Gambril's atrocities was for the time being obliterated. It was strange how a mood of happy anticipation had completely transformed the place. I had come to look upon the dreary classrooms, the playing-fields, the very elm trees as forming prison bars from which there was no prospect of escape. Now everything seemed to glow in the gentle summer haze and the immediate promise of release.

The school broke up at an early hour, and by nine o'clock nearly everybody had left. I travelled northward with two boys whose homes lay in the same direction. Neither of them was a particular favourite of mine. In fact one of them I actively disliked. But here again the magic transformation was operative. I delighted in their company on the homeward journey. They seemed to me to be not such bad fellows after all, and I felt that I had misjudged them. This new and mutual affection was further cemented by an orgy of chocolate and hard-boiled eggs.

It was delightful to find myself at home once more. Yet, after the first rapture had subsided, I began to realise that a serpent had crept into my paradise. The enjoyment of home life had acquired an additional zest through absence, just as, after travelling abroad, we return with a new appreciation of our native land. But, alas! this enjoyment had now a transient character, an all-too-briefness that the very word 'holidays' implied. Time, during the last months, had beat with a slow pulsation. Now it resumed its normal speed. School would be upon me again before very long. The thought of it haunted me perpetually.

There were also many amusements in which, now that I had been to school, I could no longer indulge because they might be considered childish, and there were certain pretences that had to be kept up for the sake of Manliness. On the very first day of the holidays my mother struck a sinister note by saying, 'You have been invited to play in a cricket match next week.' And when I began to invent excuses, she said with some surprise, 'But you have always told me in your letters that you were so fond of cricket!'

Happily the River God came to my rescue. I had learnt to swim after a fashion; well enough at any rate to satisfy my mother that I would be able to keep myself from drowning. With my savings I bought a birch-bark canoe, and I was allowed to spend most of my time on the water. The Dee was a delightful river, winding and romantic, overhung in places with rocks and trees, and complete with side-shows in the shape of back-waters, narrows, rapids and other excitements. My mother, seeing that I was happy in this pursuit and feeling no doubt that boating was quite a manly occupation, did not unduly press the cricket question. I never dared openly to confess to her how much I disliked the game, but I fancy that she understood. At all events she had ample opportunity, on the one occasion during the holidays that she saw me play cricket, to realise that I was not very good at it.

Apart from the grim foreboding of the return to school for ever lurking in the background, there was another terror that haunted me day and night. Just before the end of term I had lost a book out of the school library. The mere loss of an inexpensive book which could easily be replaced would seem to be a trifling matter, but I am sure that no criminal fleeing from justice could have gone through such agonies of mind as I did on account of that wretched volume. The book (I remember it only too well!) was *Michael Strogoff* by Jules Verne. Its title in red on a black cover remains blazoned in letters of fire on the retina of my memory. What made the matter infinitely worse was that I kept my secret to myself and brooded over it in silent misery. What is it that sometimes makes the young so chary of confiding their distresses to grown-ups? Is it childish pride? The fear of a possible lack of sympathy? The probability of finding an enemy where one hoped for an ally? I only know that my holidays were embittered by the loss of this book. When I returned to school I found it sitting calmly in its proper place on the shelf just as if nothing had happened, totally oblivious of all the fear and misery it had occasioned to one unhappy little reader.

There had been, that summer, a very welcome addition to the neighbourhood. A friend of my father's, a certain Mrs Harvey, had taken a house a few miles distant from Althrey. Her arrival made quite a stir in the county. She was widely celebrated for her beauty and her wit, and I heard her spoken of as a 'woman of fashion,' which impressed me very much. Certainly when I saw her for the first time I realised that she was quite unlike any of our country neighbours. She was always exquisitely dressed (I had never seen anyone so beautifully dressed, with the possible exception of my Aunt Flora), and, bicycling being all the rage at that time, she even contrived to look well on a bicycle, which was a great test. She had two daughters, Lydia and Christina; they were about the same age as myself and they seemed to have inherited a goodly portion of their mother's charms. Both girls had fair hair and a delicate transparent colouring. Their characters might well be described in terms of porcelain. Christina was Sèvres, Lydia Famille Rose. Lydia's personality was the richer of the two, less refined perhaps in detail, but there was more ingenuity of imaginative colouring and design. I fell passionately in love with both of them.

The Harveys were the first people of their kind I had ever met and, just as the ladies of Rose Hill had represented for me the world of continental travel, so did these new friends introduce into my life a novel and delightful aspect of the amenities of social intercourse. Although they were fond of sport (Mrs Harvey rode extremely well) I was pleased to find that they never thought of treating it as a fetish, as a touchstone of character, neither did they seem to hold the opinion that anyone who was not good at games must necessarily be inferior in all respects.

I overheard one of the neighbours say that Mrs Harvey was very 'fin de siècle.' What exactly this implied I never quite understood, but I know that she was interested in all that was going on in the world of art and literature at the time. She had known Walter Pater, Whistler, Wilde and Swinburne. But of this, of course, I knew nothing in those days, such names never having been mentioned in the family circle. My mother's culture stopped with Tennyson.

Life in the 'nineties, in a distant provincial neighbourhood such as ours, had seemed to me up till then a little devoid of charm. It was a tawdry, unprepossessing period. In the country life of the 'eighties there had been at least a certain solid grandeur, this had now given place to gimcrack. The Zeitgeist was represented by the bicycle. The costume of the period (the leg-of-mutton sleeves, the straw hats, the blouses, the masculine collars and ties worn by the women), which when reproduced on the stage nowadays raises a sympathetic smile, seemed to me at the time to be of unmitigated plainness. Interior decoration was equally depressing. Whatever the Aesthetic cult may have produced in the way of beauty elsewhere, in our neighbour-hood there was nothing but a welter of cane and bamboo furniture, draped easels, standard lamps with flounces, mirrors with roses and chrysanthemums painted on them, Moorish fretwork, Indian embroidery, pampas grass and palms; an effort, no doubt, to escape from the cumbrous smugness of the Mid-Victorian style, but which could hardly be described as successful from an artistic point of view.

I find it difficult to speak of Mrs Harvey, at this distance of time, without falling into exaggeration. The impression she made on my youthful mind is too highly coloured and gilded with the sentimental memory of the past. Her personality, when she first arrived like a meteor in our midst, seemed to me so radiant, her conversation so brilliant, that it was as though she were a being outside the ordinary range of daily life, the materialisation of some personage of fiction. I had heard it said that she was like a character from one of George Meredith's novels, and for days I struggled with *Diana of the Crossways*. But I came to the conclusion that the somewhat recondite epigrams of the heroine were not a patch on those of Mrs Harvey.

My own efforts at 'brilliant' conversation were not encouraged by my mother. Once, after I had made a particularly fatuous epigram, she said that she was afraid the society of the Harveys was having a bad effect on me and that I was growing pretentious. However, in spite of her instinctive distrust of clever people, she liked and admired Mrs Harvey and put up with a good deal from her that she would not have stood from persons of less distinction. When my mother appeared one evening at a dinner-party with a bruise on her neck and Mrs Harvey said to her, 'How disappoint-ing, my dear, that it should only be a hunting accident, I had hoped you had a passionate lover,' my mother, while expressing embarras-sed resentment, was secretly rather pleased.

I used to see a great deal of Lydia and Christina. Nearly every day I went over to their house to spend the afternoon with them, or they would come over to Althrey and we would bathe together or explore the river in my canoe. They were a little scornful of other children in the neighbourhood, whom they considered for the most part stupid or uninteresting. Between us we generally managed to dominate over them and impose upon them our own particular ideas of amusement. We had invented a variety of games both for outdoor and indoor uses. One of them, I remember, was called 'Mad Dog.' I will give a description of it, for it is a game that might prove very useful for political hostesses.

A Mad Dog was first selected by drawing lots, and then the rest of the party proceeded to hide in various parts of the house or the garden. After a few minutes' grace the Mad Dog ran amok. Anyone who was caught was formally bitten and then there were two Mad Dogs. Thus the number of Mad Dogs went on increasing and the sane ones diminishing, on the principle of the ten little nigger boys, until finally (and this was the most thrilling moment of the game) there was a howling pack of Mad Dogs in full cry after the solitary survivor.

I often wished Nesta were still living in our midst. With Lydia and Christina as allies, I would at last have got even with her. We would have stood no nonsense from her.

Another game we used to play necessitated a Medical Dictionary, which had to be surreptitiously removed from the library. You had to open it with your eyes shut and place your finger at random on a page. You were then obliged to read the passage out aloud. Many of the terms were incomprehensible to us, but they sounded very funny and we had a pleasant conviction of their impropriety. Owing to its equivocal character, this game had to be concealed from our parents and it could only be played in a restricted circle.

Soon, all too soon, the dread day arrived for my return to Elmley. Once again my mother accompanied me to London, we stayed once more in Belgrave Square and I was taken to a play, just as it had happened when I first went to school. In fact the whole process was repeated, the only difference being that, this time, I knew exactly what was in store for me.

XVIII

Masters and Boys

The most popular of the assistant masters at Elmley was undoubtedly Mr Simpson. He was primarily the Sports master,
though he taught other things as well, such as geography and
history. He was a great favourite with the boys, and he seemed
to attach a good deal of importance to his popularity. He
went out of his way to court it, and even encouraged familiarities
that might be considered unbecoming between masters and
boys.

Mr Simpson was a short, stocky little man with a heavy military
moustache that gave him a certain resemblance to Lord Kitchener.
He was never without a pipe in his mouth, and his face (like the
faces of so many of our modern English novelists) looked as though
the pipe had been there first and the face had grown round it
afterwards.

I was not sufficiently prominent in games to aspire to be an
especial favourite of his, and this naturally prejudiced me against
him. Apart from this, I instinctively knew him to be rather a
bounder. Although my feelings of class-consciousness, at that time,
were not very highly developed, nevertheless I suspected him of
being what Emma Woodhouse might have termed 'only moderately
genteel.'

Then there were two clergymen, the Reverend Mr Bevis and the
Reverend Mr Adcock. Mr Bevis was the master I preferred to all the
others. He was a gentle, scholarly man of about fifty, with a delicate
ascetic face. He was rather despised by the boys as well, I fancy, as
by the masters, for he possessed two qualities that were quite out of
keeping with the general trend of the educational policy at Elmley, a
sense of humour and a sense of beauty. He even went so far as to
emphasise the literary and picturesque side of the Greek and Latin
Classics. In his hands the *Iliad*, the *Odyssey*, the *Aeneid*, the *Odes*
of Horace became something other than mere exercises in syntax.
Alas! I was only in his class for a single term and the enthusiasm he

had succeeded in arousing for the Latin and Greek authors was speedily dispelled by his successor.

Mr Bevis cherished a secret dislike for the Headmaster, and he would now and then indulge in mild jokes at Mr Gambril's expense which met with delighted sniggers from his audience, tempered with a certain awe, for it was like watching Ajax defying the lightning.

Despite all I have said about Mr Gambril, I feel that I have only succeeded in conveying but a feeble impression of the fear this man inspired. His terrifying personality seemed to hover over the school like some obscene vulture over a flock of lambs. The rustling of his wings was for ever in the air. At any moment he might pounce. He was like the Angel of Death stalking through a plague-stricken city. No one was immune from that dreadful summons.

With regard to the other clergyman, Mr Adcock, the only thing one could say about him was that he was very old and very mad. As a teacher he was utterly useless, and I imagine that his services had only been retained for sentimental reasons. He had been a schoolmaster at Elmley for an incalculable number of years. He dated back to the prehistoric days when Mr Gambril Senior ran the school.

I don't know whether Mr Adcock had, in his early youth, lived on a farm, but he certainly had an agricultural obsession in his old age, and he was for ever using such expressions as 'putting the hand to the plough,' 'sowing seeds and reaping,' 'calling a spade a spade,' and so forth. He used to refer to boys as 'sheep' and 'cows.' When he was annoyed with you he would sometimes call you a 'bad cow.' He was a venerable-looking old man with a short straggling white beard and white fluffy hair that used to glow like an aureole when outlined against the light. Indeed he had the air of an elderly saint. Apart from the senile decay from which he was suffering, he was an amiable old man and everybody liked him. He used to praise his pupils ecstatically whenever they did anything right, and he never lost his temper or gave one punishments like the other masters. Towards the end of my time at Elmley he had grown so old and incompetent that he was at last obliged to retire. His farewell sermon was a very moving affair. He got up into the pulpit with considerable difficulty, addressed the congregation as 'My good cows,' and then burst into tears.

Mr Miles was the Mathematical master, and for that very reason especially detestable to me, for whom mathematics were anathema. He was also a prig, the type of pedantically superior, insular prig which England, above all other countries, manages to produce in its perfection. Nearly every sentence that proceeded from his lips had so exasperating a flavour that it excited a wild sense of irritation, even when one agreed with him.

I have recently discovered his exact counterpart in an English musical critic, whose name cannot be mentioned, as he is unfortunately still alive. In this man's articles and books I noticed a certain tone that reminded me forcibly of Mr Miles, so that I was curious to meet him to see if the resemblance went any further. It did indeed; and I was confronted with an almost perfect replica of the Mathematical master at Elmley. I was taken back to those far-off days and my memory was refreshed as effectively as by any of the scents, tastes and tactile aids to recollection discovered by Proust. There was the same anæmic earnestness, the same superior disparagement of things that escaped his comprehension, the same milk-and-water voice upon which a University twang lay like a thin layer of vinegar. His personality, just like that of Mr Miles, excited all those sentiments of irritation that can only be relieved by the application of a well-aimed kick. If it were not for the fact that the respective dates of births and deaths overlapped I should be inclined to believe in a reincarnation.

The master of the Second Form, Mr Grey, was a humorist. He was always making little jokes and his classroom perpetually rang with merry laughter. His jokes were not always quite on the same level, and at times the laughter was perhaps a little perfunctory. Some of them had the persistence of a recurring decimal. There was a line in Horace, 'celeri saucius malus Africano.' Whenever it occurred Mr Grey would give a wink and say, 'Now, boys, don't translate that by "Celery sauce is bad for the African." ' But he strongly discouraged his pupils from attempting to make jokes in their turn. If you ever tried to be funny yourself, he would look at you severely and say, 'You're a bit of a wag, aren't you?'

Mr Grey was a married man. When I saw his wife one day at a cricket match, I thought that I understood the reason of his intensive humoristic urge during school hours. Although rather gaudily dressed and very much beribboned, she was a severe-looking woman; she looked like a mausoleum in the flamboyant Gothic style. I am sure that poor Mr Grey was forbidden to make any of his jokes at home, so that his natural instinct could only be indulged in the classroom. However, in spite of his unflagging facetiousness, he was rather a nice little man and, after all, it was something to be able to laugh in school-time, even at a bad joke.

Mr Goddard had the distinction of being the only master upon whom the boys ventured to play practical jokes. He was evidently lacking in that subtle quality which enables schoolmasters to hold small boys in awe; a quality that is difficult to analyse. I should say its primary ingredients were a capacity for taking oneself seriously, and the magnetic power of the eye. A piercing glance can more effectively quell unruliness than any amount of strong silence. To a casual observer Mr Goddard would have appeared to be a perfectly normal specimen of the human race; he had no obvious absurdities; he neither stammered nor lisped; his appearance was plain but not ridiculous. He was not weak and foolish like old Mr Adcock, nor was he nearly so ridiculous as the French master. Yet he was ragged unmercifully. Had it not been for the ever-existent danger of the Headmaster's sudden visits to the classrooms, he would no doubt have suffered even more than he did. As it was, Mr Goddard's classroom resembled at times the harlequinade of a Christmas pantomime. Paper butterflies were released, sheaves of toilet paper were thrown into the air, explosive pens were laid on his desk and, on one occasion, his small alarum clock, which had been missing for several days, was handed to him just as he was going into chapel, carefully timed to go off in the middle of the service; which it did, with great effect.

I suppose that a sense of pride must have prevented the poor man from complaining to the Headmaster. Eventually, however (as must inevitably happen), the state of affairs prevailing in Mr Goddard's classroom attained to such a degree of publicity that he was removed from the school.

It was curious that nobody ever thought of ragging the French and German masters, for two more ludicrous creatures surely never existed. In their respective styles they were the most complete caricatures of their own national characteristics that could possibly

be imagined. One might almost have thought that they had been
very carefully selected in order to act as anti-foreign scarecrows;
their sole function being to prove to patriotic English schoolboys
the superiority of their own countrymen over their French and
German neighbours. Neither Monsieur Dupont nor Professor
Schulz seemed to be gifted with any capacity for teaching languages.
Under their tuition one merely learnt long strings of names for
which one would never be likely to have any practical use. The only
thing they did manage to do with any success was to convey the
impression that both French and German were dead languages.

At the beginning of my second term, when the school came
together for the first time in the big Assembly Room, I noticed that
the two new boys who had come that term were not present.
Remembering my own confusion and bewilderment on the first day
at school I felt sure that they had missed the Assembly through
ignorance and I began to be worried on their behalf, reproaching
myself with not having befriended them and prevented this
involuntary lapse of discipline. However, I soon discovered that
their absence was intentional; the reason for it was disclosed in the
headmaster's opening address.

'Boys,' he said, 'I have something to say to you. There are two
new-comers this term who are of a different creed to the rest of you.
One of them is a Roman Catholic, the other is a Jew. Now, boys,
you are not to allow this fact to make any difference to your
treatment of them. You must remember that they are just boys like
yourselves and it is through no fault of their own that they have had
the misfortune to be born into families who are not Protestants and,
in the case of one of them, not even Christians. You must behave to
them with kindness and courtesy. You must forget that in bygone
days Roman Catholics used to make a practice of burning
Protestants at the stake, and that the other boy belongs to the race
that crucified Our Lord.' Thus he went on, working up our feelings
against the two wretched boys and, in a spirit of Christian charity,
proceeded to rake up every imaginable grievance that Christians
might harbour against Jews and Roman Catholics. He reminded us
of a dozen incriminating facts that undoubtedly we should never
have thought of ourselves. It was a most injudicious speech.

Nevertheless, I am sure that, although he seemed bent on arousing our animosity, it was done quite unconsciously. It merely happened that, having started off in an historical vein, he was unable to resist the temptation of displaying his erudition.

Happily for the two boys the Headmaster's word was law, and no attempts were made to bully or taunt either of them, in spite of the fact that the little Jewish boy Abraham positively invited ill-treatment. He was the most repulsive specimen of his race I have ever seen, and, just as in the case of the French and German masters, one wondered if he had not been sent to the school by some anti-Semite Society as an 'agent provocateur.' He resembled an appalling caricature of a Jew, with sallow face and the traditional nose distorted out of all proportion. His skin looked as if it were perpetually exuding grease. He had thick lips and black curly hair of so repellent a texture that it at least kept people from pulling it, which they might have been otherwise tempted to do. The only redeeming feature in this lamentable ensemble were his eyes, which were large, dark and lustrous. He was nicknamed 'The Rose of Sharon' and left severely alone.

He was so uncannily awful that he fascinated me as a curiosity, and I tried to make friends with him in a spirit of ethnological research, hoping that I might perhaps be initiated into some strange Oriental mystery. But, even as a freak, he was disappointing. He turned out to be a very uninteresting, materially-minded little boy. He had to be kept in his place. If you were in the least kind to him he immediately became overbearing and impertinent. During his second term, when he had gained a little more self-confidence, he began lending money to the boys in his class, and he initiated a lottery out of which he would no doubt have made a handsome profit had it not been discovered and forbidden by one of the assistant masters.

On the other hand, the Roman Catholic, Desmond, was a rather attractive little boy. He was intelligent and amusing and there was something slightly exotic about him that made him seem different to the other boys. I remembered the horror that Lady Bourchier used to evince whenever she spoke about 'Papists,' and this prejudiced me in his favour. Moreover, he shared my dislike for Creeling, who, on his side, appeared to hold the same views as did my grandmother. Desmond did not seem to take his religion very seriously; indeed he sometimes shocked me by the irreverence with which he spoke of sacred matters. He used to take a malicious pleasure in drawing Creeling out, especially on the subject of his religious views and, having a certain dialectical skill, generally succeeded in leading him into a quagmire of argument where he would leave him floundering. Creeling used to dread these attacks, as he invariably got the worst of it; but, in the spirit of a militant Protestant, he felt it his duty to respond.

I remember one day we got Creeling into a corner and pressed him unmercifully on the subject of 'his God,' of whom he used to speak in an aggressively possessive manner.

'Tell us about this God of yours,' said Desmond. 'In what way is he different to mine? Has he got a beard?'

'No, of course not,' retorted Creeling angrily. 'He is an invisible spirit.'

'Really? No beard. Well then has he got toe-nails?'

'Certainly not!' Creeling was shocked. 'I said he was an invisible spirit.'

'That's most interesting. And tell me, where does he live?'

'He is ubiquitous. That is to say, he lives everywhere.'

'What? Not in the Headmaster's study?'

'Yes. He is everywhere.'

'Surely not in the water-closet?'

'I tell you he lives everywhere.' And Creeling broke away from us in a fury.

Desmond caught him by the coat-tails, calling to everyone within earshot, 'I say, Creeling worships a funny sort of God. No toe-nails and lives in the W.C.!'

He collected a jeering crowd round the unfortunate Creeling, until at last an elder boy intervened and told Desmond to shut up, adding that in any case he was a Roman Catholic and had better not be blasphemous.

XIX

Diversions

Small boys are apt to be romantically disposed, and they often display considerable ingenuity in extricating food for romance from the squalid ashbin of school life.

The monotonous sequence of events was, from time to time, enlivened with mysteries, strange rumours and tales of horror. The whole school would be kept agog for several days by some hidden crime. Unknown persons had been holding a smoking party in the masters' lavatories, someone had writtten an offensive word on the French master's desk, flowers had been picked in the Headmaster's garden, sweets had been bought at the village post-office and eaten secretly at night in one of the dormitories. When the culprits were successful in concealing their identity, half-holidays would be stopped in order to induce confession. On such occasions we felt as though an unknown criminal was walking in our midst, and no one was immune from suspicion. Occasionally a boy would be expelled and the reason for his expulsion never revealed.

One thing, however, was certain. Whatever crime was committed, however astutely the delinquents might scheme to escape detection, Mr Gambril would ultimately discover the truth. No ill deed had ever succeeded in baffling his lynx-like investigation. Indeed he seemed to be aware of everything that went on in the school, and one suspected that Elmley, like the Villa of the Emperor Hadrian, must have been honeycombed with secret passages whence the Headmaster could spy upon us and acquaint himself with all that was being said and done in classrooms, dormitories and offices. He was the Master Detective, Judge and Executioner in one.

In the early 'nineties, detective stories and 'thrillers' had not attained the vogue they enjoy in 1930. Sherlock Holmes, it is true, had already made his appearance in the world, but he had not yet become a figure of worldwide renown. The chronicles of his exploits were not to be found on the shelves of the school library. Nevertheless, the craving for the 'horrid' and the gruesome was just as strong among the schoolboys of Elmley as it had been, a century ago, among the young ladies of Northanger Abbey, and we were obliged, just as they were, to evolve our own 'Mysteries of Udolpho.'

In one of the dormitories there was a semi-circular protuberance in the wall that could not be accounted for by any ordinary architectural rules. Here, it was said, many years ago, a member of the school had been walled up alive, and sometimes in the depths of the night his ghost could be heard moaning and tearing at the walls of his prison with his nails.

Then there was a certain train that used to pass every evening at eleven o'clock. It was known as the Corpse Train, and was believed to be bearing corpses to the Crematorium at Woking. Nobody bothered to investigate the origin of this belief. For all I know, it may have been a perfectly commonplace goods train, but the legend, once started, became an article of faith, and the Corpse Train continued to excite a morbid curiosity, especially among the smaller boys. We used to face the fearful odds of detection and punishment by keeping ourselves awake until we heard the school clock strike a quarter to eleven (which, for us, seemed to be in the depths of the night) and we would creep out to a window in the passage from which there was a distant view of the railway line. The position of the window, from a strategical point of view, could not have been more dangerous for it was quite close to the baize door leading to the Headmaster's side of the house, through which at any moment he might himself appear. We hid ourselves as well as we could behind the curtains and waited breathlessly for the passing of the Corpse Train. Then we stole back to bed again with a thrill in our hearts at having caught a glimpse of it flashing by with a muffled roar, bearing its gruesome cargo into the night.

On the other side of the main road, opposite to the entrance to the school, there was a cemetery. A good view of it could be obtained from some of the dormitory windows on the top floor, and the fortunate occupants of these dormitories declared that phosphorescent forms could often be seen after dark flitting about among the tombstones and the yews.

The covered gymnasium adjoining the swimming bath was supposed to be haunted by a whining banshee. One evening Arthur and I plucked up sufficient courage to do a little psychic research. The great empty court looked ghostly enough in the grey twilight, and as we stood there, quivering with fear and excitement, we distinctly heard a faint but unmistakable sound of whining. If it had occurred to either of us that the uncanny sounds emanated from a dog kept by one of the assistant masters in an outhouse at the further end of the Gymnasium we would have deliberately set aside so obvious an explanation. Having obtained the thrill we were seeking, we were determined to enjoy it whole-heartedly. This kind of emotional Masochism has existed through the ages and is not confined to the very young. If a student of folk-lore were able to live for some months in a preparatory school disguised as a small boy, he might be enabled to make some illuminating discoveries as to the origin of primitive myths and the growth of primitive religions.

There was a certain boy who used to walk in his sleep. He was supposed to have been seen one night making his way along the high and perilous cornice that crowned the façade of the house. This youth, who in ordinary life was quite dull and uninteresting, enjoyed an aura of respectful publicity on account of his somnam-bulistic feats. Several other boys, excited to emulation, boasted that they also had been known to walk in their sleep. Not wishing to be outdone in this respect, I determined to give positive evidence of what others had only asserted. And so, one evening after everybody had gone to bed, I got up and set out to make a round of the dormitories with my eyes closed, moaning faintly. As I had never seen anybody walking in their sleep I can hardly imagine that the performance can have been a very realistic one. At all events nobody seemed to be taken in by it. Any success I may have had was one of low comedy and, from all sides, slippers were hurled at my person. It ended by suddenly finding myself face to face with one of the masters who happened to be on patrol and, completely losing my head, I fell back on the pretence that I was making for the lavatory. The whole thing was an ignominious failure.

The enthralment exercised over us by the supernatural had its culmination in Merton.

Merton was a boy who came to Elmley in my second term. He was a strange-looking youth. His appearance contrasted strongly with the rather mild association of his name. He might have been an Arab. He was cadaverously thin, and he had a long, hatchet-face with beetling black eyebrows that met over his nose. His eyes were very peculiar, the eyeballs showing in their entirety between the lids (an effect the ordinary person can achieve by opening his eyes very wide), giving each eye the concentric appearance of a target.

Merton was able to hypnotise. He chose for his medium a boy called Mansell. Mansell, I must confess, seemed to be almost a half-wit, but between them they gave the most remarkable performances. These séances generally took place in the boot-room, with one of us posted in the passage outside to guard against intrusion and the vigilance of masters.

Merton always used to open the séance by making a number of cabalistic passes in front of Mansell's face, and after a few minutes the medium would appear to fall into a trance. Merton would then produce a sheet of white paper and say to the medium, 'Mansell, this paper is black.' Mansell would answer in a strange, far-off, disembodied voice, 'Yes, Merton, it is black.' He would then be shown other objects and told that they were food, domestic pets or terrifying wild beasts, and he would display all the varied emotions that such things would naturally excite. He would eat blotting-paper and pronounce it delicious; he would fly in terror before a chair in the belief that it was a tiger, or stroke a football with the most ridiculous air of tenderness and call it 'Pussy.' Whilst under hypnotic influence, Mansell was said to be in a state of insensibility, and Merton would invite us to stick pins into him or to pinch him. We complied, but a little half-heartedly, for, however bloodthirsty one's disposition, it requires a certain amount of sangfroid to stick a pin deliberately into unresisting human flesh.

Our séances had to be conducted with the greatest secrecy, and this gave them an additional furtive charm, as though they were the clandestine gatherings of some occult and persecuted sect. Eventually, however, Merton's fame spread beyond our own small coterie, and hypnotism became fashionable in the school. Merton used to say that a great many more people than one might imagine possessed hypnotic powers, which could be developed if they only knew how. But obviously nobody did know how, for, although a great many attempts were made, not one of them was successful.

Even Merton himself refused to hypnotise anyone else but Mansell. This might have aroused suspicion, but he accounted for it by saying that, having found a perfect medium in Mansell, it was a useless waste of hypnotic energy to divert the force into other channels; an explanation that sounded very technical and convincing.

One day Mansell disappeared from our midst. His departure from the school remained cloaked in mystery. There was no doubt that, each day, he had been growing increasingly queer, and it was obvious that the frequent hypnotic séances had a good deal to do with this. But whether illness, misconduct or mental breakdown necessitated his removal we were never able to discover. Merton, consummate mystagogue that he was, made the most of his medium's disappearance. He implied that he had inside information on the subject and that the circumstances were too strange and terrible to discuss. In the same spirit he evolved the fiction that Mansell, although at the time far distant (perhaps even in another world altogether), was nevertheless still under his domination.

One Sunday afternoon I happened to be alone with Merton in one of the classrooms. It was growing dusk, and we had been improving the darkening hour by telling one another ghost stories. All of a sudden, Merton stopped speaking and gripped my arm. He stood up and called out in a loud voice, 'Mansell, are you there?' In the silence that followed I listened intently, quite expecting to hear the well-known voice of the medium answering out of the darkness, 'Yes, Merton, I am here.'

At that moment one of the servants came into the room to light the gas, and the spell, I suppose, was broken. I implored Merton to call on Mansell once again, but he said that the man's entry had disconnected the psychic current and it would be useless. He had, no doubt, counted on the interruption, but he managed the business very skilfully and I was profoundly impressed.

No other favourable occasion ever seemed to present itself, in spite of my continually pressing Merton to oblige. So firm, however, was my faith in Merton's occult powers that it never occurred to me for an instant to doubt their efficacy.

Since then I have often wondered to what extent Merton's hypnotic gifts were genuine and whether the whole business had not been a put-up job between himself and Mansell. Mansell was, as I have said, almost an imbecile. He was incredibly ingenuous. He believed everything he was told, and appeared to accept the most fantastic information with a sort of vacant apathy. The weakest characters are, however, not without the ambition to cut some sort of figure, and he must have realised that, as a medium in conjunction with Merton, he enjoyed a celebrity in the school such as he could never have hoped to attain on his own. But it seemed impossible that, unless he had really been hypnotised, he could have borne without flinching the pinches and pinpricks that were inflicted on him.

After Mansell's departure the craze for hypnotism began to wane. Merton himself seemed to lose interest in the subject and he began instead to develop a passion for pirates and corsairs. He told us that as soon as he left school he meant to construct a submarine (on the model of the one described in Jules Verne's *Twenty Thousand Leagues under the Sea*) with which he intended to harass the French and Russian commercial navies. As time went on, he seemed to be growing considerably less fantastic. His very appearance began to alter in the direction of normality. His eyebrows became less beetling, his eyes less piercing. He began to apply himself seriously to games and ended by growing up into a dull, quite ordinary boy. I believe he eventually went into the army.

XX

The School Concert

I have said that at Elmley the Arts were discouraged. The manner in which music was taught there was one of the methods of discouragement.

Musical instruction was in the hands of a master who was universally referred to as 'Sammy.' He may have had a surname, but I have forgotten it. Indeed, I doubt if I ever knew it. He was a comic, rotund little man with a pasty face and a small black moustache that looked as though a couple of commas had been stuck symmetrically on either side of his upper lip. His hair was black and oily, and he wore it parted in the middle. Nature had obviously designed him for a hairdresser and had given him the exterior of a slightly soiled barber's block. Why he had ever thought of becoming a music master was a profound mystery. He hardly understood the rudiments of the art and his taste was appalling.

He hated Bach, Beethoven and Mozart – in fact all the classics. He used to refer to them as 'those boring old boys.' Chopin and Schumann he considered rather too advanced for consideration, and it is quite probable that he had never even heard of Wagner or Brahms. He used to make his pupils play ridiculous, mid-Victorian drawing-room pieces, his especial favourite being a mawkish effusion called 'Les Cloches du Monastère.' (Du Maurier mentions it in *Trilby* as being one of the most bourgeois pieces of music ever written.) Sammy's pupils, one and all, had to undergo 'Les Cloches du Monastère.'

Then there was 'Home, sweet home, with variations' by Thalberg, and a series of 'brilliant' pianoforte compositions with highly suggestive titles by a composer named Sidney Smith, who, I may say, had nothing whatever in common with his more illustrious namesake. One felt that these pieces must have been written in order to enable Victorian young ladies to show off their proficiency in the drawing-room. They always reminded me of the illustrations I used to see in old volumes of *Punch* representing a crinolined damsel seated at the piano with a bewhiskered youth leaning over her, whispering sweet nothings into her ear.

I was still passionately devoted to Chopin. I possessed bound volumes of the mazurkas, the waltzes, the ballads and the impromptus, but Sammy would never let me learn any of them; he said Chopin was 'morbid' and I was obliged to study his works surreptitiously.

During the early part of my school-days there were certain artificial paradises into which I could retreat and take refuge from the petty annoyances of everyday life. Chopin's music was one of them. My interest in music had been primarily aroused by the Fantaisie Impromptu, and as no efforts had ever been made (except by Sammy) to divert my tastes into other channels, I followed the line of least resistance. Chopin's music appealed to my childish romanticism as well as to my equally childish predilection for what

looked difficult to play. I revelled in the baroque cadenzas that
glittered like the crystal chandelier in the drawing-room at Arley, in
the subtle changes in harmony that were like the iridescent hues on
the plumage of the Himalayan pheasant. In my love for Chopin
there was no doubt a literary flavour. I knew very little of his
romantic background, of the oppressed Poland, of George Sand, of
the continental life of the eighteen-thirties, yet his music aroused in
me certain vague yearnings and emotions which despite their
vagueness I could recognise as being kindred to those evoked on
previous occasions by the pictures on the screen at Arley, by the
peculiar early nineteenth-century atmosphere prevailing there, by
certain passages in my books of fairy tales and by the descriptions given me of 'abroad' by the ladies of Rose Hill; a kind of
nostalgia, perhaps, for some visionary world built up of pre-natal
memories.

Towards the end of the Winter Term there took place the annual
School Concert. A platform was erected in the big Assembly Room;
the walls were decorated with paper flowers and Japanese lanterns
were hung from the rafters. Everything was done to make the
gloomy, scholastic-looking hall look as frivolous as possible.

During the week before the concert there prevailed an enjoyable
undercurrent of excitement, even amongst those who were not
performing in the concert themselves. Parents came down for the
occasion, the day was a half-holiday, and the supper, consisting of
cakes and ices, lemonade and other non-alcoholic drinks, was
almost sumptuous. The holidays were within sight and there was a
happy breaking-up feeling in the air.

For my first appearance on the concert platform, Sammy had
insisted upon my learning a piece called 'The Lover and the Bird.'
The piece was constructed out of a single theme of nauseating
sweetness accompanied at intervals by a riot of trills and arpeggios.
If it suggested anything at all, it put one in mind of a dialogue
between a sentimental old maid and her canary. It was almost worse
than 'Les Cloches du Monastère' and I hated having to play it.
However, I learnt to execute the piece with a certain amount of *brio*.
As it sounded very difficult, my apparent virtuosity together with
my diminutive stature created a favourable impression on the

audience and the item was one of the biggest successes of the programme.

Both my mother and my father were present, and as I rather shyly acknowledged the applause I was glad to think of them assisting at my triumph. I hoped that it might perhaps reconcile them to my musical tastes. When I joined them later, I could see that my mother's pride was flattered, and even my father seemed pleased, if a little supercilious. He told me that the 'Lover and the Bird' had been one of Lady Bourchier's favourite pieces in the unregenerate days before her conversion, and that she had recently said that if she could hear it again she would die happy. He added that he hoped I would go and play it to her as soon as possible.

In the interval between the concert and supper, the boys and their parents assembled in the Lobby. My father's elegance and his slightly swaggering manner became a source of pride to me as soon as they were removed from the home circle, where I found them a trifle oppressive. Even Mr Gambril seemed to be a little overawed, and I noticed with some satisfaction that his bearing towards my father was almost servile. But what thrilled me even more was the sight of my father engaged in conversation with Longworth's mother, who was standing with her arm round her eldest son's neck. Hastily detaching myself from my mother I approached the group. Mrs Longworth made some complimentary remark and, to my amazement and delight, Longworth Major smiled at me and said 'Well played!' just as though I had hit a boundary or scored a goal. If Longworth had been Chopin himself this simple tribute could scarcely have caused me a wilder joy. The applause of the audience faded into insignificance.

In spite of the Boxhill episode and his Olympian aloofness, which seemed to create a barrier I could never hope to surmount, Longworth still continued to occupy the foremost place in my hero worship. I watched his actions with the same eager interest with which Suburbia follows the doings of royalty. I even went so far as to envisage a situation in which one of my parents (preferably my father) and one of Longworth's should be simultaneously removed, and the two that remained should marry, so that Longworth and I should become step-brothers; he would be obliged to notice me then! I had never ventured to open my heart to any of my contemporaries. Indeed, whenever anyone made a disparaging remark about the object of my secret devotion, prudence restrained me from protesting, and I was forced to content myself with the inner assurance that my adoration was justified.

Coming on top of my success at the concert, Longworth's unexpected condescension filled my cup of happiness to overflowing. Had I been in a less exalted frame of mind, I might have sobered myself with the reflection that it had been merely due to courtesy incidental to the presence of parents and to the exceptionally convivial nature of the occasion and that, on the morrow, when school life resumed its normal state, I should relapse once more, as far as he was concerned, into oblivion. But I was intoxicated by the glamour of success and I did not allow such distressing thoughts to enter my mind. That night I lay awake into the small hours of the night weaving a visionary epic of a long series of musical triumphs, interspersed with adventures in which Longworth and I were the protagonists.

On the last day of the Winter Term there took place what was known as the General Match. It consisted of a number of games of football in which the whole school participated. The teams were picked by prominent members of the school and they included boys of every form, from the highest to the lowest.

I was just as bad at football as I was at cricket. We used to have to play every week-day, but, in spite of constant practice, I never seemed to make much progress. My chief handicap (which it must be admitted, was a serious one) lay in my utter incompetence in the actual kicking of the ball. I could never be sure that it would go where I wanted it to, and sometimes I would miss it altogether. Nevertheless, by dint of an excessive display of energy, by running about and making a noise, I had hitherto managed to avoid any very conspicuous disgrace. I had always played in the lowest game, to which neither masters nor boys paid very much attention, and I was able to keep up my devices of bluff with impunity.

In the General Match, however, I foresaw that a still greater ingenuity would be required in order to keep me out of trouble, and I decided that the best thing to do would be to pursue my usual tactics on a more discreet scale and, if the ball happened to come my way, to dribble it along until it could be taken from me by some player of superior skill. The plan worked very well until just at the end of the game, when I suddenly found myself in an isolated position with the ball speeding inexorably towards me. My heart sank; I foresaw an appalling calamity. Shame and exposure seemed inevitable. A huge opponent was bearing down upon me. I shut my eyes and gave a frantic kick, and when I opened them again, I found, miracle of miracles, that I had scored a goal! My Guardian Angel, at that moment, must have been flying very low.

In the evening, when I went to say goodbye to Mr Gambril and to receive my journey money, he said to me, 'Well, young man, I hear you distinguished yourself on the football field.'

XXI

The Easter Term

The Easter Term of my first year at Elmley was one of the few really happy periods of my school-days. Athletic sports, after a couple of terms devoted exclusively to cricket and football, came as a welcome relief. It was perhaps the fault of my upbringing as an only child that I acquired a rooted dislike for teamwork and mass discipline. The adaptation of my little ego to the necessities of group psychology was one of the most laborious and unprofitable tasks of my school life. In the case of running, jumping or hurdling (known collectively as Sports) one was more or less an individual. If I came last in the hundred yards race, if I fell over a hurdle, it was my own look-out, and I was not sworn at as when I missed a catch at cricket or a goal at football.

Apart from this, there were other reasons for enjoying this particular Lenten Term. Mr Gambril's ferocity seemed to have temporarily abated. There were no floggings, canings or other manifestations of frightfulness. Before this there had indeed been one or two brief intervals of amiability, when he had appeared once more as the benign Mr Gambril I had known that first day at luncheon, but those intervals were all too rare, hasty snatches of sunshine that only served to accentuate the terror and gloom of the habitual thunder-clouds. Now, however, it looked as though the barometer of the Headmaster's temper was set for a protracted spell of fair weather. The causes, whatever they may have been, of this unwonted suavity were hidden from us in the Olympian world of adults; a success maybe of finance or love, the Promise of Spring or perhaps merely a period of relief from chronic constipation or whatever ailment it may have been that habitually embittered his nature. Anyhow, these halcyon days, while they lasted, were very delightful, and Mr Gambril's affability was not without its effect upon the school in general.

But above and beyond the mellowing influences of the Head-master's good humour, I had another and far more important source of happiness. Longworth's gracious condescension on the evening of the School Concert had not, as I had feared, proved an isolated expression actuated by unusual circumstances. On the first day of the Easter Term, when I met him in the Lobby, I had hardly dared to hope for recognition, but, as he passed, he gave me a very amiable smile and asked me if I had enjoyed my holidays. My heart beat with such violence that I could scarcely answer, and I rushed out into the playground, as a dog goes off with a bone, to gloat over my emotion in solitude. It seemed almost impossible that a thing that I had dreamt of, that I had longed for so passionately, could actually have come to pass. In my brief experience of school life I had met with so many disillusionments that I was beginning almost automatically to expect disappointment as the inevitable outcome of my ambitions.

Longworth sat opposite to me in chapel in the Monitors' pew. I glanced furtively at him and again he caught my eye and smiled. After this I lost no opportunity of placing myself, as it were by accident, in his way. My tactics were successful. With every meeting his cordiality increased, until finally, at the end of the first week, there sprang up between us a definite friendship.

It has become a little difficult in these days of intensive sex-sophistication to write about school friendships, particularly of one between an older and a younger boy. In those innocent, pre-Freudian, pre-Havelock Ellis generations how lucky were the authors of school stories! They could write of such things quite naïvely, without any fear that their readers would automatically place their tongues in their cheeks and indulge in a knowing leer. I can only say that if my feelings towards Longworth were of a sexual nature I was certainly not aware of it at the time, and I was in the ingenuous condition of Monsieur Jourdain before he realised that what he was saying was prose. I cannot, however, deny that my infatuation for this boy-hero of my school-days was accompanied by all the usual symptoms connected with sexual attraction. His image haunted my waking thoughts and my dreams. Anything in the least way related to him, however commonplace, however trivial, was imbued with an almost celestial radiance. The thought of this friendship for ever at the back of my mind was like the possession of some glorious work of art in sordid surroundings; at any moment I could contemplate it and refresh myself with its beauty. It gave a zest to the dullness of school routine, while it lent a new vitality to the things I liked. When, in the course of our Greek lessons, we read of the Homeric demi-gods, beings half human and half divine, who walked among mortals but were not of the same common clay, for me it was always Longworth who filled the picture, and the embodiment shed a radiance over the dreary hours of Greek construing. At other times he appeared to me in the guise of a Henty hero, and although I did not appreciate Henty as an author, one of his heroes in flesh and blood was quite a different matter, just as a sunset or a flower garden which, in pictorial representation, would make one shudder may be, in nature, a thing of beauty and delight.

But of what Longworth was really like I have no longer the vaguest idea. I imagine he must have been a very ordinary sort of boy, and certainly devoid of any conspicuous intellectual qualifications. I only remember that he was very good-looking, and that he excelled in all the things that make for prominence in school life. He happened to satisfy a youthful craving for some object of romantic devotion and, up till then, in the environment of my home there had been no such inspiring figure.

On the other hand, it is more difficult to understand what attraction I could possibly have had for Longworth, and what it can have been that induced him to single me out for his favour after having, for so long a period, ignored me. I can only suppose that my appearance on the concert platform must have invested me, for a moment, with a certain glamour and opened his eyes to a form of publicity in which he himself could never expect to excel. (In my own experience I have often felt a favourable reaction towards people to whom I would not naturally be drawn, when I have seen them exhibiting with conspicuous success some talent particularly alien to my own.) This may perhaps have established a sort of telepathic contact through which the sentiments I had so long and so ardently cherished for him were enabled to make themselves felt.

At Elmley friendships between older and younger boys were unusual. Age distinctions were as rigidly observed as class distinctions in pre-war Vienna, and Longworth's lapse in this respect elicited a good deal of comment. Among my own contemporaries I could see that this new intimacy gave rise to considerable irritation, and I am afraid that I took a certain pleasure in parading it. The backing of an influential protector made me perhaps even a little overbearing in my relations with boys of my own standing. At that time I had still a great deal to learn about tact, and also, alas! about human nature. The immediate pleasure the friendship afforded me tended to obscure the fact that there was in its essence something precarious, something akin to that 'putting your trust in princes' against which the Scriptures so wisely warn us. The hierarchical barrier between an older and a younger boy, temporarily displaced, may at any moment be re-established, just as a royal personage, after a moment of condescension, may unexpectedly relapse into the first person plural, the Royal 'We,' and assume once more the divinity that doth hedge a king; an experience I was presently to undergo in all its bitterness. In my first enjoyment of what I imagined to be a real friendship I naïvely imagined that such relationships could not be broken off except under the most catastrophic circumstances.

I knew quite well that Longworth was leaving the school at the end of the next term. But time at school was measured by different standards to those of ordinary life, and the end of the coming Summer Term seemed infinitely remote.

Each term had as its climax some particular form of entertainment. In the Summer Term there was the expedition to Boxhill, in the Winter Term the School Concert, and the Easter Term was enlivened by an entertainment that was known as a 'Penny Reading.'

I never understood the inner meaning of the name given to this *divertissement*, which was of a semi-theatrical character. But it seemed to serve its purpose in obviating any implication of undue frivolity, while the association of economy and literature vaguely suggested edification.

This year the Penny Reading was to consist of a lecture on Science with lantern slides, a number of recitations and three excerpts from Shakespeare – the balcony scene from *Romeo and Juliet* in which the Headmaster's daughter was to play the part of Juliet with Longworth as Romeo, the play scene from *Hamlet* and the episode of Pyramus and Thisbe from the *Midsummer Night's Dream*. The latter excerpt was destined for the smaller boys and I was allotted the rôle of Pyramus.

It was my first practical experience of Shakespeare. I had been made to learn by heart some of the more famous passages, such as Hamlet's soliloquy, Antony's speech in *Julius Cæsar*, the description of Cleopatra's barge. I had been encouraged to look upon Shakespeare as a tragic, or at any rate a serious dramatist, and the plays labelled Comedies did not seem at all to correspond to my idea of comedy. In the early stages of rehearsal the company of small boys was left more or less to its own devices. The scene of Pyramus and Thisbe, coming as it did in the midst of a rather serious entertainment and detached from its context, awoke no suspicion that it was meant to be comic. It is true we thought the punctuation of the Prologue a little odd, but we presumed it was a peculiarity of the Shakespearian method. One or two lines, notably those relating to Pyramus 'seeing' Thisbe's voice and 'hearing' her face, appeared strange, but this again we put down to the phraseology of the epoch, as also the rather unflattering comments of Theseus and his friends. We could not bring ourselves to believe that a scene containing a double suicide could be anything but tragic.

The dress rehearsal was superintended by the Mathematical master, Mr Miles. I am not sure if he realised that we had failed to grasp the true character of the piece, but I fancy that, if he had, he would have lost no time in setting us right, for he was not the kind of man who would have allowed anyone to continue in error for very long. At all events he professed himself quite satisfied with the way in which we acted our parts.

And so, when the actual performance took place, we were amazed and horrified at the spirit in which our efforts were received. Only then did it dawn upon us that the play we were enacting was intentionally comic. However, it was too late to change our methods, and our gravity, rendered still more ridiculous by embarrassment, added considerably to the hilarity of the entertainment. Our acting, at any rate, was not marred by the exaggeratedly intentional effects one is so often obliged to witness in the treatment of bygone humour on the stage, where the actors seem over-anxious lest their audience should fail to realise that their performance is meant to be humorous.

Of course none of us dared to confess that we had entirely misunderstood the character of the play we had taken part in, although one of the members of the cast was heard to say that he had not known before that Shakespeare was ever funny.

XXII

On the Roof

The following Summer Term (the beginning of my second year at Elmley) I was promoted to a dormitory situated at the end of the western wing. My bed was next to a window that looked out over some corn-fields, and a narrow lane which passed just below the house. The landscape had all the elegant rusticity of a picture by Morland or Birket Foster. Not a single note of modernity disturbed the view. The lane ran deep between mossy banks, the straggling hedges were broken at intervals by clumps of elder and hawthorn, and here and there, in receding perspective, rose the nodding green ostrich-feather plumes of an elm tree. Nothing ever came down the lane save an occasional farm cart with its heavy plodding horse and slow clattering.

For a few days at the beginning of the term a slight illness sent me early to bed, and, sitting comfortably propped up against my bolster, I could watch the sky growing a deeper purple and the lights of the small town far away on the horizon appearing one after the other until it looked as though a cluster of twinkling stars had fallen to earth. In the morning, what with the bustle, hurry and all the disagreeableness of getting up, there was not much time to meditate on the beauties of nature; but, in the evening, the placid enchantment of the scene in contrast with the basic unpleasantness of school life used to make my heart ache with a yearning after some mysterious, unknown ideal, that most intoxicating form of *Sehnsucht*, the yearning of William Blake's little figure stretching out its ladder to the moon.

If only one didn't have to play cricket: or at any rate not every day and all day! It was becoming more and more obvious that I had no talent whatever for the game. I did my best, but I found it difficult to persevere. Cricket bored me to death. Had I been really convinced by the Elmley propaganda and believed that, on the day when the vogue of cricket began to wane, the doom of the British Empire would be sealed, it is possible that the budding patriotism of my little soul might have spurred me on to further efforts.

But, apart from the fact that I was not a born cricketer, I had another very cogent reason for disliking the game. It was instrumental in separating me from Longworth. During the Easter Term, when Athletic Sports were the order of the day, boys of different ages mingled together more freely, and older boys would often take an interest in the athletic activities of the younger ones. 'Athletics' was the only form of sport at which I was any good. Longworth spent a good deal of his time coaching me, and it was largely due to his tuition that I managed to win several prizes for running, jumping and hurdling. In the cricket term, on the contrary, the distinctions of age and skill were accentuated. Boys playing on the same cricket-fields clung together and formed cliques. The only time I was able to see anything of Longworth was on Sundays, and during the short intervals between the school hours on week-days. Disregarding the official segregation, he made one or two attempts to teach me how to bowl and bat; they were not very successful and after a while he gave it up in despair. I could not help feeling that a severe strain had been put upon our friendship, and once or twice, I fancied I detected indications that the relationship between us was not quite as it had been. But I had not yet learnt the technique of manipulating a difficult situation and, when incidents arose that ought to have been a warning to me, I was as unskilful in dealing with them as, in cricket, I was clumsy in catching the ball or in wielding my bat.

In the course of the Summer Term, Longworth and some of his friends had formed the nefarious habit of going up on to the roof at night to smoke; an evil practice savouring of the worst excesses of 'St. Winifred's.' On account of their extreme daring these proceedings were naturally kept very secret. The school in general knew nothing of these midnight orgies, and I only knew because Longworth had told me under the strictest pledge of silence.

I used to lie awake at night in a state of feverish excitement, thinking of what was going on overhead while the school lay sleeping in blissful unconsciousness. It was as thrilling as being privy to the operations of a criminal gang. At moments I almost hoped that they might be found out so that, in the tremendous scandal that would ensue, I should be able to boast that I had known about it all along. Then the thought of Longworth being expelled would cause me almost simultaneously to offer a prayer for their welfare.

One evening Longworth suggested that I should, that night, go up alone with him on the roof. I was flattered and delighted by the invitation, but at the same time I was terrified at the idea of such audacity. I would have given anything in the world to refuse; yet, after the failure of his efforts to turn me into a cricketer, I felt that it might be fatal to say No. It was possible he was setting a trap to test my courage.

And so, as soon as silence reigned in the house, I crept out of my dormitory and met him on the top landing near the ladder which led out on to the roof. There was a full moon that night. This made the expedition even more alarming, and the moon kept peeping out from behind the clouds like a malevolent watchman.

We crouched in the shadow of a chimney. Longworth produced a packet of cigarettes. I had never smoked before, although I pretended to him that I had. I was afraid at first that I might not be able to get the thing to light and several matches were wasted before I was successful. It was also the first time that I had ever been on the roof. The view of the familiar corn-fields seen under the shifting light of the moon was entrancingly beautiful. My confidence was somewhat restored and I began to puff vigorously at my cigarette while we conversed in husky whispers. I was very happy. The comradeship of adventure seemed to have restored the sense of intimacy lost through cricket, and the fact that Longworth had asked me to accompany him on this perilous expedition seemed to me to be a proof of the constancy of his devotion. I wished that this *tête-à-tête* on the tiles could have been prolonged indefinitely. But, alas! the Faustian lapse ('Verweile doch du bist so schön!'), the desire to eternalise a moment of happiness, brought me ill-luck. After a while a breeze got up and it grew very cold. My nightgown flapped in the wind and my teeth began to chatter. I looked at my companion hoping that he would suggest going down. He seemed, however, quite undisturbed by the change of temperature and lay back against the roof with his eyes closed. The light of the moon fell full on his face and made it glow like alabaster against the shadowy background. Never before in my life had I seen such disturbing beauty in a human face. For a moment I forgot my acute discomfort and stared at him in wonder. He had perhaps some telepathic inkling of the wave of awe-struck admiration that swept over me, for he suddenly threw his arm round my neck and drew me closer to him. Then a dreadful thing occurred. Almost before I knew what was happening I was violently sick. Longworth sprang to his feet. 'Shut up, you little fool!' he hissed at me. But it was all very well to say 'Shut up!' I was beyond all possibility of shutting up. He snatched the half-smoked cigarette from my fingers while I lay gasping and retching at his feet. The noise I made was appalling and could not for one moment have been mistaken for the cry of a night-bird or any of the usual nocturnal sounds. But I felt so wretchedly ill and miserable that even the appearance of Mr Gambril himself would have left me unmoved.

At last I recovered a little and was able to stagger to my feet. I made for the skylight with faltering steps and managed to get down the ladder. Longworth followed me. As we parted to return to our respective dormitories he gave me a look in which fury was mingled with contempt.

XXIII

The Bible-throwing Episode

The Bible, during my early years, failed to inspire me with the proper sentiments of reverence and affection. Indeed, I regret to say I even felt an active antipathy for the Holy Book, an attitude which was largely, if not entirely, the fault of my grandmother, Lady Bourchier.

The Bible occupied so prominent a position in her scheme of life that I grew to associate it with her own austere personality and the grim little study at Stackwell. I feared that, were I to allow it to become an obsession (as it had become in her case) my own character might end by assuming that same forbidding Calvinistic tinge. I was not sufficiently cultured to be able to appreciate the beauties of biblical language, and the numerous copies of the Bible that my grandmother had thrust into my reluctant hands had been, all of them, cheap, ill-bound editions. The ugly, common bindings, the villainous print and the double columns were not calculated to arouse æsthetic interest, while the rigid numbering of the verses seemed to impart an unpleasantly didactic tone to the contents. Having been told that the book had been written by God himself, I often wondered why One who had shown himself, in most respects, lavish to the point of extravagance should have been so economical in the presentation of his literary efforts to the public.

At Elmley the Bible revenged itself upon me for my lack of consideration by becoming a positive nuisance. There were readings from the Scriptures every morning before early school, and on Sunday mornings we had to learn texts by heart and recite them in turn to the Headmaster. The Bible was thus an essential item of our morning toilet, and just as important as a collar or a tie.

Nearly every morning the wretched volume contrived to get itself lost. It would either burrow down to the bottom of my locker and hide itself under the five-gloves or the cricket bat, or else it would assume protective colouring and look exactly like a Latin grammar or a geography book. At other times it would wedge itself firmly between the back of the locker and the wall so that it could only be retrieved with the greatest difficulty. It seemed to be possessed of a definite animal malevolence and many times it made me late for school so that I got bad marks or an unjustified rebuke for slothfulness.

On Sundays, 'early school' was always taken by Mr Gambril himself. One Sunday morning towards the end of the Summer Term, whilst we were all assembled awaiting his arrival, I entered into a theological discussion with the sanctimonious Creeling, in the course of which he asserted that anyone speaking irreverently of the Bible or maltreating it in any way would inevitably be punished by God.

'What form,' I asked, 'do you suppose the punishment would take?'

'Well, you'd probably be struck by lightning, or else lose all your money.'

'What absolute rot!'

'Well, at any rate,' Creeling demurred, 'it would bring frightful bad luck.'

'Supposing,' I suggested, 'I were to get up now and throw my Bible across the room?'

'Just you try it and see!'

He was reckoning on my cowardice, a kind of assumption that arouses the meanest spirit. I at once stood up and hurled my Bible across the room.

At that very moment the door opened and Mr Gambril appeared. The book missed him by a few inches and fell with a thud at his feet. I was paralysed with horror, and he was obliged to ask twice over 'Who threw that book?' before I was able to get my voice into working order.

'Oh, it was you,' he said, in that ominously suave voice which one knew from experience was like the lull preceding the storm. He bent down and examined the book. Then the storm broke.

'The Bible!' he shouted. 'The Bible, sir! You have thrown the Bible – and on Sunday too! Stand up on the form!'

I climbed up on to the form. My knees were trembling with such violence that I had difficulty in keeping my balance. Somebody laughed.

'Silence!' said Mr Gambril. 'This is no laughing matter!

'Now, sir,' he turned to me, 'may I ask for what reason you threw your Bible?'

I hesitated. I could think of no valid reason.

'What did you throw your Bible for? Answer me at once!'

'I threw it for a bet.'

As the words left my lips I realised their infelicity. I suppose 'bravado' was the word I had meant to use, but panic confused my thought.

'For a bet? Indeed! This makes your offence even worse than I had imagined. You have the effrontery to tell me, sir, that, for a bet, which is in itself reprehensible, you actually threw God's Sacred Book across the room! Are you aware that this constitutes an act of sacrilege, liable in ordinary circumstances to be punished by a long term of imprisonment?'

I was not aware; but it seemed, at that moment, to be quite probable. I was too frightened to recognise it as merely one of those over-statements with which the Head was wont to emphasise his speech.

He turned to the assembled school. 'Never,' he proclaimed, 'in all my long experience of school life have I come across so flagrant a case of wilful blasphemy and godlessness. Boys, I am sure you are all disgusted. You will now express your condemnation of such behaviour by hissing the culprit.'

This was an entirely new form of punishment. To me, as I stood on the form with bowed head, surrounded, as it were, by a roomful of infuriated vipers, it seemed to be the most terrible thing that had ever happened to anyone, and the suggestion of mass-hatred in a peculiarly venomous shape intensified my sense of guilt. I felt as though I were branded for ever with the mark of Cain.

When the hissing had died down the Headmaster said to me in the tones of a judge delivering a death-sentence, 'You will remain standing on the form during the lesson and afterwards you will come to my study.'

This, of course, implied that a birching was in store for me. How

I got through the remainder of the lesson would be too painful to relate. There were moments when I would have welcomed annihilation. The horror of seeing what I believed to be a comparatively innocent action transformed in the twinkling of an eye into an appalling crime, followed by public shame, the experience of the pillory and finally the condemned cell. I was also smarting under a sense of injustice, complicated by the horrible doubt as to whether perhaps after all Creeling had not been right in saying that the Bible possessed magic powers of self-protection. In this case, at any rate, the insult offered to it had been followed by swift retribution.

The lesson came to an end at last. I got down from the form and followed the Headmaster out of the room in the midst of a silence that I knew to be fraught with a gloating expectancy.

As I entered the study, Mr Gambril took up one of his birches and laid it on the table. He then proceeded to deliver a forcible homily on sacrilege and wickedness in general, in the course of which he expressed grave misgivings about my future career. But although he fingered the birch and, from time to time, shook it at me menacingly, he finally dismissed me without having used it. The implication was that my offence had been far too serious for mere corporal punishment and that I was lucky to have escaped expulsion. I only thought that I was lucky to have escaped the birch.

It may perhaps seem difficult to believe that so trivial a misdeed as throwing a Bible could have provoked all this fury. But schoolmasters, like many other people in responsible positions, are often overcome by the tedium of their duties, and at such moments, I imagine, they gladly welcome any excuse for working up a violent emotion. It relieves their feelings and acts as a moral pick-me-up. Thus it sometimes happens that small boys, to whom the psychology of their elders is a sealed book, are left with a confusing idea of the relative magnitude of their crimes.

On returning to the schoolroom, I was relieved to find that my act of sacrilege had not really damaged me very seriously in the eyes of my schoolfellows. The hissing was, of course, a perfunctory affair, entered into with zest because the act of hissing was in itself rather enjoyable. Furthermore, it had been a 'command performance' and not in the least a genuine manifestation of public opinion.

As a matter of fact, in school life, spectacular disgrace generally produces a reaction of popularity, and I was at once surrounded by an interested crowd. There was, I am bound to say, some slight disappointment when it transpired that I had escaped a birching. However, the sense of being, for the moment, in the public eye helped to dissipate the cloud of guilt that hung over me, and my spirits rose again. Indeed I felt myself almost a hero. My thoughts turned to Longworth. I hoped that my act of audacity might perhaps tend to counteract the lamentable impression left by the incident on the roof. But I could find him nowhere.

The bell tolled for morning chapel. I knew that I should see him there, for his place was directly opposite mine on the other side of the aisle. We had been in the habit, ever since the beginning of our friendship, of enlivening the service by exchanging signs and grimaces, flicking pellets of paper at one another, and seeing how far we could go without attracting the attention of the masters. But now I noticed, with growing concern, that Longworth was deliberately trying to avoid looking in my direction. I was bewildered by his behaviour and I found it impossible to believe that the Bible-throwing business could have anything to do with it. Hitherto he had never betrayed any symptoms of excessive piety.

As we left the chapel I at last managed to catch his eye, but, to my horror, I was met by so chilling a stare that it gave me the sensation of a door being slammed in my face. If I had only had more self-assurance and less amour-propre, I should have accosted him then and there and asked for an explanation. But amour-propre, alas! is for ever getting in the way and complicating human relationships. In the interval between chapel and the luncheon hour I came face to face with him in the Lobby. I was not going to risk the humiliation of a public rebuff, and so I deliberately cut him.

It was a decision taken in a lost cause, and, as it often happens in such cases, I was haunted for a long time afterwards by vain regrets. I would re-enact again and again in my memory the circumstances of this fateful meeting, wondering whether, if I had made a last frantic effort at reconciliation, it might perhaps have altered matters. But, at the moment when it occurred, it seemed as though fatality lay heavy on me. It was useless to struggle against it and the only thing left for me to do was to eclipse myself as gracefully as possible. I made no attempt to approach Longworth through an intermediary. There was nobody I felt I could trust to act in this capacity, nor did I wish it to be known that I 'minded.' The position of one who has been dropped is humiliating, and it was particularly so in this case. The friendship with Longworth, and my own rather injudicious attitude in the matter, had not endeared me to some of my contemporaries, who did not hesitate to parade the malicious pleasure my fall from favour afforded them. It was impossible to disguise the fact that it was Longworth who had decided the rupture of our relations; had it been a case of friendship between equals I might perhaps have pretended that it was I who had taken the initiative, or, had I been more sophisticated, I might even have invented an incident which called for a display of outraged virtue.

I heard, later on, the reasons that Longworth gave for having broken with me. He said that he at last realised that it didn't do for a fellow in his position to be intimate with a mere kid, that I had shown a tendency to presume on his friendship and that I had been getting too 'cheeky.' He said that the Bible-throwing business had given him a good excuse to put an end to the affair.

It had been obvious to me from the beginning that the Bible-throwing had been a mere pretext. I was continually haunted by the thought that if I had only been less obtuse, if I had realised more fully how precarious my relations with Longworth had been growing during the last few weeks, perhaps this disastrous climax might have been averted. I reviewed in my memory each single event that had taken place during the previous months, pondering with self-torturing intensity upon each word or action that might have hastened the friendship to its end, leading up to the culminating episode on the roof which had given it its death-blow. My reflections inevitably ended in the sorrowful conclusion that I had lost Longworth through some inherent defect in my character, a defect that it might be impossible to remedy and one which, throughout my whole career, would stand, like the Angel with the flaming sword, in front of every paradise I sought to enter. I called to mind all the humiliations I had suffered during my short life, all the people who had disliked or despised me – Nesta, Cousin Emily, Mademoiselle Bock – and they seemed to circle above me in the dusky air like the Eumenides, pointing at me fingers of scorn.

The remainder of the Summer Term was utter misery. Longworth's friendship had been the one bright flame that lit up my dreary existence at Elmley and had made school life glow with a pleasant radiance. I fell into a state of deep depression. Even Mrs Gambril noticed that something was amiss. She sent for me and inquired if I had any secret trouble. She asked me if I were being bullied. This I indignantly denied. That was, in any case, a thing that one would never admit. She plied me with questions and finally, in desperation, ordered me a tonic, to be taken daily after meals. Its bitter taste was a daily complement to the bitterness of my heart. I wished that it could have been the waters of Lethe. Each day there was the recurrent agony (like a vulture tearing at my liver) of being obliged, in chapel, to sit opposite the cause of all my misery and to meet with never a flicker of recognition on that once so friendly face. Now, whenever his eyes chanced to meet mine, I encountered the cold, inhuman gaze of an archaic statue.

XXIV

Dissolving View

A few days before the end of the Summer Term I heard that my grandfather Mr Farmer was dead. When I came home for the holidays I found that my mother had gone to Arley. Neither I nor any of my small cousins had been summoned to the funeral, it being considered wiser, I suppose, to spare us the depressing ceremony.

This was the first time, within my experience, that anyone with whom I was nearly connected had died. But Mr Farmer's death had taken place at a distance and the only emotion that I can remember feeling was one of slight annoyance at not having been invited to the funeral. For the first time, also, I found myself alone at home without a parent or a governess to control my actions, and, in the enjoyment of this novel experience, I remember thinking how pleasant it would be to have no parents, to be one's own master, free to do just whatever one liked. After letting my thoughts revel for a while in an orgy of imagined liberty, I suddenly recollected how devoted I was in reality to my mother. I was seized with remorse, and discovering a new form of self-pity in the idea of being an orphan, I burst into floods of tears. One of the servants, through an excusable misunderstanding, sought to console me with the information that 'Grandpapa had gone to heaven and was now among the angels.' As I had only known 'Grandpapa' while he was afflicted by his strange mental derangement, this conjured up a rather ludicrous picture, and I wondered what the angels would think of some of the curious language he used during his more violent outbursts.

My grandfather's death left an unsettled state of affairs at Arley, and so we did not go there as we usually did during the summer holidays. For some time afterwards, in this devoted family circle, so closely held together by ties of loyalty and affection, the air was full of the jealousies and recriminations that so frequently follow on the reading of a will. During the visits of various relatives to Althrey during the summer months I was continually overhearing comments on the injustices the will contained, so that I eventually came to believe that it must have been a monument of posthumous malice.

With regard to Arley itself it was finally decided that my grandmother should stay on there, together with Aunt Flora and Uncle Luke. My mother's eldest brother, who should by rights have taken up his residence at Arley, having apparently a deep-rooted aversion to the Gothic style, preferred to remain in the Georgian house in which he had been living up till then.

I was very relieved to think that there was to be no alteration in the conditions at Arley. The picture of Arley as it had appeared to me in my early youth was one that neither time nor circumstances had succeeded in obliterating, and although school life had transformed my outlook to a considerable extent and had now become more important to me, a more serious affair than home life, nevertheless, the peculiar atmosphere of Arley, which I have attempted to convey in the opening chapters, remained the foundation upon which the fabric of my later impressions rested.

I looked forward to my next visit to Arley (which was to take place at Christmas) with an anticipation intensified by a longer absence than usual.

Once more, after I had crossed the river and got within sight of the grey towers looming through the trees in the twilight, I was seized with that same ecstasy of anticipation I had always experienced as a small child. I even felt that, with my grandfather gone, the place might assume a gayer and still more lovable aspect.

But as soon as I set foot inside the house I began to realise that a curious transformation had taken place. At first I attributed it to the natural aftermath of sadness consequent on my grandfather's death, a cloud of melancholy not yet dissipated by time. There was, without doubt, a subtle alteration in the atmosphere, indefinable in its quality, but which none the less seemed to have affected even the material aspect of things, just as scenery on the stage is transformed by a change in the lighting.

During the last years of my grandfather's life, my grandmother had come to rely more and more for the management of the household upon my Cousin Emily, who had taken up her residence permanently at Arley and had been given a small suite of rooms in one of the towers. But it had always been found necessary to keep her out of my grandfather's sight as much as possible, for he detested her, and her mere appearance was sufficient to provoke one of his fits of violent, incoherent rage.

Latterly Mr Farmer had grown quite incapable of taking any part in domestic affairs, of giving an order even; nevertheless, so long as he remained alive, the patriarchal spirit continued to prevail. He was still the nominal head of the house; his authority remained in theory the ultimate appeal; the primeval leadership of the 'Old Man' was still an important convention. Emily therefore played the part of an unobtrusive housekeeper and remained in the background.

At the age of thirty, Emily had developed into a prematurely aged, wizened little creature. Her beady eyes had just a little more expression than those of a frog and slightly less than those of a parrot. Her pursed-up mouth gave her a tightly shut appearance, as though she were bolted and barred against all external influences, and her closely-buttoned-up tailor-made costumes seemed an appropriate sartorial accompaniment to her features. She affected a type of headgear known as the 'pork-pie' hat. When she went out she invariably carried a bulging, Robeyesque umbrella, no matter how fine the weather. This implement I came to regard as Emily's own special symbol, just as the chimonanthus shrub stood in my imagination for Aunt Flora. In Emily's hands the umbrella seemed a natural weapon of defence against all the things in life that were in the least removed from the commonplace.

When I was a small child, Emily had, from time to time, endeavoured to adopt repressive measures; she occasionally 'sneaked' about me to my grandmother and managed to get some of my simple but slightly subversive amusements forbidden; but, as I grew up, her interference became less effective and finally she relapsed into a malevolent quiescence.

Since she was my grandmother's protégée, the attitude of the rest of the family towards her (with the exception of my cousins and myself) was one of indulgent toleration. Mrs Farmer used to say that she found her invaluable, but it is difficult to imagine that anyone so averse to constructive effort could possibly have coped with the complicated domestic arrangements at Arley. It was always presumed that the clock-work efficiency with which the house was run was in reality due to the capable management of the housekeeper, Mrs Matchett. However, Emily succeeded in making my grandmother believe that she did it all herself, and my grandmother's compassionate nature prompted her to take the most favourable view of anyone she protected.

As soon as my grandfather had disappeared from the scene, Emily began to exercise an uncanny dominion over the household. My grandmother, Uncle Luke and Aunt Flora were none of them very vital characters, and they were unable to hold out for long against Emily's system of negative attrition. By methods of subtle insinuation she managed by degrees to discourage their few modest ambitions until finally she contrived to reduce them to a condition of inertia similar to her own.

Her increasing domination over Arley and its inhabitants was like some strange, insidious mildew which ended by pervading every cranny and corner of the place. She seemed to have woven a spell that held it in a lethargic thrall, and before long it became

overgrown with weeds and brambles of a more deadly kind than
those that infested the palace of the Sleeping Beauty. The very
rooms began to change their characters. The library lost its air of
luxurious comfort; the reading lamps burnt less brightly in their
emerald shades; the busts of the Eminent Men of Letters scowled
from their niches in evident disapproval, and the porphyry urns on
the mantelpiece began to assume a funereal aspect. In the
blue-and-gold drawing-room some of the most agreeable landmarks
began to disappear, the Himalayan Pheasant and the scrapwork
screen. Even Aunt Flora's sitting-room had suffered a change. I
noticed that the dome-shaped cage with its twittering birds was no
longer there. 'Emily says that they are unhealthy,' Aunt Flora
explained. 'Perhaps she is right.' And she smiled rather sadly. One
began to wonder whether Emily did not possess hypnotic powers,
for in normal circumstances Aunt Flora would never have allowed
herself to be deprived of her birds. Now, however, she seemed quite
resigned.

The most drastic change of all had taken place in the housekeeper's room. It was a change that I felt more acutely perhaps than
any other. Mrs Matchett had gone. Whether she had been sent
away, or whether she left of her own free will, I was never able to
discover. It is probable that she felt disinclined to face the effects of
Emily's growing despotism. Her place had been filled by a
meek-faced woman with whom, out of loyalty to her predecessor, I
never attempted to make friends.

In dealing with her different victims Emily varied her methods.
She had managed to impress my grandmother with the idea that she
was very old. It became an obsession, and the poor lady now spent
the greater part of the day resting. Uncle Luke, who always had a
tendency to hypochondria, was induced to believe that almost any
form of activity was bad for him. Aunt Flora, who was a genuine
invalid, was encouraged to think that, if she were to renounce
certain of the pleasures of her already sufficiently limited existence,
she might possibly get better. And so the birds had been banished
from her sitting-room under the pretext that their continual
twittering was injurious to the nerves and that the cage was
insanitary. The number of the flowers in the room was diminished;
it was supposed that they poisoned the air. As poor Aunt Flora had

few interests beyond her flowers and her birds, she ended by passing most of her time in aimless meditation on the sofa. I imagine that she was still interested in clothes, but now that I had grown older she no longer took me into her confidence.

At the time the first symptoms of this baleful transformation at Arley began to appear, my analytical powers were not sufficiently developed to enable me to trace them to their true origin. I could not, of course, help noticing the mysterious decay that seemed to be undermining the place; but some time elapsed before I came to connect it definitely with Cousin Emily. On the surface she seemed to be as unimportant as ever, and, as far as visitors were concerned, she still kept very much in the background. The only thing that I noticed during the first visit after my grandfather's death was that she seemed to be a little less obsequious in her manner towards my mother, in whose person she probably scented danger. My mother's energy and active disposition might have stirred the spellbound inhabitants of Arley to some form of activity which would have shaken Emily's regime of stagnation. Towards myself Emily's attitude was, as it had ever been, one of controlled aversion.

My mother's contempt for Emily was so profound that, with her tendency to disregard all facts that did not fit in with preconceived theories, she could not at first bring herself to admit that anyone she held in such low esteem could possibly play so decisive a rôle in the life of a family of which she herself formed part, and, even if she had any suspicion of the true state of affairs during that winter visit, she still considered me too much of a child to be taken into her confidence with regard to the doings of grown-up members of the family. She even went so far as to defend Emily (whom she disliked as much as I did), when I once began to unburden my heart on the subject. 'You must remember,' she said, 'that Emily is an orphan and that she is your cousin.'

Albeit, the 'orphan cousin' eventually succeeded in practically excluding my mother and myself from the place which held such happy associations for both of us; not indeed by direct methods, but by so transforming the atmosphere of Arley that it became no longer a pleasure to go there.

Beyond an occasional malicious insinuation, there was nothing in Emily's demeanour to which one could possibly take exception, and it remained just as difficult as ever to believe that so colourless an individual could exert an influence over anyone or anything. But in the end one was forced to the conclusion that, beneath that façade of physical and mental sterility, there lay a will of iron. Her very lack of character she seemed to employ as a weapon. It was impossible to reason with her. There was no use in attempting to convince a person who met every argument with a tightly shut mouth and an offended air. Towards almost everything of a positive nature Emily adopted an attitude of passive resistance. The suggestion of any innovation, however innocuous it might be, appeared to wound her moral susceptibilities. I remember that once, when my mother suggested some new variety of flower for the garden, Emily pursed her lips and said, 'I have never heard of it,' just as though my mother had put forward a proposition that was vaguely obscene.

In the early Roman mythology, where every aspect of life had its tutelary Genius, Emily would have aptly figured as the Goddess of Vis Inertiæ.

XXV

Epilogue

I should prefer to give this record of my childhood a happy ending, and I am loath to close it in a minor key, on a note of disillusion. But to pursue my career further into a brighter mode would be to transcend the limits I have set myself. I consider that my childhood comprises my early years at home and the first four terms at Elmley; for, although I remained at Elmley for four years in all, those first four terms seem to me to contain all that is necessary to elucidate the psychological history of my early years. The remainder of my time there brought me no new spiritual adventures, and the period represents, as it were, a 'marking time' in my mental development.

The break-up of my friendship with Longworth and all its attendant humiliation and misery affected me deeply. But I fancy that the dissolution of Arley had an even stronger influence, all the more so because it was not so obvious. The Longworth episode was at least a tangible one. I realised it clearly as a source of sorrow and anguish; but with regard to Arley the issue was more obscure. I hardly understood at the time that places could be more important than people. (This somewhat exaggerated sentiment for places may perhaps be a peculiarity of my nature, and when I hear cats spoken of slightingly as 'being more attached to places than to people' I always feel a little conscience-stricken.)

After all, Arley had formed the background to the first stages in the evolution of my character. It was the soil in which my personality had begun to sprout; so that, when it was transformed, under the influence of Emily, so as to be scarcely recognisable as the Arley I had known and loved in the first years of my life, it was (to continue the horticultural simile) as though the earth had been scraped away from my roots.

The combination of these two discouragements, the Longworth episode and the change at Arley, cast a benumbing spell upon the closing years of my childhood, and it was not until I left Elmley for Eton, which coincided with the transition from childhood to adolescence, that a new and more vigorous chapter in my life began.

FAR FROM THE MADDING WAR

CONTENTS

As every character in a work of fiction is bound to have some characteristic that is characteristic of someone, the author will be obliged if his friends will not attempt to recognise themselves or each other in these pages.

I

Emmeline's War Work

Miss Emmeline Pocock sat, intently bending over a large piece of embroidery, surrounded by good taste and silence. The room she sat in was as elegantly appointed a room as anyone could wish to see, although a highly attuned connoissance of decorative subtleties might detect, here and there, a blemish; a somewhat too deliberate juxtaposition of objects; colour arrangements that envisaged artistic ideals without quite achieving them. But, on the whole, the general effect was one of harmony, discretion, lack of pretentiousness, and there was none of that absence of comfort that good taste so often entails.

The room was also sound proof. Emmeline, when her father took up his residence as Warden of All Saints, had caused the walls of her room to be padded with cork and sea-weed, and she had installed double windows, so that she should not be disturbed by the cries of undergraduates, by their practising of musical instruments (some of which were of a very disagreeable nature), by the distant rumble of traffic and, above all, by the perpetual buzzing of aeroplanes.

The sky, above the old university town, seemed to have become a rendezvous for aviators, a kind of non-stop meet; they were for ever circling, wheeling and diving overhead and the ancient walls never ceased to vibrate with their droning. To many this might be a promise of protection; to Emmeline, the sound was a reminder of the precarious age we live in.

Her dislike of disturbing noises was not, however, due to a love of meditation. On the contrary, when she was alone in her room, she preferred to indulge in complete mental repose. Her faculties of association were perhaps unduly sensitive and insufficiently controlled. The shouts of undergraduates would evoke, in the manner of Gray, a poignant reflection on the exuberance of youth and its impending doom; the sound of a hunting horn echoing through the quad, an *espièglerie* to which representatives of the higher social

strata were much addicted, recalled to her alternatively the follies of
the aristocracy, or modern music, which she much disliked.

To her, a place where she could spend a certain portion of her
time in the absolute quiescence of her consciousness was a necessity.
'Life,' she used to say, 'is so difficult to cope with that I find I can
only do so by fortifying myself with long periods of respite from
thought.'

People to whom she had made this confession had recommended
other ways of banishing thought: games, household duties, gardening, charitable works, or reading her father's philosophical books,
which were so difficult to understand that it was no use trying. But
she preferred her own methods.

Let us consider Emmeline's appearance in order. The first
impression was one of gentleness and modesty. Then you began to
realize that she was extremely pretty. Some even considered her
beautiful. But her features were too retroussé to conform with the
canons of classic beauty. Emmeline herself believed that it was
better, for all practical intents and purposes, that a young woman
should be pretty rather than beautiful, and made no attempt to
assume the airs that so often accompany the fatal gift. She was of
rather diminutive stature, but her body was so well proportioned
that she appeared taller than she really was. Her hair, as a poetical
undergraduate had once said, was reminiscent of a cornfield at
daybreak. Her complexion was of that fairness that invites freckles,
but as she never exposed herself to the sun that was not a serious
defect. Her type was more suggestive of the eighteenth century than
of the present day. She looked like a nymph in one of the less
licentious pictures of Fragonard. Her manner was aloof and
dignified. In fact she was not the sort of girl with whom you might
be tempted to take liberties without encouragement. And encouragement in this respect was one of the things that Emmeline
never gave.

The war had come upon her as a very unpleasant surprise. The
twenty years of her life had been spent in the company of eminently
sensible people. Her mother, now deceased, had been a very
sensible woman. Her father, who was a philosopher, had always
appeared to possess a fund of common sense, and the few who may

have held different views had never betrayed them in her presence. Being neither a keen nor a very conscientious student of politics, she had put her trust a little too implicitly in the words that fell from the lips of some of the eminent statesmen who occasionally came to her father's house. And as such people often speak quite reasonably, however much their subsequent policies become distorted by the exigencies of political strategy, she was deluded into rather too optimistic an outlook. In a phrase so frequently used in the newspapers, she allowed herself to be lulled into a false sense of security. With a naïve faith she had clung to her belief in the ultimate triumph of reason.

After going through a few weeks of dismay and depression, during which she gathered from the conversation and the activities of her friends that she was expected to alter her rather indolent mode of life, she determined to apply herself to some form of war work.

But what on earth, she wondered, was it to be? She dreaded the thought of an uncongenial task. She did not see herself in a munition factory or in a hospital; performing clerical work in a Government office, driving an ambulance or even doling out sausages and tomato soup in a canteen.

Engaged in these speculations, she suddenly thought of an immense and valuable piece of embroidery stowed away in her bedroom. Why it should have come into her mind at that particular moment she could not imagine. The associations of our thoughts, as Emmeline had often discovered, are sometimes so unexpected and obscure that they defy analysis. The connecting links flash by with the rapidity of a cinema reel, so that it becomes impossible for the memory to record their succession. But Emmeline was not concerned just then with analysis. She hailed the intrusion of the piece of embroidery as an inspiration. 'That,' she said, 'will be my war work.'

She went upstairs and took it from the shelf where it had reposed ever since, some years before, it had been bequeathed to her by an aunt, an old lady who, in spite of a moderate outlay, had succeeded in amassing a collection of objects of considerable artistic value.

During a visit, at a moment when conversation had lapsed and Emmeline had felt the necessity of making some sort of remark, a contingency that is, more often than not, fraught with danger, she had expressed an exaggerated appreciation of the embroidery (which as a matter of fact she did not greatly admire), with the result that it had been left to her in her aunt's will in the place of some other legacy that she would have preferred.

It was a very fine piece of work, but, notwithstanding its great rarity and value, Emmeline had found no place for it in her decorative scheme. It was too ostensibly precious, too obviously a museum piece, and would have struck a false, or rather too high a note, in a room which was meant to be lived in agreeably rather than scrutinized by the eye of a collector. Emmeline had often thought of presenting it to some museum, but had refrained from doing so, partly from indolence and partly from delicacy of feeling with regard to a legacy, especially as her aunt had often expressed her dislike for museums and referred to them as 'those mausoleums of beauty,' a phrase that very exactly described her own house. Similar considerations precluded the idea of selling. It would have been repellent to her to make a profit out of a token of family affection. Thus it had become something of a white elephant, and at moments she was disturbed by the thought that she ought to have it insured.

Returning to her room, she spread out the embroidery over the back of a sofa. It was certainly a remarkable piece of work. An expert to whom she had shown it had pronounced it to be German, probably of the fourteenth century, bearing traces of Byzantine influence. It represented incidents in the lives of the saints, interspersed with lettered scrolls and devices composed of flowers, foliage and animals. It was wonderfully preserved. The colours were still fresh, and glowed with a sombre radiance.

She wondered where and in what circumstances her aunt had picked it up. She knew that the old lady had neither the means nor the inclination to pay a very high price for anything she bought. Emmeline regretted that she had not made enquiries while her aunt was still alive. In view of what she was about to do, she longed to know its history, and she wished she had made investigations while there was yet time.

Focusing a swivel lamp on a corner of the embroidery, she took up a small pair of scissors and, drawing up a chair, she sat down before it and began slowly, deliberately to unravel the tiny threads of silk, offering a mental prayer to God to grant her the requisite strength to persevere in her minute labour of destruction until not a single thread remained of this unique, almost monumental, work of art.

II

A Dinner Party at the Warden's

After toiling strenuously for several hours and finding that at the end of that time she had only succeeded in unravelling about a quarter of a square inch, Emmeline was disheartened by the difficulty and magnitude of the task she had undertaken. When she was obliged to unpick some of her own embroidery she had always found it an unexpectedly lengthy business. But here her difficulties were increased a thousandfold by the fact that time had coagulated the silken threads into an almost solid mass, and she was obliged to excavate carefully with the point of her scissors in order to detach each thread. 'I am sure,' she said to herself, 'it must be like picking oakum, only worse.'

She was determined, however, not to evade the minutest intricacy of her work. If she were to do so, the whole point of it would be lost, and she might as well throw the whole thing into the fire straightway.

The views she had now evolved on the subject of war work were very definite. Above all it should not be pleasurable. The proper spirit was one of austerity; and she disapproved of the way in which some of her friends seemed to be enjoying their work. Had she herself taken on a job in a hospital or in a government office, had she applied herself to any of the more normal forms of war activity, she might conceivably have come to enjoy them too. She knew that the work she had chosen would never be anything to her but tedious, laborious and heart-rending.

She found her views confirmed by the speeches of some of the cabinet ministers, an almost gloating insistence upon the nation preparing itself for hardships and suffering, by the admonition of

Marshal Petain, 'Trop de plaisirs,' and by the exhortations she read
in the newspapers that people should destroy their asparagus beds.

The more she thought on the matter the more convinced she
became that her choice had been appropriate and comprehensive.
The spirit of sacrifice was represented in the destruction of a
valuable possession; the spirit of self abasement in the fact that she
had joined the ranks of the Great Destroyers and was deliberately
courting the same kind of odium that had been incurred by
Herostatus, who burnt the temple of Artemis at Ephesus, or Lady
Burton, who tore up her husband's manuscripts. Yet, she felt, she
was not quite as one of these. Herostatus had been actuated by a
craving for immortality, Lady Burton by prudishness. Their
motives, at any rate, were less elevated than hers.

Temperamentally she was averse to destruction. As a child she
had never pulled the wings off flies or broken her toys. But now
destruction was in the order of the day. That the embroidery
happened to be of German origin did not appeal to her as a point in
her argument, though it was one that might perhaps meet with the
approval of the rabidly patriotic. It was a pity, of course, that what
she was doing could not possibly help to win the war, but then the
same thing could be said of a great deal of war work that was very
much applauded.

As a rule she was not intimidated by unfavourable criticism, but
she was easily fatigued by reiteration. Many of her friends, she had
noticed, did not content themselves with expressing their opinions
once and for all. They were inclined to go on and on about them. In
spite of her confidence in the fitness of her choice, she suspected
that, by even the most inveterate of vandals, it would be
condemned. Thus she foresaw the necessity of keeping the nature of
her work to herself. She would not be able to boast about it or bore
people with it, as did some of her friends. It would be better to incur
the reproach of doing nothing whatever in the war than to expose
herself to constant recriminations, and possibly to be ticketed with
the label of eccentricity. It occurred to her that certain war
occupations were of so secret a character that they could not be
divulged. That, she decided, would be the line that she would take
about hers.

It was nearly dinner time. She remembered that Mr Jericho had been invited, and that he had a habit of bouncing into her room unheralded. She gathered up the embroidery and stowed it away out of sight. She was not a wink too soon.

It was characteristic of this ebullient personality that you rarely heard or saw him coming. He appeared quite suddenly, like a pantomime demon or a cuckoo out of a cuckoo clock. His departures were equally sudden and, unless he happened to be in a situation from which he could not decently escape, he would, like the cuckoo, after sounding the requisite number of notes, vanish with a snap.

Mr Jericho was blond and rather Flemish looking. His person presented a strange combination of asceticism and sensuality. A spiritual gourmet, he suggested an inspiration of Fra Angelico executed by Rubens. He wore very large steel-rimmed spectacles, through which his eyes focused you with an alarming intensity. You felt that there was nothing they missed, and, indeed, that they often saw a good many things that weren't there.

He was tutor of modern history at All Saints and was said to be one of the most brilliant exponents of that equivocal science, the philosophy of history. His interests centred also in the less serious weaknesses of mankind, and particularly in those of his colleagues. No intrigue, no drama, no love affair, however recondite, could occur within the precincts of the university without his immediately becoming possessed of its every detail. He seemed to hold a divining rod for anything that savoured of scandal, and it was perpetually turning in his hands.

Emmeline was not particularly interested in college gossip, but she enjoyed hearing it recounted and embellished by Mr Jericho. The most trivial, the most anodyne item of personal news was transformed by his exquisite artistry into a little masterpiece of psychological literature.

He was preparing to regale Emmeline with an account of the latest elopement of Mrs Postlethwaite, the only don's wife who had pretentions of being a 'grande amoureuse', when the Warden tapped on the door and called out that dinner was ready and that Professor and Mrs Trumper were waiting below.

'Oh, damn,' said Mr Jericho, for he knew that the presence of the Trumpers was going to spoil the evening.

As they sat down to dinner, Emmeline reflected, as she often had occasion to do before, on her father's peculiar ideas of entertaining. He enjoyed the company of intelligent and amusing people and he liked his dinners to go with a swing. But some strange kink in his nature, some blind spot in his social vision, caused him too frequently to ruin a promising list of guests by the insertion of one or two people who, he must have known, would infallibly wreck the party. There was no lack of such people in the town, but if he felt it his duty to ask them, he could have easily invited them all together and made a holocaust of it.

Mr Jericho had a theory that it was Doctor Pocock's love of experimental research that impelled him to find out whether certain combinations of people would always go badly. The Provost of Unity, who was also interested in the whys and wherefores of human behaviour, had put foward the suggestion that it might be due to a philosopher's mistrust of perfection, to his belief that no rose should be unaccompanied by a thorn. Emmeline herself was disinclined to discuss the matter with her father. Since the death of Mrs Pocock, they had reached a tacit understanding never to comment on each other's idiosyncrasies.

Professor Trumper was large and ungainly. His rugged features looked as if they had been carved by an indifferent sculptor out of some very unpleasant species of granite. He was reputed to be one of the rudest members of the university. But it was difficult to know whether his rudeness proceeded from arrogance or from stupidity, a form of discourtesy that sensitive people found hard to deal with. To Mr Jericho in particular, the Professor's rudeness was an irritating problem. He prided himself on a capacity for encountering any abnormal manifestation of behaviour, whether it took the form of extreme rudeness or excessive politeness. In the case of Professor Trumper he never knew whether his repartee should be inspired by anger or pity.

Professor Trumper was one of the few dons of the higher order (excluding, of course, those coming from Scotland or the Dominions) who was willing, in a purely social gathering, to speak for any length of time on his own particular subject. This habit was deplored by many of his colleagues, who held that your 'subject' should only be spoken of in the lecture room, in intimate discussions with colleagues or on rare occasions in order to impress some important guest. An ordinary stranger venturing to probe into the nature of a don's scholastic activities would be viewed with suspicion. One was reminded of the anecdote about a personage of the nineties who, asked by a cabman to what address he should drive him, replied: 'Why should I reveal to you the whereabouts of my glorious home?'

Professor Trumper, however, was not a prey to such inhibitions. Indeed, one often wished that he were; that he could be psycho-analysed in an inverse sense and given a few.

The Professor had a powerful voice and a manner of clearing his throat that acted like a mine-sweeper. He was able to talk any one down, and his wife often thought that he resembled Doctor Johnson.

Mrs Trumper was physically unlike her husband. She was small and fragile looking, and she had an air of faded sweetness, which, however, was soon found to be deceptive. After getting to know her a little more intimately you came to the conclusion that she was like marmalade that had gone sour.

She was an international idealist, and, although she never seemed to be doing anything to further it, she was a great believer in what she called 'the nations getting together.' 'If only,' she would lament, 'the nations would try to understand each other's psychology! It is because the different countries take no trouble to get to know one another that international security has become imperilled.' 'Tout savoir c'est tout pardonner' was a phrase that was constantly on her lips. Maddened one day by its reiteration, Mr Jericho had remarked that it would be truer to say: 'Tout savoir c'est tout condamner.'

She was crazy about small nations, the smaller the better. She often wrote articles in the more intellectual periodicals. In her literary activities, however, she was apt to be dogged by misfortune. Her opinions and her prophecies were continually being refuted by facts before the article was published. Just before the war she had written a letter to the *New Stateswoman* which ended with the words: 'If only Hitler would speak all would be well.' It appeared on the day after the Fuehrer had made one of his four-hour speeches and all was not well.

Mrs. Trumper had been connected at one time with the League of Nations. She had spent a year at Geneva and had never quite recovered from it.

Resigning himself to the prospect of not having the kind of conversation he would have enjoyed, Mr Jericho decided to turn the party into a sort of game in which he would employ his wits in heading off Professor Trumper from one of his customary dissertations on marginal utility, imperfect competition, vertical disintegration, and other weighty aspects of economics. However, the Professor, that evening, seemed to have made up his mind to speak about nothing but the war.

Doctor Pocock did not encourage discussion of the war at his dinner parties. He was at heart a little gloomy as to its ultimate issue, and he did not wish to lay himself open to the charge of being a defeatist. Unlike some of his colleagues, he hesitated to express views that were not sincere, and he had resolved to adopt the same non-committal attitude as an eighteenth century sage had done on the subject of religion. If questioned as to his opinions, he would reply that they were those of every sensible man and were opinions that every sensible man kept to himself.

But he did not enjoy having to be silent, and, when anyone spoke at too great a length about the war, he grew restive. Unlike Mr Jericho, he did not possess the requisite conversational strategy to circumvent subjects that were distasteful to him.

Mr Jericho, being once more disappointed in the nature of the game he had prepared himself to play, being confronted with cricket instead of chess, was playing it carelessly and with a lack of concentration that enabled Professor Trumper to rumble on unimpeded.

To Emmeline it was a slight source of consolation that the Professor that evening was not in one of his jocular moods. He was being wholly serious. He gave his hearers to understand that, although nearly overwhelmed by the weight of the world's affairs, he was nevertheless able to deal with them. He had them well in hand. And from time to time Mrs Trumper would insinuate that, in a modest way, she was of some assistance to her husband; that (as in the oriental cosmogony) she was the tortoise that supported the elephant that supported the world.

It was the Professor's jocular moods that Emmeline dreaded. They reminded her of a placard she had seen on a road announcing a 'steam roller at work,' and she had thought at the time how much more alarming a proposition would be a steam roller at play.

'When the output of such commodities as civilian clothing for the home market is curtailed, there will be a danger of the vicious spiral of inflation. The Government can either attack the inverted pyramid of credit at the base or withdraw purchasing power by compulsory saving or arrange for a valorisation of prices by the cartelisation of each industry separately – '

Listening vaguely with one compartment of her brain and pursuing her own thoughts with the other, Emmeline pondered on the many conversations that had taken place in her father's house. She reflected that, whether they had been brilliant and witty or laborious and dull, always they had seemed to be impregnated with a curious sense of sterility; they never appeared to lead anywhere. There must, she thought, be some kind of inhibitory influence in the air that prevented people from ever really disclosing their points of view. It is true that Professor Trumper never showed any hesitation in this respect, but then his verbal activities could hardly be described as conversation.

She had once ventured to discuss the matter with her father, and he had explained to her that it was probably due to a code of manners that had become established in the days before dons were allowed to marry, before domestic life had come to disturb the monastic routine of the university. When the same people dined night after night in the hall or the common room, it was found that discussions inevitably led to the same conclusions and frequently ended in great discourtesy, just as certain chemical combinations inevitably produce the same results accompanied by explosions. In order to obviate a monotonous breach of good manners, any subject likely to lead to controversy came to be avoided, and the too naked exposure of a point of view was looked upon as an indecency.

Emmeline did not entirely accept her father's explanation. In her school days she had read much about conversations in eighteenth and nineteenth century salons. She had read Boswell, in which the conversation recorded, although not always polite, was at least substantial and incisive. She had read the Journals of the Goncourts and the novels of Anatole France. She had expected too much, perhaps, from the intercourse of clever men round a dinner table. She began to fear that what people had said was true and that the art of conversation, like that of letter writing, had succumbed to the stress of modern civilization. These are not thoughts, you will say, of a highly original nature, but they helped Emmeline to bear the tedium of the Professor's monologue.

'And there is yet another way in which I consider the vicious spiral may be checked. Those who are responsible for our economic policy must firstly take into consideration – '

Noting the growing symptoms of fatigue on the faces of her father and Mr Jericho, Emmeline felt it her duty to try and do something to relieve them. She took advantage of a momentary lull in the Professor's soliloquy, which up till then had been running on, like Sanscrit, without punctuation. 'What,' she enquired, turning to Mr Jericho, 'do you really feel about the architecture of Kimble College?'

Emmeline as a rule did not take a very prominent part in the talk at her father's dinner parties. Indeed, she very rarely opened her mouth. When she did so, and asked a seemingly innocent question in a very sweet voice, it produced the effect of a saccharine bomb, and everyone was startled into attention. Even Professor Trumper was momentarily disconcerted and Mr Jericho was able to say what he thought of it.

The architecture of Kimble College was a bit of a problem to the small section of the university that took an interest in such things. Built in the seventies of multi-coloured brick, and in the Gothic style, it had been a source of controversy ever since. It had been violently attacked and as violently defended. Of late the balance of taste seemed to be inclining in its favour, and an eulogistic article had recently appeared in the Architectural Review.

'One has only to stand,' wrote the enthusiastic critic, 'in Kimble main quad when a sunset has drained the colour from the bricks, to see how admirably the chapel and hall and surrounding buildings are proportioned to the sunk expanse of the quad. It is a whole that hangs together, the chapel dominating everything, as it should, in a college which was founded for perpetuating academic education definitely based on the Church of England. Whatever criticisms admirers of the Renaissance may level against Kimble College, they cannot say it is a copy of anything. It is not the product of an antiquarian, but of an architect. Sir Gilbert Scott, whose work is all too prominent in England, was a copyist. The architect of Kimble was an inventor.'

The passage is quoted at length, as it will dispense of my recording Mr Jericho's reply. His view reflected those of the article which he had read.

Professor Trumper and his wife, who were not particularly interested in architecture, had nothing to say on the matter, and the Professor was engaged in summoning up his strength for a crashing return into the conversational field. When he did so it was obvious that his nerve had been a little shaken by this aesthetic digression, and both Mr Jericho and Doctor Pocock were able to interpose an occasional remark. The conversation drifted to the topic of fifth columnists, and Professor Trumper said that every man of them should be taken out and shot. Mr Jericho agreed with him, and said that most of the fifth columnists were to be found in the Civil Service, and that the Civil Service was in itself a fifth column and a valuable asset to the enemy.

'You forget,' said Mrs Trumper, 'that my son is in the Civil Service.'

Mr Jericho had indeed forgotten, but he was sure that Mrs Trumper thought he had not. He feared lest Emmeline and her father might believe him guilty of a deliberate error of tact and a lack of courtesy to his host. If Mr Jericho suffered from any social defect, it was rather from excess of tact than its absence.

Everyone suddenly felt a little tired. Even Professor Trumper's flow of rhetoric was beginning to ebb. The conversation flagged again and again, until it resembled the moribund flickerings of an electric torch. The black moth of somnolence settled on Emmeline. In one last flicker Mr Jericho turned to the amours of Mrs Postlethwaite, a theme that was invariably resorted to when all other subjects of conversation failed.

Mrs Postlethwaite had just perpetrated another of her elopements. They had now become of such regular occurrence that they had ceased to cause the stir they occasioned at the outset of her amorous career, and were only censured by those in whom custom could not stale their infinite morality, or by ladies who feared for the safety of their husbands. In her love affairs Mrs Postlethwaite took the initiative. Her natural selection, however, did not appear to be governed by a preference for strength and cunning, or, indeed, for any physical or mental superiority. Her choice was marked by a lack of discriminaion, and it was said of her that her tastes were so catholic as almost to amount to indifference. To Mr Jericho she was something of a harpy, a female satyr. 'What young men loth! What struggle to escape!' And he would imply that her siren lurings were all too often frustrated by the ear-stoppers of Ulysses.

Though Mrs Postlethwaite's elopements were numerous they were surreptitious and brief. They never attained the proportions of a major scandal, such as might have become for the authorities a matter of concern. After a week or two of uneasy bliss, she would return to her husband, who was a biologist, and, more preoccupied with scientific research than conjugal relationship, pretended not to have noticed anything.

'I am not very good at keeping count of such things,' said Doctor Pocock. 'Were I to keep a social diary I fear it would be marred by many lacunæ. But I fancy this must be at least her third elopement within the last year.'

'Nothing of the sort,' said Mrs Trumper, 'I saw her only this afternoon, and I think it is monstrous the way people go on about that unfortunate little woman. She has every excuse, I am sure, with that preposterous husband. Personally I am devoted to her, and she feels just as I do about small nations. Even if what people say about her were true, I should consider it my duty to deny it. Besides, if we dons' wives didn't stick together where should we be?'

Doctor Pocock repressed the impulse to assure Mrs Trumper that, whether the dons' wives stuck together or whether they disintegrated, her own position would remain unaffected.

Mr Jericho jumped up and made one of his cuckoo-clock exits.

It was a well-known characteristic of the Trumpers that, having established an atmosphere of gloom and stagnation, they seemed to enjoy sitting on in it indefinitely. Emmeline felt they were never going. They appeared to be impervious to silences, yawns and references to the lateness of the hour. At last, as even bad things must eventually come to an end, they left. But their leave-takings, unlike those of Mr Jericho, were as protracted as the finale of a Brückner symphony.

After kissing her father good night, Emmeline dragged herself wearily to bed. 'I must really speak to him about his dinner parties,' she thought, as she climbed the stairs, 'but I know I never shall.'

III

Emmeline's Visitors

Emmeline, hitherto, had never subjected herself to the discipline of a methodical routine. Her daily life had been conducted more or less according to moods and circumstances. In the ordering of her day caprice had reigned supreme.

Now all that sort of thing was going to be altered, and she set herself to draw up a schedule of her working hours. It was not, she found, an easy thing to do. It required a great deal of planning and she was a novice in the art of organization. At last she evolved something that seemed to her workmanlike, the kind of thing one might see posted up in a school or an office.

Rise 9 a.m. for 10.15 a.m.

10.15 a.m. to 11 a.m. Interval for breakfast.

11 a.m. to 12. Correspondence and perusal of The Times.

12 to 1 p.m. War work.

1 p.m. to 2.30 p.m. Interval for lunch.

2.30 to 3 p.m. Rest.

3 p.m. to 4 p.m. Interval for recreation.

4 p.m. to 5 p.m. War work.

5 p.m. to 6.30 p.m. Interval for tea.

6.30 p.m. to 7 p.m. War work.

After some deliberation she cut the last item on the programme. Her friends, when they came to tea, often arrived late and were apt to stay on till nearly dinner-time, and it might be difficult to get rid of them. Besides, she might want to hear all they had to say. Now that she was taking an active part in the war she felt it was important to keep in touch with the outer world. A duty not only to herself, but to her country. She might perhaps one day write an article for the newspapers: 'What a Don's Daughter thinks about Peace Aims.' Furthermore, she was afraid that her war work might be completed too soon, and she dreaded the idea of having to look out for another job.

'It makes a pretty full day,' she reflected, as she pinned up the schedule over her writing-table.

After adhering rigidly to it for a week or two, she began to feel the benefits accruing from a well-ordered routine. She now understood why people found it a cure for neurosis and introspection.

Only an hour, you will notice, had been set aside for recreation. For the sake of her health, Emmeline decided to spend it in the open air. She had never really enjoyed walking in the town, and she disliked having to greet her acquaintances when she met them in the streets. It seemed so pointless. One might just as well nod and smile at any well-known building one passed. The contemplation of architecture was far pleasanter and more profitable than any desultory conversation one was likely to hold in a chance encounter in the streets. In order to avoid this she had, on many occasions, been obliged to rush suddenly into shops and buy things she didn't want. As her father had exhorted her to practise strict economy, she took to walking in the meadows instead. When she did so, she was accompanied by an imaginary dog. Upon the approach of anyone she knew, she would cry: 'Toby! Toby!' and plunge into a shrubbery.

Executing one afternoon an evasion of this kind, on seeing someone she thought she knew, she was surprised and annoyed at finding herself pursued. She was preparing, at the risk of considerable personal inconvenience, to make her way still further into the bushes when she recognized the voice of her friend Caroline Paltry (it was unmistakable), and she knew that from her, as from the Hound of Heaven, there was no escape.

Lady Caroline Paltry was one of her old school friends. She had always been distinguished for her great vitality and overwhelming persistence. Even in the face of fearful odds she always succeeded in getting what she wanted, whether it were the friendship of another girl or a motor car.

'What on earth are you doing?' she asked the dishevelled Emmeline as she emerged from the bushes; 'and I never knew you had a dog.'

'I haven't a dog,' replied Emmeline. 'I was only trying to avoid you – I don't mean you in particular – just anyone.'

'Oh, my dear, I hope you aren't getting morbid. You aren't depressed by the war, are you?'

Emmeline begged her not to continue the conversation. 'Please don't speak to me here,' she implored. 'Come and have tea with me some afternoon, and we can have a nice talk.'

'I am only here for a few days. I'm looking for a house.'

'But you won't find one here,' said Emmeline with a desperate desire to hasten her departure. 'There's nothing here, only trees – and, of course, nature in a sort of way,' she added, casting a deprecating glance at the laurels.

Caroline disliked being mystified, and began to feel that she was wasting her time. 'I'll come and see you to-morrow at five, you quaint old thing,' and tweaking Emmeline by the nose, a gesture reminiscent of their schooldays, she hurried away.

On the following afternoon Caroline arrived on the stroke of five.

'Well,' she said, 'I've found a house. It's about three miles from the town. It's modern and has very nice bathrooms and a good kitchen garden, and it's even described in the agent's catalogue as historical.'

'Why historical?'

'It appears the Duchess of Windsor once looked at it and said: "What an ugly house." As a matter of fact it *is* rather ugly and it's hideously furnished, but it will suit my purposes well enough.'

'What are your purposes, Caroline?'

'Oh, I'm running a canteen, looking after evacuees, organizing work parties and recreations for the troops, and then there's the Women's Guild.'

'Stop,' cried Emmeline. 'You're making me giddy.'

'And blood transfusion. Have you given your blood, Emmeline?'

'Now, Caroline, let us make the position quite clear. If you're going to start asking me questions about what I'm doing, giving me advice or trying in any way to run my life – '

Caroline did all these things instinctively and unconsciously, but if confronted with revolt she was disposed to be reasonable.

'I never interfere with people's lives,' she protested. 'I only try to do good and make others happy. I suppose you think that's silly?'

'No, dear,' said Emmeline. 'I think it's optimistic.'

'Are you doing anything in the war?' Caroline continued. 'Oh dear, I suppose I'm not to ask you that. I'm sure you aren't. But I don't care. I'm not taking a strong line about it. I'm too busy just now to bother about shirkers.'

Stung by the word 'shirkers', Emmeline said, 'I'm sure I don't know why you should imagine I'm not doing any war work.'

'Well, are you?'

'Of course I am.'

'And may one be permitted to enquire what, exactly, it is?'

'Please don't talk like Henry James, Caroline, and I'm afraid I can't tell you what, exactly, it is.'

'I don't know Henry James,' Caroline replied. 'And why ever not?'

'Well, you see, it happens to be rather secret.'

'Oh, it's that kind, is it?' said Caroline, a little contemptuously.

Knowing Caroline's persistence in asking questions and what she called 'getting to the bottom of things,' Emmeline thought it advisable to change the topic.

'How is Nathaniel?' she asked.

Nathaniel, from Caroline's habitual way of speaking about him, might have been a dog or a pet rabbit, but he was actually her only child, aged three. She was bringing him up in her own way. When he was a baby she had taken him about with her everywhere in a dog basket, even to dinner parties, where she would deposit him in a corner of the room, and when the time came, would leave the table to feed him from the breast, a proceeding that some of her fellow guests were apt to consider eccentric. He was now being nourished exclusively on carrot juice and given psychological toys to play with. These consisted of things of different shapes that had to be put into holes, and it seemed probable that, later on, a severe course of psycho-analysis might be necessary. He was already beginning to show signs of phobias and repressions.

'Nathaniel?' Caroline repeated, as though trying to recall him to mind. 'Oh, Nathaniel. He's all right, thank you. Francis is taking him to Southampton. I want him to get accustomed to the sound of bombs.'

Francis was Caroline's husband. He was a composer; the white hope (thus a critic had described him) of English music. His compositions, though slightly lacking in originality and inclined to be long winded, were very much appreciated by the more serious of the English musical critics. He had originally embarked on a diplomatic career and had abandoned it in favour of music, but in so doing he did not abandon the principles of diplomacy. He set out to get to know all the most influential musical authorities in the country. He professed great humility, sought their advice, listened to their opinions and made Caroline ask them to luncheon. Although Caroline herself knew very little about music there was no greater propagandist of his work. She would run round and insist on music-shops displaying his wares in the window, she would expatiate on his genius to all and sundry, and she would bully reluctant conductors into performing his music. In fact, she took his musical career in hand (she took it in her stride), and the Provost of Unity had once suggested that Francis's compositions should be published under the title 'Lady Caroline Paltry. My husband's works.'

Caroline's parents, Lord and Lady Otterboy, were not at all like their daughter. They were very quiet people, and they lived in Ireland. Indeed, they were so quiet that Caroline, when she married Francis Paltry, forgot to invite them to the wedding. She afterwards reproached herself with this lapse of memory (as a rule she never forgot things) and wrote them a very nice letter.

The parlourmaid announced Mrs Postlethwaite. It was this lady's custom, on her return from one of her elopements, to show herself about the town, to pay a round of visits, adapting in each case her demeanour to the character of the person on whom she called. To the romantic and compassionate she would pose as the erring wife who had repented. To the more austere she would speak of her great devotion to Herbert Postlethwaite. With Emmeline she took a rather more intimate line.

Caroline, unaware of Mrs Postlethwaite's romantic reputation, thought her just a silly little woman and was bored by the intrusion.

'I must go now,' she said, 'I've got the hell of a lot to do to-morrow. All the goats are arriving and the wagonette and Mamma and Papa and some of the evacuees, and I've got to start planting potatoes on the lawn.'

Emmeline put out her hand to ward off the tweak. She feared Mrs Postlethwaite might be shocked by the familiarity of this farewell gesture.

As soon as Caroline had left the conversation assumed the character of a confession.

'Don't ever have anything to do with men, Emmeline,' Mrs Postlethwaite urged. 'They bring nothing but trouble and disappointment into one's life. People call them "gay deceivers." They may be deceivers but they are seldom gay. Dreary and egotistic they are for the most part.'

'Why don't you write a book about them?' asked Emmeline. 'I'm sure you could.'

'Oh, but I have, my dear,' replied Mrs Postlethwaite, looking surprised. 'I'm always writing about them.'

Emmeline had forgotten that Mrs Postlethwaite was, among other things, an authoress. She had written several novels and a volume of short stories. They were not very good. Although full of dramatic incident, they were apt to be marred by too persistent an undercurrent of nostalgia. She was a woman of varied talents, which she exploited at moments when she was not wholly engrossed in love. Before she married Herbert Postlethwaite she had kept a perfumery shop in Cheltenham. Her business, after quite a brilliant start, had languished and eventually collapsed. She had studied perfumery with the intention of putting some of her own creations on the market. But these, like her novels, were of so nostalgic a character that they proved too much altogether for the retired colonel's wives who frequented her shop.

Herbert Postlethwaite, on a visit to his sister in Cheltenham, had rescued her from the debris of her scent shop. Spiteful people had said that the marriage had been chiefly due to his biological interest in the lesser apes. And indeed there was something rather monkeylike about Mrs Postlethwaite. She had a spiritual prehensile tail that was always getting hold of things by the wrong end, and, mentally, she was apt suddenly to stop and scratch herself. You wouldn't be in the least surprised to find her hanging from the chandelier, indulging in disjointed introspection. Now, in the more subtly cultured atmosphere of the university, she was engaged in making ornamental articles for domestic use, which consisted for the most part in fanciful garments designed for covering things up: teapot and telephone cosies, embroidered covers for address-books and railway guides, hand-painted gas-mask containers. She appeared, with regard to inanimate objects, to be inspired with an almost abnormal modesty.

Recently she and Mrs Trumper had formed a great attachment for one another. The friendship was a strange one, and it was difficult to see what these two women could possibly have in common. Mr Jericho, who had an explanation for almost everything, said it was the expression of a secret prurience on the part of Mrs Postlethwaite for culture and respectability, on that of Mrs Trumper for sex.

'Mrs Trumper is taking me to a lecture on Federal Union this evening,' Mrs Postlethwaite announced. 'I suggested she should come here and fetch me. I hope you don't mind, Emmeline.'

Emmeline did mind, but it was not her habit to betray her opinions about other people's friends.

'I never knew you were interested in politics,' she said.

'Oh, but I am, Emmeline. I'm interested in everything. That's why I'm always so happy. And I'm sure that you, too, dear, would be happier if you concerned yourself a little more with things of the outer world.'

'I'm quite happy, thank you, Mrs Postlethwaite. I'm sure Federal Union wouldn't make me any happier than I am already.'

'Oh, I don't mean only Federal Union. I meant you ought to go about more and see more people. You sit all day in your room. You've become almost a recluse, and it's bound in the end to make you introspective and neurotic. Woman is by nature a gregarious animal. Herbert says so.'

'Even though I don't go out very much, Mrs Postlethwaite, I hear a good many things.'

'Yes, indeed. I know you see a lot of Mr Jericho, and the Provost of Unity, I hear, telephones to you every day. But that's not enough. There are so many clever and interesting people in the town, such thrilling people, dear. You ought to profit by them while you can. And won't you call me Antoinette? We know each other so well now that it seems quite absurd for you to go on calling me Mrs Postlethwaite.'

Emmeline thought that it would be equally absurd to call her Antoinette, especially as her identity card had revealed the fact that her name was really Mabel.

Mrs Trumper put in her head at the door.

'I've just popped in,' she said, 'for Mrs Postlethwaite. I find I have made a miscalculation of the time, and the meeting isn't till half past six. I thought I'd just look in and have a little chat.'

Instinctively Mrs Trumper chose the one uncomfortable chair in the room. Her spartan temperament impelled her always to make herself uncomfortable, and, incidentally, others as well.

'Won't you have a nicer chair, Mrs Trumper?' said Emmeline, preparing to give up her own.

'No, Emmeline. This one does very well for me. I am constitutionally incapable of lounging.'

Emmeline, as she looked at her, wondered on what principle she chose her clothes. It was obvious that vanity played no part in her choice. Knowing Mrs Trumper's ascetic disposition, she concluded it was the nearest approach she could make in modern times to sackcloth and ashes. It was only in the event of a dinner party or a grand political meeting that she would attempt to decorate herself, and would then appear in a grey silk dress with, poised precariously on her sparse grey hair, a single diamond star that looked as if at any moment it were going to shoot. On these occasions she also wore a mantle of dejected white fur that had been removed from one of her husband's disused ceremonial gowns.

'Your room is so peaceful, Emmeline,' she said, looking round her disparagingly; 'a real haven of rest, a veritable sanctum.'

'It's because of the double windows,' Emmeline suggested.

'No, my dear. It's because of your own personality. The Provost of Unity, who, as far as I can make out, never says anything sensible, made a remark about you that for once in a way was quite true. He said you reminded him of the Nereid Gallene, the personification of the smooth and smiling sea.'

'That was very kind of him,' said Emmeline. 'I suppose I am rather lethargic, and mother often used to tell me that I smirked.'

'Oh, he didn't mean that,' Mrs Trumper interposed hurriedly. Although outspoken, she never willingly made mischief. 'He didn't mean that at all. He meant that you give one an impression of calm and repose. You seem so aloof from this world of turmoil and strife, so wrapped up in your own quiet thoughts.'

'I often feel,' said Mrs Postlethwaite, 'that she would have made a wonderful nun.'

'Nonsense,' said Mrs Trumper. She was a religious woman, but she had no use for nuns.

'Although I can well sympathise with your disinclination to expose yourself to the rough and tumble of an active social life. (I mean social, of course, in the proper sense of the word.) I often wonder if it is good for you.'

'It is not always easy to know what is good for one,' said Emmeline.

'No doubt,' said Mrs Trumper; 'but I always say that we must have something definite to live for, whether it is politics, religion or art. I hope you will pardon me for saying so, Emmeline, but I sometimes feel that your mode of life is just a little – shall I say aimless.'

'I suppose it is. I am sorry, Mrs Trumper.'

'Oh, don't apologise to me, by dear child. It's yourself I'm thinking about. I often wonder if you are really happy. I don't see how anyone can be really happy leading the kind of life you do. Perhaps you have spiritual consolations. Excuse me for asking rather a leading question, but have you ever tried to find God?'

'Oh, yes, Mrs Trumper, I have indeed. At least I did once. But, like the people who looked for the Holy Grail, I felt I wouldn't know what to do with Him when I had found Him.'

'Oh, hush dear,' exclaimed Mrs Postlethwaite.

'Now, Emmeline,' said Mrs Trumper, 'you're not to talk like that. I won't have it. I know your father is an atheist, but that is no reason why his daughter should be blasphemous.'

'Father isn't an atheist,' Emmeline protested, 'and I didn't intend to be blasphemous. I only meant that I wasn't able to develop a talent for religion. It is possibly the fault of my upbringing, but I don't want to blame Papa and Mamma for anything. I have always had wrong-headed ideas about God. It seems to be in my nature. When I was a child I used to think that the Day of Judgement meant that we were all going to judge God, and I still don't see why not.'

Mrs Trumper was rather taken aback by this curious point of view. She attributed it to an inadequate comprehension of the nature of original sin, and was preparing to explain it. But Emmeline had decided that it was time to put an end to what, she felt, was beginning to amount to religious persecution.

'I think, Mrs Trumper,' she said, 'it is wiser for us not to go on talking about religion. It is obvious that our views would not be the same. Besides, it is boring Mrs Postlethwaite – I mean Antoinette,' she corrected herself with an internal giggle.

'Not at all, Emmeline. I always enjoy a serious discusson.'

'This is hardly serious,' said Mrs Trumper, looking at her watch, 'and in any case it is time to be going.'

Mrs Trumper left with the uneasy feeling that she had been worsted by an inexperienced girl, a thought that was galling to one accustomed to hold her own in debate. She also left Emmeline in a state of uneasiness. 'This sort of thing,' she thought, 'is disturbing to my peace of mind. It will have to be stopped. If people start coming into the house and probing into my soul, life will become unbearable.'

Had she known it she would have felt that she was being, at that moment, amply revenged.

On arriving at the Pandemonian, Mrs Trumper and Mrs Postlethwaite found that the meeting had been postponed for an hour. The place was dark and deserted, and, in spite of Mrs Trumper's persistence, remained as impregnable as a mediæval fortress. It had begun to rain. They were far from the houses of anyone they knew and they were unable to find a taxi. There was no shelter in the immediate neighbourhood except a public-house, into which their position in the university debarred them from penetrating. And so the two ladies were obliged to wander about disconsolately in the rain until the doors opened.

IV

Two Telephones and an Intermezzo

The Provost of Unity had acquired, a little irrelevantly perhaps, a reputation for eccentricity. A Head of a college, on attaining an advanced age (and the Provost was well over seventy) has only one alternative before him: either to end his life in an amiable dotage or else to assume an aura of oddity. He must either become a 'dear old man' or an eccentric. The Provost, with his malicious understanding of human nature, his irascibility and his impatience of bores, could never have settled down into being a dear old man. He was therefore inclined to welcome the reputation that had been thrust upon him, and he knew that eccentricity covers a multitude of sins.

Of late this once almost too prevalent trait has become increasingly rare, and those who lament the preponderance of the humdrum, who are on the look-out for symptoms of crankiness in their colleagues, are apt to clutch a little too eagerly at any straw.

It was said that some years ago the Provost had become entangled in a communist procession in the High Street and had been hailed as friend and comrade by some undergraduates from Corpus Diaboli. After this incident he was supposed to have made a vow never to cross the High Street again and had, ever since, remained immured within the precincts of Unity College.

It was also alleged that he had fired a number of shots from his window at the venerable Dean of Dimchurch.

Like many legends, both these stories had some foundation in fact. It was true that the Provost had been hustled during a communist demonstration, but the reason why he stayed so much at home was because he preferred doing so. When he heard of his supposed vow, he made no efforts to deny it, foreseeing that it would provide him with an excellent excuse to refuse the invitations of certain dons who lived on the further side of the High Street. It was also true that he had fired a gun out of his window, but it was at a grey squirrel in his garden, not at the Dean of Dimchurch, and the Dean, who happened to be in the neighbourhood, had been startled.

Though avoiding the hospitality of others, the Provost was far from being a recluse. He was fond of company. He liked seeing people, but he preferred seeing them in his own house. He was essentially a host.

It has been said that humanity may be roughly divided into hosts and guests. A psychologist has explained the types as representing two kinds of will, the will to power and the will to subjection. In the case of the Provost the explanation is undoubtedly a sound one. In his own house he had people more or less at his mercy. If they annoyed him he could be rude to them and, if their physique permitted, kick them out. In other people's houses he was bereft of the necessary authority to deal with any unpleasantness which, in his own, he was inclined to welcome. And that is why he invariably refused invitations, even to the homes of the grand and the agreeable.

He spent most of his time in his vaulted neo-Gothic study, surrounded by early editions and fragments of Greek archaic sculpture, writing his memoirs in a large volume bound in vellum. It was unlikely that these could be published until after his death, and when they were, they would undoubtedly cause a certain amount of surprise and annoyance to a great many grandchildren.

In spite of a pronounced disregard for the feelings of others, the Provost concealed beneath a certain spikiness the sensitive and kindly nature of the hedgehog. He was inclined even to sentimentality. Of this he was fully aware and he considered it an inappropriate weakness that did not fit in at all well with the character he had evolved for himself. The ruthlessness, of which even his best friends often had cause to complain, was in reality a sort of anti-aircraft barrage against the insidious attacks of sentiment. It was a great tribute to the Provost's charm and entertainment-value, as well as to the excellence of his cuisine, that people put up with as much as they did.

In his youth he had been considered one of the best-looking young men of his day. Now, at the age of seventy-three, his features, though battered by time, still resembled those of the Greek head on his mantelpiece given him many years ago by an admirer 'because it was so like him.'

He was a man of varied interests. He had a great capacity for enjoyment. Latterly his chief enjoyment seemed to be conversing with his friends on the telephone. He was in the habit of ringing up every day one or two of a chosen group of confidants, and with these he would talk on any subject in which, at the moment, he happened to be interested: it might be Greek antiquities, a question of moral philosophy or more often merely local gossip. He found that conversation was more untrammelled when the people to whom he spoke were invisible. The contact was impersonal and less likely to arouse emotions inimical to intellectual discernment. It was a transaction satisfactory to both parties. Unable to see his victims wince, he was less tempted to wound, and conversation was carried on in a kinder, less provocative tone.

It was to Emmeline that the Provost telephoned most frequently. He was devoted to her. He liked to hear the gentle, drowsily malicious intonations of her voice. She was also the only one of his friends whose feelings he never felt impelled to hurt. Perhaps because he knew that she would be the last person to try and take advantage of any display of tenderness. And, even if she had, he would perhaps have welcomed it. The self-portrait he had so carefully composed would appear all the more realistic if there were in it just one weak spot.

Emmeline had not yet quite recovered from her resentment of Mrs Trumper's catechism and, when the Provost rang her up, she complained bitterly of the indiscreet questionings she had been subjected to.

'Your little controversy,' said the Provost, 'takes me back to the days of my youth. I so rarely hear His name mentioned nowadays. Even in the newspapers His role seems to have been taken over by Time. In the last war they were always saying: "God is on our side." Now they say: "Time is on our side." No doubt, having been told that He is on the side of big battalions, they feel that nothing much can be expected of Him until we attain parity of armaments. By the way,' he broke off, knowing that the topic often led him into a vein of rather facile humour, 'I had a visit yesterday from Lady Caroline Paltry and her parents. That is to say she left them with me while she went to do her shopping. They are an amiable couple, but their views, such as they have, seem a trifle out of date and, like the Eminent Personage we have just been discussing, they seem to know very little about what is happening in the world. Lord Otterboy asked me if we had had any visits from the Zeppelins.'

'Poor things,' said Emmeline. 'Caroline never tells them anything and they only read *The Times*.'

'I dare say she hasn't the leisure. She appears to be a very active young woman. Indeed all the ladies here, with the exception of yourself, seem to be displaying great energy, and Mrs Postlethwaite, I understand, is writing another book.'

'Oh, dear,' said Emmeline. 'I hadn't heard.'

'Poor William Organ,' continued the Provost, 'will, I fear, once again be embarrassed by his disciple.'

'Her first book was, I remember, dedicated to him.'

'And her style was so closely modelled on his that one of the critics took it to be a parody. It is the only literary success that poor Mrs Postlethwaite has ever had. It is pleasant nowadays, when authors are so conceited, to find such a touching example of literary devotion. Where you or I would have at our bedside a volume of Lucian, Voltaire or Simenon, at hers you will find The Portrait of a Genius, The Fountain-Pen or the Journey of a Soul. I lay no claim to having penetrated into the lady's bedchamber. The information was given me in a moment of abandon by Herbert Postlethwaite. He told me that he frequently found her asleep with one of these volumes open in her hands. A charming picture.'

'She doesn't often speak to me about her literary work,' said Emmeline, 'but she did once tell me that what appealed to her in his books was the refined and spiritual manner in which he handled her favourite theme – and you can guess what that is.'

'Oh, good heavens,' exclaimed the Provost. 'That reminds me. It was really the reason I rang you up. A most astonishing piece of news. So astonishing, in fact, that, as in Madame de Sévigné's famous letter, I ought to herald its announcement with a thousand adjectives of amazement.' He paused. 'I do hope Jericho hasn't told you already. I don't wish to be the purveyor of a twice-told tale.'

'I can't say until I know what it is.'

Detecting a note of eagerness in Emmeline's voice, the Provost displayed further hesitation.

'It's such an important piece of news (almost a military bulletin), that perhaps I oughtn't to tell you without further confirmation.'

'As you please,' said Emmeline. He was being too much like Juliet's nurse.

At that moment a tumult arose in the passage outside Emmeline's room. Caroline appeared, pushing before her an elderly and bewildered couple. 'Do you mind my leaving Papa and Mamma with you for a few minutes?' she asked. 'I've got to rush round to the Blood Transfusion Office and give some blood. I shan't be long. It's just round the corner. I tried to leave them with your father, but he said he was going out.'

The Otterboys seemed very glad to sit down.

'We are not as young as we were,' said Lady Otterboy, 'and Caroline is always on the dash.'

They were rather pathetic, Emmeline thought. Every idea they had ever had about anything seemed to have been, at one time or another, demolished by their daughter. Now they were left with no ideas at all and Lord Otterboy appeared to have lost his memory.

'We are returning to Ireland tomorrow,' said Lady Otterboy. 'We had thought of making a longer stay, but we find everything here is so very uncomfortable.'

'Would you believe it?' said Lord Otterboy. 'No marmalade.'

'Yes,' said Lady Otterboy. 'Ever since he can remember, Otterboy has been accustomed to have marmalade for his breakfast, and here there is none to be had. Even Caroline can't get it. We were warned about the butter and we brought a large quantity from Ireland, but Caroline has given it all to the evacuees.'

More and more they reminded Emmeline of the Babes in the Wood.

'It seems nice and quiet here,' said Lady Otterboy. 'It is not so quiet in Caroline's house. I thought I heard some bombs falling last night, but it turned out to be Caroline banging doors upstairs.'

'Everything is so different here from what it was when I was an undergraduate,' Lord Otterboy complained.

'My dear,' said his wife, 'you know perfectly well you were at Cambridge.'

'I mean to say,' Lord Otterboy persisted, 'the type of under-graduate has very much altered since my day. A more weedy looking set of fellows I never saw.'

Emmeline was debating whether it were part of her duties to defend the undergraduates when Caroline returned.

'They wanted me to lie down after giving my blood,' she said. 'I told them I never lay down during the day, and anyhow I hadn't time.'

'My grandfather always used to recommend bleeding,' said Lady Otterboy.

'And really,' continued Caroline, 'one does meet people in odd places nowadays. I should never have expected to find the "versatile peer" working in the Blood Transfusion Service.'

'What peer is that?' enquired Lady Otterboy.

'Lord FitzCricket,' said Caroline.

'Old Puggy's son,' was Lord Otterboy's comment.

'Don't you remember, Mamma? He came to our wedding wearing a mask.'

'We weren't there,' said Lady Otterboy.

'Come on,' said Caroline. 'We've got to get back before the black-out.'

A growling noise was coming from the telephone. Emmeline, at the moment of Caroline's irruption, had forgotten to replace the receiver. She was reminded of the sensational piece of news that the Provost had promised her and was anxious to hear it. She reflected however that, in omitting to put back the receiver, she had probably prevented him from making any further calls for some considerable period and consequently he would not be in the best of tempers. She thought of Mr Jericho. She was a little ashamed of her curiosity. She liked to be told news, but she preferred not to have to ask for it. At the same time she knew that Mr Jericho would be very pleased to tell her, and would moreover be able to supply a more comprehensive selection of details than the Provost.

Mr Jericho understood at once.

'You mean the Trumper scandal.'

'?'

'Professor Trumper.'

'What has he done?'

It appeared that one day, when Mrs Trumper was in London and Mr Postlethwaite had gone to Cheltenham to see his sister, the Professor and Mrs Postlethwaite were seen lunching together at the Beehive, a small restaurant in an obscure side street to which people went when they didn't wish to be seen, so that to be seen there was almost a confession of guilt.

'It is certainly strange,' said Emmeline, 'but I don't see that it implies anything.'

'Ah, but that is not all,' went on Mr Jericho. 'You know that awful little Montmorency boy. He is continually stopping me in the street to tell me some scurrilous tale or other. It is most humiliating and makes me feel as if I had the reputation of being only interested in trivial things. His stories are very often untrue, but what he told me the other day was so strange and fantastic that I don't believe he has the imagination to have invented it. What would you say was the most incongruous, the most uninspiring spot for a lovers' rendezvous?'

'I'm unlikely to know,' said Emmeline. 'I haven't much experience in such matters.'

'Well, you might perhaps guess. For now I come to think of it, given the persons concerned, the place might be considered extremely suitable.'

'The pathological laboratory?' suggested Emmeline.

'Very near,' said Mr Jericho. 'No, it was the University Museum.'

The University Museum faces Kimble College, and had it been of later date might appear to have originated in a determination on the part of its architect to go one better. It is with the interior that we are concerned, and here the architect has fairly let himself go, and given free rein to his Gothic imagination. The visitor penetrates through Venetian mauresque cloisters into a spacious garth, lit from above by a diamond-paned glass roof supported on slender iron columns and arches decorated in the Gothic style. The place is crowded with cases containing fossils and stuffed birds interspersed with gigantic reconstructions of the skeletons of prehistoric monsters. A strong aroma of taxidermy prevails throughout and the ensemble creates the impression of a joint design by Darwin and the Tractarians.

'I will try to make my narration as dramatic as possible,' said Mr Jericho. 'One afternoon, Montmorency and two of his friends paid a visit to the Museum. Overawed by the strangeness of the scene, they contemplated it for a while in silence. At first they thought the place was deserted, but hearing suspicious sounds coming from behind one of the fossil cases, they approached stealthily. Peering through the skeleton of the dinoceras, or it may have been the iguanodon, they espied the Professor and Mrs Postlethwaite fondling one another.'

To Emmeline's sensitive imagination the vision was repellent.

'There are some ideas,' she said, 'that are too preposterous to be entertained – even in war-time.'

V

Visit of an Eminent Politician

Saturday night at Cato's Restaurant was always a very jubilant affair. Since the closing down of the dining clubs, it was the only place where conviviality could still be found. Sometimes, however, it was apt to be overdone, and the meditations of visiting journalists were disturbed by community singing or the throwing about of comestibles. It was certain that, within this festive hall, tragedy was never allowed to rear its ugly head and, however bad the news might be, the radiant faces and the shrieks of merry laughter created always the impression of a victory dinner.

Billy Montmorency was entertaining a party consisting of four or five undergraduates and a middle-aged gentleman whose portly sprightliness and very deliberate manner of speaking proclaimed him a personage of some importance.

Billy had come to the university at the beginning of the war with the intention of reviving the spirit of the nineties. It had been conveyed to him discreetly and, in one or two instances, painfully, that it was neither the time nor the place and that, in any case, he did not possess the requisite personality to carry out so ambitious and difficult a project. He had been, for a time, one of Mr Jericho's pupils, but, instead of availing himself of his tutor's extensive learning, he preferred to regale him with information of rather too personal a nature, and Mr Jericho had thought it wiser to discontinue his tuition. Billy's efforts to attain social prominence by other methods having failed, he was obliged to content himself with giving dinner parties to undergraduates who allowed him to pay the bill without thinking it necesary to pay any further attention to him in return.

The important middle-aged guest was no other than the famous Mr 'Lollipop' Jenkins. ('Lollipop' was the nickname he was known by in the House of Commons.) He had been invited by Jimmie Guggenheim Junior, an American undergraduate who, though continually exhorted by his parents to return to America, had remained obdurate to their entreaties and was staying on to 'see the old country through.' He was very much impressed by Mr Jenkins and indeed Mr Jenkins had all the qualifications for impressing an American undergraduate.

Mr Jenkins had been an undergraduate at the university himself and his record had been extremely brilliant. He had gained a considerable reputation by the mock-heroic speeches he was in the habit of making at debates and dining clubs.

On leaving the playground of the university and embarking on the more serious activities of political life he continued to fulfil the promise of all that had been expected of him. In the course of an unchequered career he had been in turn author, journalist and member of Parliament and now he was all three at once. His political novels, his biographies of statesmen ran into countless editions; high prices were paid for his articles, his conversation was listened to with respect at London luncheon parties. In the eyes of the world he was a success. Yet as he approached middle age his more thoughtful friends began to suspect that something was going a little wrong. Although outwardly the rose retained its rubicund exterior intact, they scented the presence of the invisible worm.

It was to be expected, of course, that as he grew more successful and more important he should put aside something of the sparkle and gaiety of youth. He seemed, however, reluctant to abandon altogether the role of *enfant terrible* that, as a young man, he had played in so engaging a manner, and people began to feel that there was something really rather terrible about an *enfant terrible* who was growing middle-aged and slightly pompous. The mock-heroic speeches he had made as an undergraduate he now delivered in deadly earnest. They were still enlivened with little jokes. Formerly designed solely to amuse, their function was now to prove a point and they were sometimes a little laboured.

However, there was one very endearing trait in Mr Jenkins' character, and that was the sentimental affection he felt for his old college. Whenever his activities permitted he would revisit the place and relive the memory of his undergraduate days. 'You can't think what this means to me,' he had said to Mr Guggenheim Junior as they passed through Dimchurch Quad, and the tone in which the words were spoken had given that tough young man a lump in his throat.

It was also to his credit that he seemed to prefer the company of quite unimportant young men to that of many of his wealthy and influential acquaintances. He appreciated the necessity of keeping in touch with the representatives of the coming generation so that when they knocked on the door he would be there to greet them.

It will be unnecessary to describe the rest of the party in detail. It consisted of typical undergraduates such as you will find in the pages of any recent fiction dealing with university life, and nothing very striking in the way of novelty has sprung up since the war. Appearances, perhaps, have had a tendency to grow a little less distinctive. One young man, chinless and rather inane looking, was a pure mathematician. Another, who had the air of a faded debutante, was a rugger blue or something of the sort.

'You can imagine,' said Billy, 'what a shock I got when I caught sight of them through those bones.'

'Cut it out Billy,' snapped Mr Guggenheim. 'We've had enough of that yarn.'

'Oh, all right,' said Billy plaintively. 'But you can understand my feeling sore. Before she took up with old Trump I rather fancy she had her eye on me.'

Mr Jenkins gave him an angry look. It was intolerable that, while everyone else at the table was treating him with due deference, his conversation should be continually interrupted by this young man's fatuous remarks.

Mr Jenkins was not entirely satisfied with the way in which the university was taking the war. His visit, this time, had been made in the interests of mass observation. He was, perhaps, a little over-burdened with a sense of responsibility. He had convinced himself that it was largely owing to his vigorous articles and speeches that his unarmed and apathetic country had at last been persuaded to stand up to the dictators. There was a story in circulation that, on being rebuked by an elderly general in a train for not giving up his seat to a man in uniform, he had exclaimed: 'If it had not been for me you would never have had your war.' The story was no doubt untrue, but it was symbolical.

He had visited his former tutor, the Provost of Unity, a man he had idolized in his undergraduate days, and had found him a little unresponsive. The evening before, Mr Jenkins had given a lecture at the Pandemonian to an audience composed chiefly of dons and their wives, members of Cheatham House and people from the various government departments evacuated to the city. Towards the end of his lecture, carried away by his eloquence, he had exhorted them to meet the foe with blazing eyes. The Provost had complimented him on the success of his oratory and said that he heard that so many people were now walking about the streets with blazing eyes that torches were no longer necessary in the black-out.

It was sad, thought Mr Jenkins, that a man whose intellect he had once so greatly respected should have degenerated into a flippant buffoon. He had met with other disappointments. He had failed to persuade Mr Jericho that, although the philosophy of history was all very well in peace-time, his talents would be better employed in the army, and Doctor Pocock had firmly refused to discuss politics.

'Yes,' said Billy, 'I fancy she had her eye on me.'

Mr Guggenheim Junior tried to kick him under the table, but kicked the pure mathematician instead. The pure mathematician, who was getting a little tipsy, suddenly produced a chin and assumed an air of truculence. Mr Guggenheim Junior knew that on Saturday nights dinner parties were apt to end in dissension, and a large piece of Yorkshire pudding, apparently aimed at Billy, had just landed on the table. 'It's getting a bit noisy here,' he said to Mr Jenkins. 'Shall we go over to my rooms right now – I mean now?' he corrected himself.

Mr Jenkins was loth to lose the rest of his audience. 'Perhaps some of you fellows will come and join us?' he said, emphasising the word 'some' in a way that rather markedly excluded Billy. To reinforce his point he shook hands with Billy and thanked him for an agreeable evening. At that moment the press photographer Mr Jenkins had ordered suddenly appeared and took a photograph of him in the act. The photograph that was subsequently published in several of the illustrated papers was a source of gratification to Billy, but of some embarrassment to Mr Jenkins.

VI

The Lives of the Saints

As Emmeline progressed with her work she found herself taking a growing interest in the figures of the saints she was engaged in destroying. She knew very little about their lives and habits, and as she examined more closely their sheep-like faces and their stiff byzantine draperies she began to wonder what manner of men and women they had been.

Her interest in them was somewhat akin to the melancholy concern she used to feel for the fine old houses she saw being pulled down in London in the days before the war. Of course, in her case, the destruction was not to make way for some hideous hotel or for a block of modern flats, and it was justified by the fact that it was war work. Nevertheless she was beset by a slight feeling of compunction. People, she thought, so often destroy things light-heartedly, without ever bothering to find out anything about them. However useless her war work might be, she was determined that there should be nothing about it that could be considered frivolous or light-hearted.

She went to her father's library to see what books she could find on the subject of hagiology. They were most of them rather bulky, but there was one, the Reverend Alban Butler's 'Lives of the Saints', that was a little shorter than the others, and she noticed on the title page that it had been published with the direct sanction of Cardinal Manning.

Once, as a child, during a slight attack of religious mania, she had been very much taken with the idea of becoming a saint herself. She had consulted a Roman Catholic governess about it and had been told that, in order to do so, at least two accredited miracles would be necessary. This seemed a serious drawback, but not an insuperable one. There would no doubt be witnesses who could be bought. After dallying with the idea for a time she had abandoned it in favour of becoming a political hostess. Later on, when she came to read Shakespeare, she decided, on the advice of Cardinal Wolsey, to fling away ambition altogether.

Emmeline had no very great aptitude for research work, and it was perhaps for this reason that the impressions she gathered from her reading were inclined to be superficial. She also had a tendency to concentrate on the female saints, and she rather deliberately avoided those that were better known, lest she should be unduly influenced by the glamour of their reputation. In her initial investigations she was not very fortunate.

St. Gertrude, she read, although possessed of the greatest natural talents, was penetrated and entirely filled with the deepest sentiments of her own nothingness. She longed for death and spent most of her time sighing. In the author's words. 'The Saint, as a chaste turtle, never interrupted her sweet sighs and moans.' Emmeline thought she must have been a rather trying woman to live with, and passed on to St. Hedwig, Duchess of Poland. This saint also professed great humility and was often seen to kiss the ground where a virtuous person had knelt in the church. No provocation could ever make her show the least sign of emotion or anger. She, too, must have been a rather irritating woman, Emmeline thought. After persuading her husband to build a monastery for nuns at Trebnitz, St. Hedwig refused to live with him any more and would only meet him in public places. She ate very little and dressed so badly that even the nuns complained about it.

Emmeline turned to an earlier period. Saint Olympias, who lived in the fifth century and was described as 'a widow', never had a bath and, like St. Hedwig, was very badly dressed. She suffered a good deal from the gossip of her neighbours and frequently appeared in the law-courts. On one occasion she had the bailiffs in the house. All these things induced a chronic state of melancholy. The only bright spot in her life appeared to have been the nice letters she had from St. Chrysostom exhorting her to cheer up.

The character of St. Jane was a little more spirited. At the age of eight she rose from her father's table on perceiving a heretic among the guests. Emmeline couldn't help thinking that she must have been a nasty little prig and that probably the heretic was very glad when she left. 'If I were to do that here,' she said to herself, 'I should never get a square meal at all.' She had a poor opinion of St. Paula, who was in the habit of hiding her inability to argue under the cover of violent public abuse. Whenever anyone asked her embarrassing questions about the damnation of unborn babes and the nature of the resurrection, 'from henceforth she so detested that man and all of the same opinions that she publicly proclaimed them to be enemies of the Lord.' Emmeline knew of a great many artists, scientists and politicians who behaved just like this and were never likely to be canonized.

Emmeline tried hard not to allow herself to be prejudiced and she feared that she had somehow missed the point of these people's lives. As she made a habit of reading for edification as well as for instruction, she persevered with her studies, hoping eventually to come across some useful example, some helpful rule of life. Mrs Trumper's reproach still rankled. She realised, of course, that the author had been a little too insistent on certain episodes in the lives of the saints that he would have been better advised to gloss over and that he was more preoccupied with questions of doctrine than with morals and manners. She wondered if it might not have been wiser to have consulted some record that was more direct and less coloured by the author's personal views. Yet the book had been approved by Cardinal Manning and the facts at least must be correct. She thought that it might be more profitable to pay less attention to biographical aspects and to study the main characteristics of saintliness and the qualities by which these men and women had achieved canonization.

Asceticism, she knew, was one of the most important of these and she took great pains to try and understand the difference between the austerities practised by dervishes and fakirs and those practised by the saints. She remembered that St. Paul had said that asceticism was not much good without charity and yet this was a quality in which most of the notable ascetics appeared to be lacking. In many cases mortification of the flesh seemed to her to have been a little overdone and not very different from the asceticism of the fakirs, but she was pleased by the account of a female saint who despised her body to such an extent that she offered it to all comers. If Mrs Postlethwaite, she thought, were to adopt that line, she too might achieve sainthood. And she was personally encouraged by the description of the Fathers of the Desert who 'trained not only to hard manual labour, but to that which was apparently as useless as it was hard, often unmade at night the mats they had plaited during the day.' As for mortification of the spirit, she suspected that it was too often a form of inverted snobbishness and led to an inward conceit that was worse than indulgence.

The martyrs, of course, were in a different category. But there had been martyrs on both sides, and those who eventually got the upper hand distributed the praise.

However, at the end of her investigations she had to admit that she had come across one or two characters who answered to her personal conception of saintliness, but there were far too many of whom she wondered how they had managed to be made saints at all. She attributed it to backstairs influence or to a talent for publicity.

She came to the conclusion that the Community of Saints was an essentially Catholic institution, a sort of Upper House like the Senate or the House of Lords, and that there were no conspicuous examples of virtue and courage that could not equally well be found in the annals of secular history. Anyhow, she told herself, in a work of destruction the innocent and the guilty must suffer alike. And she continued, with equanimity, to unpick the column of St. Simeon Stylites.

VII

The Professor's Love Story

The 'affaire' between the Professor and Mrs Postlethwaite was, according to rumour, beginning to assume the proportions of one of the great romances of history. References were made to Eloise and Abelard, Numa and Egeria, Pericles and Aspasia. The Provost thought it resembled the story of Hero and Leander, the Hellespont being represented by the Professor's physique.

There were speculations as to whether Mrs Trumper and Mr Postlethwaite had any idea of what was going on. It was almost certain that Mr Postlethwaite had not, and that, in any case, he would not have very much cared. He was more interested in the experimental researches he was carrying out with the assistance of his goats, guinea-pigs and monkeys. It was even said of him that he was more solicitous of their welfare than of that of his wife, and indeed at times they gave him far more anxiety. They were apt to play too prominent a part in college life.

As a special privilege, because he was engaged in work of national importance, he was allowed to keep his animals in an outhouse adjoining Dimchurch College. But the permission was very often on the point of being withdrawn. Owing to imperfect supervision on the part of the scout deputed to tend them, they were continually getting out of their cages. A guinea-pig that had secreted itself in Mrs Postlethwaite's bicycle basket had nearly caused a serious accident by suddenly appearing while she was bicycling down the High Street, and Mrs Trumper had been butted by a goat on her way to early communion. But it was the lesser apes that caused the greatest trouble. On one occasion they had managed to find their way into the Dean of Dimchurch's study. Being very short sighted, he had at first mistaken them for a deputation of undergraduates and had been much annoyed at having wasted an unctuous welcome.

The Provost of Unity had decided to give a luncheon party for the Trumpers and the Postlethwaites, together with three observers in the shape of Mr Jericho, Emmeline and her father. Emmeline had at first declined the invitation (Live and let live was her motto), but the Provost had insisted so vehemently that she had ended by accepting.

The gathering had something of the character of an inquisition.

The Provost was resolved that there should be no lack of material aids to the investigation of truth, and produced for the occasion a rare and heady vintage, with which the glasses of the guests were constantly replenished.

The first thing to be noticed was that the Professor was less talkative than usual. It is true that the Provost was perhaps the only member of the university by whom the Professor was a little intimidated. Too often his monologues had been abruptly cut short by one of the Provost's trenchant remarks. It was also noticed that he avoided addressing Mrs Postlethwaite and that he displayed an unusual tenderness towards his wife.

Mrs Postlethwaite seemed a little nervous, and her simian restlessness was very much in evidence. She was dressed more quietly than usual. There were none of the bright colours in which she habitually disported herself. None of the glittering gipsy-like beads and feathered fantasies.

'Have you ever been to the University Museum, Mrs Postlethwaite?' asked the Provost. 'It is a curious place and well worth a visit. I ask because so few people seem to know it. Although I am not an admirer of reconstructions of prehistoric skeletons I am forced to admit that in these Gothic surroundings they acquire a certain beauty.'

'I have never been there,' said Mrs Postlethwaite.

'You should go,' said the Provost.

'How is your book getting on?' asked Emmeline.

The change of subject seemed more welcome to Mrs Postlethwaite than to the Provost. 'Oh, thank you, Emmeline,' she cried with evident relief. 'It is very kind of you to ask. It's getting on very well. I've nearly finished it.'

'I always enjoy your love scenes,' said Mr Jericho.

'Oh, nonsense, Mr Jericho. I'm sure you never read anything so frivolous as my poor little books.'

'Indeed I do,' said Mr Jericho, 'and I certainly don't consider them frivolous. If anything, they err too much on the serious side.'

'I find it hard,' Mrs Postlethwaite sighed, 'to strike a happy medium.'

'That,' said Doctor Pocock, 'is a difficulty we all suffer from.'

'May I say that I also enjoy Mrs Postlethwaite's books,' said the Provost, 'and even the earnest Trumper no doubt –'

'He never has time to read novels,' interposed Mrs Trumper hurriedly. 'You couldn't expect it of him. And I myself find very little time for light literature, especially now that I am working at Cheatham House.'

'Tell us, Mrs Trumper,' said the Provost, 'between four walls, what it is you really do at Cheatham House? I know you are bound by the strictest secrecy, but you might perhaps give us some rough idea. I always long to know what goes on inside that mysterious building.'

Cheatham House had been evacuated to the university at the beginning of the war. It was supposed to be a kind of sublimated branch of the Foreign Office and was said to be concerned with theories rather than realities. From time to time questions had arisen as to its utility, and letters were written to the newspapers complaining of a waste of public money. The only signs of extravagance that were visible to the outside world were the lorries that were continually seen leaving the building with large quantities of waste paper. Investigations, however, proved that, athough the institution did not appear to be doing much good, it was doing very little harm, and it was allowed to continue its activities. Latterly the secrecy that surrounded it had been redoubled. A stockade had been erected outside the main entrance, passwords were required to gain admittance, and the building had become more mysterious and impenetrable than ever.

Mrs Trumper was torn between the desire to maintain an air of secrecy and at the same time to prove how useful she was being.

'Well,' she said, 'I can't tell you very much. I have to read a great many foreign newspapers.'

'That must be nice,' said Mrs Postlethwaite.

'And of course,' continued Mrs Trumper, 'one has the usual difficulty in getting one's views accepted.'

At that moment Mr Postlethwaite, who had appeared to be in a state of coma, suddenly woke up and gave a stirring account of the polemics of his early life. It was interesting, but, under the circumstances, not at all what was wanted. Fortified by the Provost's good wine, nothing could silence him. His narration continued throughout the rest of the luncheon, and all efforts to divert the conversation into more relevant channels were vain.

'Well,' said the Provost to Emmeline, who had remained behind after the others had left, 'I fear we have got no further than we were before.'

'I often wonder,' said Emmeline, 'if it isn't a mistake to try and find out too much about things.'

'Little obscurantist,' said the Provost.

VIII

Poltergeist

Doctor Pocock had been suffering from an attack of influenza. He was now convalescent and was sitting in his oak-panelled bedroom propped up on his pillows. Emmeline sat at his bedside, reading aloud to him from a book by Gertrude Stein.

'In sometimes there is always and a little more than Arthur if they are mating and there are exceptions. Rules are not what are not sometimes and always with feathers and parallelograms are longer and not warmer when exceptions are there. A cucumber can be its own father if wanted and not wanted and not not wanted so a cucumber can be its own father if fathers are wanted and not wanted and a father can be its own cucumber if feathers are wanted and not exceptions. Exceptions are circular and have little extremities that shake and are less than more and fewer than something.'

'Thank you, dear,' said Doctor Pocock. 'That is enough for the present. I find I am unable to take in very much at a time.'

Emmeline closed the book and was preparing to return to her work when Mr Jericho appeared. He was very excited about the accounts that had just reached him of sensational happenings at Cheatham House. A poltergeist had broken into the place and was creating havoc there. The most extraordinary and unaccountable things occurred every night and sometimes during the day. All the books in the reference library were found to have been taken out and replaced upside down. Important maps had been defaced by ink. Secret and confidential documents were littered all over the garden and had been picked up by unauthorized persons. Sentences were scribbled on the walls in a language that not even the most erudite professors could understand. Some of the rooms had been rendered uninhabitable by the most appalling smell. The telephones were constantly ringing and, when answered, rude words were shouted from the other end, and when the Dean of Dimchurch (whom Destiny seems to have selected for an Aunt Sally) arrived for purposes of exorcism, he had been struck down by a heavy volume of code. Investigations led to the conclusion that these things could not possibly have been done by any human agency.

Mrs Trumper had discovered, in a scientific work on the subject, that a poltergeist was nearly always associated with the presence of an idiot child, and had insisted on several junior members of the personnel being removed. Beyond creating a certain amount of ill-feeling this measure had not had the slightest effect. The poltergeist continued to haunt the building and seemed to be doing everything within its power to make the lives of the inmates a burden to them.

Doctor Pocock was very interested. His philosophical doctrines did not preclude belief in the supernatural as long as his own particular theories were not embarrassed.

'Mr Sacheverell Sitwell,' he said, 'has recently written a book on the subject. I wonder if they have thought of calling him in.'

'I fancy he has only a literary interest in the matter,' said Mr Jericho. 'I don't think he has had any practical experience. And I feel that if Mrs Trumper is unable to deal with the situation, nobody can. In any case I don't suppose they would care to have their troubles settled by anyone from outside. I hear they have refused offers of assistance from the Society of Psychical Research.'

'It is dreadful to think of their peace of mind being disturbed in this way,' said Doctor Pocock. 'I fear it may have serious repercussions on our foreign policy.'

'I imagine that poltergeists at the present moment must be

suffering from an inferiority complex,' said Mr Jericho, 'and possibly Cheatham House is one of the few places left where they can really feel at home.'

'It is very trying for poor Mrs Trumper to have this added to her other troubles,' remarked Emmeline. 'I hear she seems very depressed. I must say I find it hard to believe that Professor Trumper should be able to make any woman unhappy.'

'It may not be entirely on that account,' said Mr Jericho. 'I understand she was very much upset at having a contribution to the *New Stateswoman* rejected, an article proving that in no possible circumstances could Italy enter the war.'

'I have noticed,' said Doctor Pocock, 'that Mrs Trumper, in the architecture of her theories, is more concerned with logical accuracy of structure than with the solidity of its foundations. Her conclusions are correctly derived from unsound premises. And although, in the world of politics and theology, happy results are often obtained in this manner, they do not appear to be obtained by Mrs Trumper.'

'You mean, Father,' said Emmeline, 'that Mrs Trumper talks nonsense.'

'Thank you, my dear,' said Doctor Pocock, 'for explaining to me what I mean and expressing it so concisely. You must remember that we philosophers never like putting things simply. Philosophy is concerned with the search for truth, and this does not lend itself to simple phraseology.'

'That is no doubt why Pilate left in a hurry after asking his famous question,' remarked Mr Jericho.

'I must be leaving you, too,' said Emmeline; 'it is time for my afternoon walk.'

IX
Lord FitzCricket

There had been lately so great an influx of refugees into the town that Emmeline, obliged one day to visit the shopping centre, could hardly make her way through the streets. Czechs, Austrians and Germans crowded the pavements. Chattering Frenchwomen were to be heard complaining in high staccato voices about the black-out and other inconveniences. Corpulent Jewesses in trousers, armed with string bags, descended on the food shops like locusts. Women from Whitechapel treated their perambulators as tanks and mowed down everything before them.

At first this alien population confined itself to the shopping centres and did not penetrate into the streets and sanctuaries of the collegiate portions of the town. Latterly, however, it had shown a tendency to overflow into the meadows, and Emmeline now took her daily exercise in the spacious garden of All Saints.

This, for her, was no deprivation. She loved the garden, with its wide expanse of lawn, flanked on one side by the old walls of the town, on the other by the grey edifice of All Saints, half hidden by the elm-trees, above which towered the spire of St. Ethelburga's. A very pretty picture of it by a Royal Academician, entitled 'Haunts of Ancient Peace', with a quotation from Tennyson attached, hung in the Warden's dining-room. But Emmeline was not a believer in Wilde's theory of nature copying art, and it did not interfere with her own impressions of the place. However, she would have enjoyed going there more if the same curious thing had not happened to her every afternoon.

It was her custom to walk several times round the little mound in the centre of the lawn that seemed destined for a temple that had never been built. After a while Emmeline found herself becoming hypnotised by the tranquillity and timelessness of the place. It induced a sort of trance in which her steps were always led, as if by an invisible guide, to a corner of the garden in which there was a gloomy little rockery devoted to the cultivation of Alpine plants.

Here she would come to with a slight shock and return to the Warden's lodgings obsessed by a feeling of depression.

That afternoon, on waking up at the rockery, she found a man standing before it in an attitude of despondency. He turned, and she saw it was Lord FitzCricket. She had met him once before in her father's house. She had sat next to him at dinner and had thought him agreeable, if slightly absurd.

'Are you fond of Alpine plants?' he asked her.

'I think perhaps they would be better in the Alps,' replied Emmeline. 'They might be less in evidence.'

'It would be hardly worth while going to the Alps to find out,' remarked Lord FitzCricket. 'I have never felt the charm of the Alps, even on picture post cards. Though even the Alps just now –' He broke off. The thought of foreign travel seemed to be too much for him.

'Would you mind my taking a turn with you?' he asked. 'I feel unusually lonely this afternoon.'

'I was just thinking of going home,' Emmeline replied. 'Won't you come back and have some tea? I am sure Father will be delighted to see you.'

She felt sorry for him. He looked so unlike the grinning photograph she had once seen in the *Tatler*.

When she got back to the Warden's lodgings she was told by the parlourmaid that Doctor Pocock was asleep and that the tea had been prepared in her room.

Lord FitzCricket was a stocky little man with a countenance that varied rather considerably with the mobility of his features. Quiescent, they appeared saturnine, but when animated, they took on an air of benevolence. He had now become completely bald, and when he was annoyed he looked like a diabolical egg. He possessed, however, no inherently satanic characteristics, and the impression was merely due to a peculiar slant of the eyebrows.

He was always referred to by gossip-column writers as 'the versatile peer', and indeed there was hardly a branch of art in which he had not at one time or other dabbled. He composed music, he wrote books, he painted; he did a great many things with a certain facile talent. He was astute enough to realise that, in Anglo-Saxon countries, art is more highly appreciated if accompanied by a certain measure of eccentric publicity. This fitted in well with his natural inclinations.

He had a collection of strange masks that he used to wear when motoring. He dyed his fantail pigeons all colours of the rainbow, so that they flew over the countryside causing bewilderment to neighbouring farmers. He was always surrounded by odd animals and birds. When travelling on the Continent he had a small piano in his motor car, and on the strength of this he was likened in the popular press to Chopin and Mozart. Someone had even suggested a resemblance to Lord Byron, but for this he had neither the qualifications of being a poet nor a great lover.

Animated by the tea and the atmosphere of Emmeline's room, Lord FitzCricket began to speak of his first reactions to the war.

'For a time,' he said, 'the war knocked me out. I felt as if I had been pole-axed. I was unable to do anything at all. I offered my services, but I was advised to go on doing what I was doing, and God only knows what that was. I couldn't compose music, I couldn't write or paint. It all seemed to have become so pointless. I believed it was the end of everything and certainly of people like me. You see, I'm all the things that are no use in war. My character is essentially pacific and hedonistic. I like everything to be nice and jolly and I hate to think of people hating one another. I've never been any good at anything practical. I'm an amateur, and fundamentally superficial. I am also private spirited. I have never been able to summon up any great enthusiasm for the human race, and I am indifferent as to its future. I have always led a self-centered, sheltered life, and my little world consists of my hobbies and personal relationships.

'In moments of despair I often take a book, it may be the Bible, or Virgil, or even the Encyclopædia Britannica, and open it at random, hoping to find a message of help or comfort. This time it was the Fables of Lafontaine. I opened it at the fable of the grasshopper and the ant. It was not very encouraging, for I realized that what I am is a grasshopper, and it's now the turn of the ants. The world has no use at present for middle-aged grasshoppers.'

'You seem to be suffering from a sense of guilt,' said Emmeline. 'Have you thought of trying psycho-analysis?'

'That is an idea,' said Lord FitzCricket. 'Thank you for suggesting it. As it is, I feel better already for having unburdened myself, even to an amateur. You may not believe me, but this is the first time since the war that this has happened. There must be something odd about this room. It strikes me as a place in which one could almost write a sincere autobiography. I feel I'd like to sit here for ever, talking about myself. But I don't suppose you'd care for that. As it is, I fear, I have bored you with my whining.'

'Not at all,' said Emmeline politely. 'I hope you'll come again.'

Emmeline did not often proffer such invitations to people she hardly knew, and after Lord FitzCricket had gone and she settled down once more to her work she found herself wondering why she had done it.

X
Potpourri from a College Garden

Some concern was beginning to be felt in the Provost's intimate circle about the curious attitude he had recently taken up with regard to death.

The Provost had always confessed that the death of a friend gave him a secret feeling of satisfaction. It appealed, he used to say, to his sense of composition. Completing the individual's life, it enabled him to judge it as a whole. It also, he said, appealed to his predilection for tidiness. He was pleased to think that the poor fellow's affairs were at last in order and that there would be no further shocks and surprises. He felt as Shelley had felt about Keats.

> He has out-soared the shadow of our night,
> Envy and calumny, and hate and pain
> And that unrest that men miscall delight
> Can touch him not and torture not again.

But now death only seemed to appeal to his sense of humour. When the demise of any of his friends was announced to him it appear to affect him with a malicious glee and was the occasion for an outburst of sardonic hilarity.

'When he enquired of me the other day,' said Mr Jericho, 'whether I had heard of any funny deaths lately, I told him that one of the things that kept me alive in these gloomy days was the fear of my death becoming the subject of his witticisms. He seemed surprised and even a little hurt.'

That the Provost was becoming slightly unbalanced was manifest in other ways. He had, of late, grown more acutely irascible. His rendings of inoffensive persons had taken on a ferocity worthy of Tiberius or Caligula, and his rudeness to mild undergraduates reminded one of Jowett. As time progressed he grew more and more misanthropic, and now only saw people whom his official position made it necessary for him to see. Beyond telephoning occasionally to Emmeline or to Mr Jericho, he seemed desirous of cutting himself off completely from all communication with the outer world.

He was not best pleased therefore when Mr Lollipop Jenkins appeared, one day, in his study.

Mr Jenkins was full of a book called 'Chronicles of Guilt'. It was published anonymously and was a vehement indictment of a number of politicans whom the author considered responsible for the actual state of affairs. It was comprehensive, though there were one or two diplomatic omissions.

He had just arrived with a great many copies of this book, and was busy distributing them among the dons and the undergraduates and seeing that they were properly displayed in the bookshop windows. He had brought a specially bound copy to present to his old tutor, for although Mr Jenkins considered that the Provost's intellect had sadly degenerated, he could never forget all that he had meant to him in the old undergraduate days.

When the Provost looked up from his writing-table, where he was engaged in composing his memoirs, and saw Mr Jenkins advancing upon him in sprightly pomp, he felt murder in his soul. A murder had just taken place in his own college. One undergraduate had shot another. He feared that the infection might spread and felt that, at all costs, he must control himself.

'I have brought you a book that I thought you might like to read,' said Mr Jenkins.

'I am not reading very much just now,' said the Provost. 'What is it about?'

'It's about all the damned fools who have landed us in this mess,' replied Mr Jenkins.

'Are you in it?' asked the Provost.

Mr Jenkins gave a deprecatory snigger. It was as well to let the Provost have his little joke. 'I think it will amuse you. And it puts the case very clearly.'

The Provost eyed him with disfavour.

'I don't think the subject is one for amusement. And is there anything to be gained by recrimination?'

Mr Jenkins was becoming unnerved.

'It's not very long. You won't have much difficulty in getting through it.'

'The Imitation of Christ is not very long,' said the Provost, 'but I have never been able to get through it.'

Mr Jenkins persisted.

'Oh, but this is much shorter.'

'Then it can't be very comprehensive. In a case like this we are all of us guilty. I would sooner read the telephone directory. You can keep your book. Goodbye.'

Mr Jenkins failed to realise that he had got off very lightly.

There had lately been one or two cases of war neurosis among the undergraduates. Luckily, except in the shooting affray at Unity, the effects had not been serious. A theological student at Corpus Diaboli had opened his veins in his bath, but had been rescued in time and was now recovering. Beyond a certain annoyance expressed by the Blood Transfusion Service at the waste of good blood the incident had no further consequences.

In a lighter vein, Billy Montmorency had at last achieved the notoriety he had longed for, and had been sent down. Having grown weary of the ingratitude his entertainments seemed to inspire, he gave no more dinner parties. But being full of invention and hope, he had set out to devise other ways of making himself conspicuous. For a while he had taken up religion. Enlisting the services of Father MacOrkney (from the Collegio Beda in Rome), he held theological debates in his rooms, but as these were supplemented by an excessive consumption of liquor they ended either in stupor or horseplay and had to be discontinued. He then attempted to form flamboyant romantic attachments with some of his friends, but desisted on being told rather brutally by Jimmie Guggenheim Junior that sentimental friendships were no longer considered chic. At last in desperation he took to communism. He became a violent defeatist. He went round saying the most malicious things about the war, calculated to spread alarm and despondence. And finally, at a debate got up by Mr Jenkins on 'What Britain is fighting for', he had interrupted that gentleman's opening address by crying out: 'We are fighting to put back the clock'. Whether it was for this, or for some more serious delinquency, that he was sent down, nobody knew nor cared. He left the university unwept. His father, who was a prominent member of the Ministry of Information, was furious and threatened to disinherit him. Billy thought that, in the present circumstances, it didn't much matter whether he were disinherited or not, and he had the satisfaction of feeling that in one respect at least he resembled Shelley.

'I have a theory about the Provost,' said Mr Jericho. 'There is something that has puzzled me for a long time, and I believe I've at last discovered what it is.'

'This dreadful searching for truth,' said Emmeline. 'Why can't we leave her at the bottom of her well, which is her proper place?'

'Don't you want to hear?' asked Mr Jericho.

'Of course I do. Please go on.'

'Well, you see,' said Mr Jericho, 'we have known the Provost and loved him, and taken him for granted – '

'Yes,' Emmeline assented, 'we have certainly taken him for granted.'

Mr Jericho had developed a new gesture. He would suddenly whip off his spectacles, polish them with his handkerchief, replace them, and stare through them with a greater intensity than before. The gesture was accomplished in a single rapid movement.

'Please don't do that, Mr Jericho,' said Emmeline. 'I find it hard enough to pursue a consecutive train of thought in conversation as it is. You can do it to Professor Trumper if you like, but not to me.'

'I am sorry, Emmeline. You will pardon me for pursuing my own train of thought. We have taken the Provost for granted. We have always known that his eccentricity was a mere sartorial detail, like a funny hat or a peculiar overcoat.'

'You must admit that it suits him.'

'Everything suits him,' said Mr Jericho. 'He has seen to that. He has painted his own portrait with the skill of a Holbein – but have you ever wondered if it is the portrait that nature would have painted if she had been allowed to have her own way? I believe that he has achieved the difficult feat of having altered his predestined character.'

'That is certainly a difficult feat. I have never succeeded in altering mine – but then I'm not sure that I ever really wanted to. Where I was at school there was a mistress who used to say that God gave us our character and it was blasphemous to try and change it.'

'The aphorism,' remarked Mr Jericho, 'seems to me rather inadvisable for a schoolmistress, but on the whole I believe it to be true.'

'We had a parrot,' Emmeline continued. 'Father used to say it hated being a parrot. It certainly looked as if it did. But, poor thing, what could it do except make the best of it?'

'Let us avoid question of free will and determinism,' Mr Jericho urged. 'I believe that the Provost was intended by nature to be a man of action and not a scholar. Gifted with great intelligence and will power, he has managed to make a success of the career he has chosen, but I believe it was not the one designed for him by destiny. He was born to be an eagle, but he has succeeded in deliberately transforming himself into a parrot, a charming, wise and fascinating parrot.'

'And now he hates being a parrot,' said Emmeline.

'Now he hates being a parrot,' repeated Mr Jericho. 'But it is too late. The eccentricity that is growing on him is not the case of a fictitious reputation becoming real. It arises from a repressed sense of dissatisfaction and vain regret. Had he been a statesman, a man of business, or a military leader, we should no doubt have lost an agreeable friend – however, we must not only think of ourselves.'

'I'm afraid I always think of myself,' said Emmeline; 'and I prefer him as he is.'

XI

The Rustling of Wings

Emmeline had hoped that the finicky and laborious nature of her work would enable her to enjoy at least the respite from thought that was so necessary to her mental and physical well-being. But she found that, on the contrary, it often gave rise to the most disquieting flights of fancy and led to meditations on problems that, owing to a lack of philosophical training, she was unable to solve. The latter consideration was neither a solace nor a deterrent. Once she started thinking about anything, she was unable to stop, and her persistence in trying to reach a conclusion often gave her a headache. She hesitated to ask her father to help her with her intellectual difficulties because his explanations generally made them more incomprehensible than they were before.

That afternoon she was troubled by a problem suggested by the design of the embroidery. She remembered having read somewhere that the world showed incontrovertible evidence of having been designed. She wondered whether the God or Demiurge who was responsible for the design was beginning to find that it was not coming out quite as He had hoped and whether He were not at present engaged in destroying it bit by bit just as she was destroying the embroidery. It was a disturbing thought. Nevertheless it was nice to think that her work, humble as it was, might have so distinguished a parallel.

Her cogitations were interrupted by the arrival of Lord Fitz-Cricket.

Some time had elapsed since their last meeting, and Emmeline was a little piqued at his not having responded to her invitation more promptly. In the meantime she had found herself thinking about him, more often perhaps than seemed necessary. Of course, he was an absurd little man and frightfully futile. Nevertheless, he had aroused in her a certain interest. He appealed to the motherly instincts which, in spite of an almost militant virginity, she was unable at times to repress. Had she been the Caroline Paltry type of woman she might have felt impelled to look after him, to take him in hand and smooth out for him his muddled difficulties. Most of the people she knew were almost too efficiently capable of looking after themselves, and it was a welcome change to have at last met someone who wasn't.

'Do you find,' Emmeline asked, 'that when you think about anything for any length of time you always end by taking a personal view or getting back to first causes? It is most annoying.'

'I never think about anything for any length of time,' replied Lord FitzCricket. 'It doesn't suit my temperament. Thinking about frivolous things sometimes gives me pleasure, but when I think about serious matters I get discouraged. The only solution is to have something to do that stops me thinking. Lots of people are like that. They're all right until they begin to think.'

'Yes,' said Emmeline, 'that is what I have discovered, and I thought I had found something that would stop me thinking, but I'm beginning to realize that it doesn't.'

She immediately regretted having mentioned her war work and feared lest Lord FitzCricket might become inquisitive.

'You're looking much more cheerful than when I last saw you,' she said.

'Yes,' said Lord FitzCricket. 'I took your advice and am being psycho-analysed. I really think it is doing me a lot of good. Psycho-analysis has the same sort of charm as going to a fortune-teller. You lie on a sofa and talk about yourself for hours and hours. That in itself is exhilarating for the Ego. All sorts of curious things were found in my Unconscious; a stuffed bird, a pair of gloves, a black rubber mackintosh, in fact the whole contents of a jumble sale. No wonder I felt queer.'

'And have you got rid of them?' asked Emmeline.

'I hope so. Of course, they may come back, but in future I'll know what to do about them.'

'Apart from a sense of guilt,' said Emmeline, 'I didn't notice that you were suffering from any very serious complexes. But then I'm not very observant.'

'It's rather in my family, you know,' said Lord FitzCricket. 'My grandmother suffered from very bad agoraphobia. She couldn't stand being in large open spaces. She was very fond of travelling, but of course she couldn't go to the desert, or the Savannahs or the Tundras or the Steppes. When she went to Russia her doctor said to her: "Mind the steppes". His puns, I'm told, were better than his pills. I used to suffer from agoraphobia myself in a mild way. My psycho-analyst tells me it is a form of the back-to-the-womb complex.'

'Good heavens! What is that?' asked Emmeline.

'Oh, don't you know? It's a thing we're all supposed to suffer from more or less. Our first impressions of the world are so disagreeable that we want to pop back again at once. Birth is a shock that very sensitive people never get over. American women have womb-chambers constructed in their houses so that they can shut themselves up in them whenever the complex gets bad. I remember, in the Stuyvesant-Kruger divorce case, one of the principal grounds for divorce was that the wife always found her husband sitting in the womb-chamber when she wanted to go there herself.'

'Surely they could have afforded two,' said Emmeline.

'One would have thought so. But rich Americans often have very odd economies.'

'Tell me more about your psycho-analysis,' said Emmeline. 'It's very interesting. I'm beginning to wonder if perhaps I oughtn't to be analysed myself.'

'Well,' said Lord FitzCricket, 'another thing the analyst found out was that my death-instincts were getting the better of my pleasure principle, and that it was something to do with my Œdipus-complex. It just shows how mistaken one can be about oneself. When I used to feel like that before I always thought it was my liver.'

The telephone bell rang. It was the Provost of Unity. He seemed to be in high spirits.

'Emmeline,' he said 'I've got a very funny piece of news for you. Prepare yourself for a good laugh. Mrs Trumper has hanged herself.'

Emmeline was silent. From the other end of the telephone the Provost sensed that she was not taking the news quite in the way he had expected.

'What?' he said. 'You don't think it's funny? How extraordinary! Nobody seems to think it funny. I must say I am disappointed in you, Emmeline. I thought that you, at least, had a sense of the comic.' And he hung up the receiver.

Emmeline remained standing before the telephone for a few seconds and then returned to where Lord FitzCricket was sitting.

'How dreadful,' she said. 'Poor Mrs Trumper has committed suicide.'

'It is dreadful indeed,' said Lord FitzCricket. 'I never met Mrs Trumper, but it always upsets me to hear of anyone committing suicide. I once thought of committing suicide myself. Have you any idea why she did it?'

'No,' said Emmeline; 'I simply can't believe that it was because the Professor was carrying on with Mrs Postlethwaite. I should hate to think it was that.'

'In nine cases out of ten,' said Lord FitzCricket, 'people commit suicide not at all for the reasons one thinks. It may be that she was suddenly overwhelmed by a sense of discouragement. Or perhaps she was merely tired of having to dress every day, like the suicide in Mark Twain, who left a note "Tired of buttoning and unbuttoning." '

'You might have thought so if you had seen her clothes,' said Emmeline. 'Oh, dear, I suppose I shall have to write to Professor Trumper. It will be a very difficult letter. I dare say I had better get Father to do it.'

Emmeline seemed very distressed, and Lord FitzCricket, feeling that the incident had put an end to any futher levity in the conversation, withdrew.

XII

Lady Caroline's Activities

Lady Caroline Paltry was, as usual, very busy. The evacuees she had taken in at the beginning of the war left after a few weeks. They complained that the house was too far from the town, and Caroline, who was not given to considering other people's tastes, refused to let them have tinned salmon and fed them almost exclusively on fresh vegetables, porridge and rabbits. They found her domineering and altogether too whimsical in matters of diet.

The schoolmistresses who succeeded them proved even less of a success. They deplored the absence of intellectual atmosphere, they were shocked by Caroline's physiological frankness and were annoyed by her discouragement of political discussions during meals. So in their turn they left, and Caroline had now filled the house with poor relations. She charged them very little for their keep, but, in return, she made them help with the housework, look after the goats and the chickens, clean the car and the wagonette, dig in the garden and perform any other useful jobs she could think of. When evening came they were so exhausted that they retired to bed at an early hour and gave no further trouble. Caroline felt that she had at last got a billeting arrangement that was fairly satisfactory.

In the town and in the neighbourhood she had found scope for her usual activity. She had doubled the number of work parties and canteens, she had designed a new uniform for the Women's Guild, and although she did not fully appreciate the sociological value of art, except in so far as her husband's music was concerned, she made Francis give concerts for the entertainment of the troops.

She was now engaged in arranging for a performance of his new symphony at the Pandemonian. The use of the place for musical purposes involved certain formalities, but Caroline had succeeded in browbeating the authorities concerned into acquiescence and, as a work of supererogation, she had forced her parents, who had no very great love either for music or for their son-in-law, to come over from Ireland for the occasion.

Emmeline was now seeing quite a lot of Lord FitzCricket, and he had taken to accompanying her on her afternoon walks.

Lord FitzCricket, since his residence in the precincts of the university, had grown more earnest, and suggested that their outings would be improved if some definite object were involved. And so nearly every afternoon they would visit some architectural feature. But after a time, although there were many interesting and beautiful buildings in the town, they found that the repertory was becoming a little monotonous.

'I'm afraid it's not true,' said Lord FitzCricket, 'that a thing of beauty is a joy for ever. That is the worst of poetry. One is inclined to believe a thing just because it sounds nice.'

'I never did believe it. There was a girl at my school who was a thing of beauty, but she certainly wasn't a joy for ever. I don't think anything can be a joy for ever. That's the trouble about heaven.'

'One doesn't want any kind of monotony. Perhaps heaven will turn out to be a sort of sublime variety show.'

'I don't fancy the idea of variety going on for ever,' said Emmeline. 'And if we are going to keep our personalities, how is it going to suit everyone's taste? There'll be just as much boredom and complaining in the after-life as there is in this one. And people who go to heaven are bound to be rather exacting. Things in this world are in a pretty good muddle, but it's nothing to what it will be in the next.'

'And theology holds out no hope of a different stage manager. I expect that's why so many people are in favour of annihilation.'

'That sounds dull to me,' said Emmeline, 'but of course there'd be no dressmakers' bills, no Professor Trumper, no war. But one doesn't want to be looking forward to something one can't define, and even Father can't define non-existence. I once asked him if a thing could be non-existent and he said: "How many non-existent things do you think there are in this room?" '

'And how many were there?'

'I don't know. I suppose I had formulated my question wrong. That often happens in philosophy.'

'There's not much to be gained by formulating questions about the unknowable. That's what Kant said.'

'I dare say he did. Father says he was a great one for platitudes.'

'I think it's a mistake to be priggish about platitudes. Speaking as a man of the world I'd rather be guided by a few honest platitudes than by any amount of metaphysics. Let's leave the unknowable to philosophers and theologians and get on with our work, cultivate our garden.'

Emmeline's thoughts grew personal.

'Or destroy it. Wouldn't that do as well? It would keep one busy, I mean.'

'It depends on the garden. There are some I know that would be none the worse for being destroyed. And I don't suppose you're advocating indiscriminate destruction.'

'No,' said Emmeline. 'Only things that are out of date and no more use. Museum-pieces for instance. What is the good of having them about? They only discourage people or incite them to make bad copies, and a lot of time and trouble is wasted in keeping them up.'

'I'm afraid I'm a museum-piece myself,' said Lord FitzCricket, 'and I still believe in tradition.'

'Tradition is nothing but a graveyard,' said Emmeline. 'I was told that by an undergraduate.'

'Destroying the graves won't abolish the necessity for graveyards. And we seem to have got away from the point.'

'One always does here,' said Emmeline, 'and in any case I must hurry home. Caroline Paltry is bringing her parents to tea. There's a couple of museum-pieces for you, and you had better come and compare notes. Only they're not your period. They're much, much earlier.'

Caroline arrived with Lord and Lady Otterboy in a small open car. She had some difficulty in extricating them from among the objects with which it was packed – a bird cage, a gramophone, a sack of potatoes and a number of agricultural implements. She had also brought her husband.

Francis Paltry and Lord FitzCricket did not get on very well. Their temperaments and their æsthetic views were poles apart. Lord FitzCricket was a dilettante and had always been interested in the pleasurable aspects of art, and he thought that a work of art should never be tedious. Francis, on the other hand, held that art should be austere, and he felt that he himself had a mission. Lord FitzCricket said that Francis believed in catharsis through boredom.

Francis had once written rather rudely about Lord FitzCricket's compositions. The article was unsigned, but Lord FitzCricket knew that Francis had written it and Francis knew that Lord FitzCricket knew.

'I hope you're coming to the concert,' Caroline said. 'Francis's symphony is really magnificent. Don't you think so Mamma?'

Lady Otterboy was evasive. 'It seemed very nice, but then I have only heard it on the piano.'

'I don't suppose FitzCricket would care for it,' said Francis.

'I am sure that I should enjoy it very much,' said Lord FitzCricket. 'But I am not certain if I shall be able to go to the concert.'

'Nonsense,' said Caroline. 'I'll take you.'

'Is your symphony very long?' asked Emmeline.

'Certain people might consider it long. It lasts about an hour and a half, and it's in one movement. If a man has something to say, he must take his time about it. I haven't been able to acquire the modern knack of developing a theme in a few minutes or not developing it at all.'

'I think you're wise,' said Lord FitzCricket. 'If you're setting up to be a national composer. The English have a tendency to judge art by size and weight.'

'We aren't a nation of shopkeepers for nothing,' said Emmeline.

'Napoleon said that,' remarked Lord Otterboy. He would show them that he, too, could join in a highbrow discussion if he chose.

'Why don't you modernize your room, Emmeline?' asked Caroline.

'Caroline, will you please leave me and my room alone. I've spoken to you once before about interfering.'

'I like it,' said Lady Otterboy. 'It's a nice quiet room. Caroline's house is so noisy.'

'Oh, don't go on about the noise, Mamma.'

'Don't you know there's a war on?' Francis enquired facetiously.

Lady Otterboy thought his remark was directed against herself and was offended.

The atmosphere, though not exactly electric, was becoming a little strained. Lord FitzCricket was not good at coping with dissonant personalities, and although he would have liked to examine the Otterboys more closely, he felt that he would have preferred to do so in the absence of Caroline and her husband.

'I must be going,' he said.

'Are you still working in the Blood Transfusion Service?' asked Caroline.

'Yes, that's where I'm going.'

'Then I'll come with you. There's a new method of storing blood I want to tell them about. Why don't you marry Emmeline?' she asked as soon as they had got out of the room.

'Why don't I what?'

'Marry Emmeline. She's a very nice girl and she wants taking out of herself.'

'But do you think that's necessary?'

'Well, you might try. I'm not coming with you really. I only wanted an excuse to get you alone. Think it over.'

'I knew that fellow's father,' said Lord Otterboy. 'Old Puggy we used to call him. He was a splendid old chap, a fine shot he was and rode well to hounds. Does this fellow hunt?'

'I believe he used to.'

'Why did he give it up?'

'I think he took to writing music.'

Emmeline's remark was intentionally mischievous. She was anxious to divert attention from Lord FitzCricket and she had taken a dislike to Francis.

Lord Otterboy grunted and glared at his son-in-law.

Caroline turned to Emmeline. 'Why don't you marry him?'

'Marry who?'

'Lord FitzCricket, of course. It's quite a good title.'

'Oh, Caroline, dear,' said Lady Otterboy.

Emmeline flared up. 'Caroline,' she said, 'this is the second time this evening that you have given me ridiculous advice. If you do it again I shall have to ask you to go.'

'I'm going anyhow,' said Caroline. 'And, my goodness, you are getting bad tempered.'

'I'm sorry, Lady Otterboy,' Emmeline apologized, 'but you must admit that Caroline at moments is maddening.'

Whatever Lady Otterboy thought, she refused to commit herself. 'She didn't mean it, dear,' she murmured in an aside.

Caroline was not particularly interested in match-making. It was a matter of indifference to her whether Emmeline and Lord FitzCricket married or not. But seeing two unattached people in a room together had upset her sense of organization.

XIII

The Love Life of Socrates

Mrs Postlethwaite's novel, that had just appeared, was a new departure in the way of style and background. The scene was set in ancient Greece, and the story was a love romance between Socrates and a fascinating hetaira. The authoress made no attempt to embellish the physical appearance of Socrates, but she had taken a certain amount of liberty with his conversation, which was not at all like that recorded by Xenophon and Plato. There was also an undue insistence on his 'voices'; they were continually making the most improbable suggestions.

The hetaira herself was a lady of considerable charm and determination, and she was inclined to thrust herself into unhistorical situations. She succeeded in persuading Socrates, in spite of his well-known dislike for the country, to go with her and live a pastoral life in a secluded valley in the manner of Daphnis and Chloe. During his trial she burst into the court, made an impassioned speech to the judges and ended by taking off all her clothes. The device did not appear to have been so successful as in the case of Phryne, and although several of the judges were very much affected, Socrates was condemned all the same. She made a final irruption into the cell where Socrates was awaiting his death and, at his personal request, handed him the cup of hemlock.

Xantippe did not figure very largely in the book. It was implied that she was a bit of a drag on her husband, a hindrance to his philosophical activities and, in the description of her exterior, acute observers might detect a slight resemblance to the late Mrs Trumper. Owing to an oversight on the part of the printer and the proof reader she appeared for the first time in the book as Christiantippe.

The only other event, at the time, that stirred the even tenor of university life was the invention by Mr Jericho of an important military device. It appeared that, unknown to anyone, he had been working for some time on a weapon of lethal character which, after considerable opposition on the part of the War Office, had at last been adopted and was proving to be of considerable value.

Having achieved a utilitarian act of national importance such as to preserve him for ever from the charge of frivolity, Mr Jericho gained in self-assurance. He acquired once more his pre-war ebullience, and no longer attempted to conceal his interest in the more trivial aspects of human life.

Mr Jericho had bought a copy of Mrs Postlethwaite's novel and was reading passages from it to Emmeline and Lord FitzCricket.

'Overhead was the blue sky, and through the silver filigree of the overhanging olive branches the sunlight fell in dappled plashes on the succulent turf and smote the ripples of the quick-flowing stream into a thousand facets of glittering diamond. Aglaia was sitting on the banks of the Ilyssus and, with one foot, was lazily caressing the water weeds.

' "You say, Socrates," she murmured, and her voice was limpid, like the clear-flowing water. "You say that Nature has no call for you, that you can learn nothing from the fields and trees, the mountains and the many-sounding brooks?

' "I know a little glade far off from the bustle of the city, far off from the distractions of social life. There we could live for ever happy, disturbed only by the bleating of the lambs, the hum of the bees and the twittering of the birds."

'And that night, tossing sleepless on his couch, above the lowing of the oxen and the clattering of the heavy wine-carts as they laboured over the marble pavements of the city, above the cries of the drunken helots returning from the dicteria, Socrates heard his

Voices calling to him softly: "Go to the country, Socrates, go to the country." '

'Read us the part where she takes off her clothes,' said Lord FitzCricket.

' "Do not condemn this just man," she cried. "What has he ever done to you or to the people of Athens? You say he is a corrupter of youth. I am young and Socrates has loved me. His teaching has taught me nought but ideals of nobility and purity. Here I stand, a living testimony to the falseness of your accusation."

'Loosening her girdle, she let fall her chiton to the ground and stood before them, an alabaster amphora of purest design. Would that Pheidias and Praxiteles had been there to see!

'Dazzled by the milk-white radiance of her perfect form, a gasp ran round the court. Meletus, in awe of so much beauty, placed his hands before his eyes, and the face of Xantippe skulking behind a column assumed a sour expression.'

'I wonder if she has sold the cinema rights,' remarked Lord FitzCricket. 'There'll be a good deal of competition, I should imagine.'

Mr Jericho closed the book.

'I am worried about the Provost,' he said, 'Have you heard anything, Emmeline?'

'No. I have telephoned several times, but there was no answer.'

'Ever since my little contribution to the war he seems to have taken a dislike to me, and he never once referred to it, even sarcastically. I heard he was ill and went to enquire. I was met on the doorstep by a hospital nurse. She was like Cerberus in her manners. "You are the last person he would wish to see," she said and practically slammed the door in my face. Since then I haven't persisted.'

'Oh, dear,' said Emmeline; 'it's dreadful when one's friends get so queer.'

XIV
All Clear

It now seemed certain that Mrs Postlethwaite had broken off relations with Professor Trumper and that their romance was at an end. No doubt, after the tragic incident that had occurred they both of them thought it wiser to discontinue their intimacy. It was also possible that Mrs Postlethwaite may have felt that, like d'Annunzio and Goethe, she had purged herself of passion through literature. When that lady paid her a visit one afternoon, Emmeline guessed it was something in the nature of an all-clear signal.

Mrs Postlethwaite was dressed in the deepest mourning. Emmeline wondered how she was going to treat the subject of Mrs Trumper's death.

'For several days,' Mrs Postlethwaite said, 'I was simply prostrated. It was, as you can imagine, a fearful shock. You knew, of course, that poor Pixy was my dearest friend.'

Emmeline appeared a little bewildered.

'Yes,' Mrs Postlethwaite continued, 'that was her pet name. She was always called Pixy by her family. Though you may not perhaps agree, I think it suited her. In spite of her serious outlook on life I always felt that there was something about her that was a little "fey".'

Emmeline felt that she had not been sufficiently acquainted with Mrs Trumper to go into that aspect of her character.

'And Professor Trumper?' she enquired. 'How is he taking it? I suppose he is quite heartbroken, poor man. She was such a help to him.'

Mrs Postlethwaite assumed a detached air.

'I really don't know. He has a hard, selfish nature. I never really liked him. She was, of course, my great friend. Poor Pixy! I fear she was never a very happy woman, in spite of all her political interests. Her ideals were too high. It was a mistake, in this cruel, evil world of ours, to have too high ideals. One meets with so many disappointments. Well, she is at rest now. She was buried, you know, in St. Luke's in the West, such a charming, peaceful little churchyard. I like to think of her lying there. It appears she had always set her heart on being buried at St. Luke's, and I believe they had to get special permission as it's practically full up. I wanted to design her tombstone, but that horrid old Professor vetoed the idea. All this has upset me very much, and I should like to go right away somewhere and forget things. But I feel my duty is to stay with Herbert just now. He is working so hard and, although he hasn't much time for poor little me, I know he likes to feel I am there. And oh, he has given me such a wonderful idea for a novel –'

'I liked your last one,' Emmeline interrupted. 'It was so full of poetry.'

'Oh, nonsense. That was just a trifle. This one is going to be really serious. It's all about evolution. May I tell you? I always find if I talk about my plots it gives shape to my ideas. The action takes place in the Darwin period, when there was all that controversy about evolution. My hero is a famous biologist, and I shall make him just a wee bit like Herbert. At first he was very religious and believed in the Bible, but after a great deal of mental wrestling and agonies of conscience he ends by believing in evolution, and it comes to mean everything to him. Then one day, while poking his fire, he finds a human tooth embedded in a lump of coal. You see that would upset the whole theory of evolution and ruin his life's work. It would be too cruel, especially after his having given up religion.'

'Good gracious!' exclaimed Emmeline. 'What does he do then?'

'I haven't quite made up my mind. I had thought of making him commit suicide, but poor Pixy has rather spoilt that idea. I shall have to think of something else.'

'Couldn't the housemaid have dropped it?' suggested Emmeline.

'Oh, no,' said Mrs Postlethwaite. 'It was a fossilized tooth, and, besides, it wouldn't be a serious ending.'

Lord FitzCricket arrived.

'We were speaking of biology,' said Emmeline.

'Oh, hush,' cried Mrs Postlethwaite.

'Biology?' said Lord FitzCricket. 'That is one of the subjects I never tried to tackle. I've always had a thirst for knowledge and felt I wanted to get to know a little about everything. But my experience with physics upset me so much that I had to abandon the idea.'

'You mean things blowing up?' asked Mrs Postlethwaite. 'No, that's chemisty. But biology's quite safe, except that you're liable to be bitten by monkeys.'

'It was not explosions or monkeys that I was afraid of,' Lord FitzCricket explained. 'It was something more subtle and far more disconcerting. When you're as sensitive as I am, you are liable to get acute inflammation of the sense-data. After studying physics for a while, I began to feel the electrons inside me jumping from one level of energy to another, and I became a martyr to Heisenberg's Principles of Uncertainty. I had a nervous breakdown and was obliged to do a rest-cure. I fear something similar might happen if I were to take up any other branch of science, and that is why I have confined myself to the arts.'

From below came the sound of the hall door being closed.

'That must be Father,' said Emmeline. 'He has been to see the Provost. Will you please excuse me for a moment. I want to hear his news.'

She ran downstairs and found her father taking off his overcoat and scarf.

'Did you see him, Papa?'

'Yes, dear,' Doctor Pocock replied. 'It was very sad, but at the same time I felt slightly consoled. He seemed much calmer than I have known him for many years. He was sitting out in the garden under an ilex tree. It is a nice establishment and the atmosphere is very peaceful. The doctors and the nurses all seem very sensible people. I don't fancy he recognized me, but he talked quite coherently. He seemed to take great pleasure in the flowers. I never knew he was interested in horticulture, but he appeared to know the Latin names of all the flowering shrubs. The nurses seem very fond of him and they told me he gave very little trouble. But they said he grew very agitated at times and kept crying out for a machine-gun.'

When Emmeline returned to the drawing-room she found Mrs Postlethwaite expatiating to Lord FitzCricket on the pleasures of conjugal life.

XV

The Garden of Sleep

Whether it was due to Caroline's propaganda or to the fact that, of late, musical entertainments had been few and far between, on the afternoon of Francis's concert the Pandemonian was crowded. All the musical élite were there, and even Professor Trumper, who very rarely went to concerts, was present.

Caroline was sitting with the Mayor and the Vice-Chancellor. She had invited Emmeline and Lord FitzCricket, but they preferred being nearer the door.

'There's always something a little depressing about musical audiences,' remarked Lord FitzCricket. 'At a concert I often find myself envying King Ludwig of Bavaria.'

'They're no worse than people at race meetings or political gatherings,' said Emmeline, 'or any other crowd of people who are interested in the same thing. It's seeing them all together.'

'Yes, I suppose so. Individually they're all right. There's Mr Jericho over there. He looks just as bad as anyone. Crowds have a faculty of reducing individuals to the lowest common measure. It may well be that the proper study of mankind is man, and the study of mankind is discouraging.'

Fragments of conversation emerged from the general chatter. They were mostly complaints.

'They've made Marjorie a corporal. It's sickening.'

'All the windows were blown out, and the doors too.'

'The greenfly on our roses this year was something terrible.'

'She actually had the cheek to say I was gamma-minded.'

There was a sudden hush. Francis had appeared on the conductor's platform and tapped with his baton.

The first item on the programme was Brahms' Tragic Overture. Then came the Symphony.

Pale, watery sunshine falling through the high windows, illuminated Francis as if with semi-official limelight.

'There's no doubt,' said Lord FitzCricket, 'that he's destined for the Musical-Laureateship.'

When the Symphony was over, he suggested to Emmeline that they should not wait for the rest of the concert. 'I think we have done our duty by music for the day.'

On their way out they met Mr Jericho.

'It supplies a long felt want,' was his comment.

'I'm afraid it does,' said Lord FitzCricket. He was a little embittered by the rapturous applause with which the Symphony had been greeted.

'Shall we go to St. Luke's in the West?' Emmeline suggested. 'It was where Mrs Trumper was buried. But that's not my reason for proposing it. I think we may find it restful after all that strenuous music and it's quite near.'

'The reason why I dislike Francis,' said Lord FitzCricket, as they walked along, 'is that he's a prig. Priggishness is the one human failing I have never been able to stomach. For all I know I may be a prig myself. I don't think I am, but if you're irritated by some characteristic it often means you've got it yourself.'

'You are perhaps a trifle conceited,' said Emmeline, 'but I don't think you're a prig.'

'There have been too many prigs let loose on us lately,' Lord FitzCricket went on. 'It has become almost a public danger. But the English, I believe, are aware of it. The abuse directed against highbrows doesn't imply an aversion for culture, as some people seem to think. It is the old terminological trouble, and when they say highbrows they really mean prigs. All the same, the public is often taken in by them. Priggishness is insidious and, in cunning disguise, insinuates itself into art, politics and religion with disastrous results. There ought to be a Viligance Committee of Prig-detectors.'

St. Luke's in the West is an ancient church, standing in a graveyard planted with rose bushes, Irish yews and a few shady trees. Although situated in the centre of the town and close to one of the main thoroughfares, the place has a rural, out-of-the-world air.

'The Provost used to say he liked walking in cemeteries,'

remarked Emmeline as she opened the gate. 'He said it gave him pleasure to think that so many people were dead.'

'The thought doesn't give me pleasure,' said Lord FitzCricket, 'but it might help to reconcile one to death.'

'Don't let us talk about death,' said Emmeline. 'It is a very dull subject. Destruction is a much more exciting problem.'

'It's certainly a very actual one. If it goes on much longer there'll be nothing left except military objectives.'

'Oh, I don't mean war-destruction.' Emmeline sat down on a tombstone. 'I mean something far more universal. I mean the destruction that is going on for all time and is the fate of all created things. It'll take millions of years perhaps, but in the end there'll be nothing left at all – not even military objectives. It makes everything seem so silly. Shakespeare was worried by the problem, too. "The great globe itself shall dissolve and leave not a rack behind," but if it was a consolation to him that our little life is rounded with a sleep, it isn't to me, much as I enjoy going to bed. I shan't be happy until I get a really good working theory. Please help me, Lord Fitz-Cricket.'

'I'd really rather not think about it today, if you don't mind,' said Lord FitzCricket. 'I'm a mental coward and I can't face theories.'

The wicket-gate opened and a woman appeared. She was dressed in deep mourning and was accompanied by a young man. She was carrying a large bunch of flowers. They saw it was Mrs Postlethwaite, and the young man was Mr Guggenheim Junior. Emmeline and Lord FitzCricket had a simultaneous thought that the meeting might prove embarrassing and hid themselves behind one of the Irish yews.

Emmeline peeped through the branches.

'She's laying flowers on Mrs Trumper's grave,' she whispered.

'The Altar of the Dead,' said Lord FitzCricket.

After the rite had been performed and Mrs Postlethwaite and her companion had left the churchyard, Emmeline resumed her seat on the tombstone. Lord FitzCricket sat down beside her.

'Will you marry me, Emmeline?' he asked.

'Oh, no, Lord FitzCricket, I couldn't really.'

'I was afraid you might say that. I know I haven't much to offer you.'

'Oh, it isn't that,' Emmeline protested. 'It's not that at all. It's simply that I'm not a marrying woman.'

'Well,' said Lord FitzCricket, getting up from the tombstone, 'perhaps I'm not a marrying man either. And in any case if I marry I suppose it ought to be someone who could look after me. You couldn't do that, Emmeline, could you?'

'No,' said Emmeline, 'I don't think I could.'

When Emmeline returned to her room it was growing dusk. She drew the curtains, turned on the swivel lamp and took out the embroidery. But that evening she had great difficulty in settling down to her work. Thoughts kept buzzing about in her brain like a swarm of flies.

'I couldn't possibly marry him,' she said to herself, 'but it was nice of him to ask me. I don't want to marry anyone. I shall never fall in love, I'm sure. Passion seems alien to my nature and I really haven't the energy. I just want to be left alone. But if Father were to die, what would become of me? Anyhow, he isn't dead yet, and what's the good of bothering about the future? Anything may happen. And then there's this tiresome destruction problem. I can't get on with my work until I've cleared it up. Lord FitzCricket wasn't very helpful, and it's no good asking Father; he would only make it worse. I shall have to puzzle it out for myself.' She made a great mental effort. 'Some people seem to think that life is a striving for positive perfection. Perhaps they've got it the wrong way round, and perfection is really negative. All created things are doomed to change and decay and only destruction can give them immunity. And so the impulse to destroy is more reasonable than the impulse to create. Perhaps another day I shall think of something better. It will have to do for the present. I really must get on with my work. Oh, dear!' she cried, as she poked her scissors into the breast of St. Agatha. 'If only one didn't have to think.'

Portrait of Elgar
Second Edition

Michael Kennedy

Portrait of Elgar, first published in 1968, was acclaimed as a 'brilliant biography', an 'admirable, absorbing book', and 'an important and engrossing contribution to the Elgar library'. Since then much new biographical information has come to light. This new edition takes full account of recent research and includes a number of new illustrations.

OXFORD PAPERBACKS

Edith Sitwell

A Unicorn Among Lions

Victoria Glendinning

Winner of the Duff Cooper Prize and the James Tait Black Memorial Prize for Biography

'*I find it difficult to overpraise Victoria Glendinning's work . . . This is biography at its best . . . If you are at all interested in literature, this superb book should be on your shelves.*' – Frank Delaney on *Bookshelf*

'*It's hard to imagine a life of Edith Sitwell that could surpass it.*' – John Carey in the *Sunday Times*

OXFORD PAPERBACKS

Some People

Harold Nicolson

New introduction by Nigel Nicolson

The story of author and diplomat Sir Harold Nicolson's relationship with his wife, Vita Sackville West, was described by their son Nigel in his celebrated book *Portrait of a Marriage*. Nigel Nicolson has now written an introduction to *Some People*, his father's highly original autobiography of his childhood, years at Oxford, and career in the Foreign Office. In nine brilliant vignettes Harold Nicolson puts 'real people in imaginary situations, and imaginary people in real situations' to create a careful self-portrait and an acute, sometimes mordant, commentary on people he had known, and on fashionable life in the 1920s.

The Gates of Memory

Geoffrey Keynes

'*Less an autobiography than a valuable piece of social history . . . a portrait of an age.*' – Anthony Storr in the *Sunday Times*

Sir Geoffrey Keynes's remarkable autobiography was published just a year before his death in 1982 at the age of 95. Brother of the celebrated economist Maynard Keynes, friend of the Bloomsbury Set, distinguished surgeon and pioneer of the use of blood transfusion, he was also a dedicated bibliophile whose definitive editions of the works of William Blake were responsible for the rediscovery of that long-neglected genius.

OXFORD PAPERBACKS

Saki

A Life of Hector Hugh Munro
with six stories never before collected

A. J. Langguth

'A Saki biography at last, and surely a definitive one' – Emlyn Williams

Under the *nom de plume* of Saki, H. H. Munro wrote three novels and a host of witty, unnerving short stories that have won him a permanent and unique place in English writing. The facts of his life are sparse, but through A. J. Langguth's detective work a convincing portrait of this intriguing figure of the pre-1914 literary scene has at last been established.

A complete list of Oxford Paperbacks, including books in the World's Classics, Past Masters, and OPUS series, can be obtained from the General Publicity Department, Oxford University Press, Walton Street, Oxford OX2 6DP.